POOR MAN'S JUSTICE

BY
D. H. MITCHELL

To Jeff, Aimee and Steven,

Keep your world filled with innocent fascination and childhood dreams. Embrace life. Don't wait for it to cross your path; reach out and carry it over the rainbow to glory. Now and for years gone bye, I'll be watching, listening, and embracing your unfolding story with unconditional love.

Thank you, kids. Love, Dad.

To my mother, Shirley,

I am extremely proud to be your son. The kids and I thank you for all your loving support.

Thank you, mom. Love, your son David.

Acknowledgements

This book has been written without prejudice or malice. All characters in the book are real, although a few names, which cannot be recalled, have been inserted where necessary (*). Court transcripts, National Parole Board hearing tapes, and other recorded interviews used in the book have been edited only where clarification was deemed necessary. Some dates and times of events may be approximate, unless confirmed by diary notes, transcripts, tape recordings, or other legitimate means of identification.

I would like to thank my editor, Audrey McClellan, for her patience and intuitive perspective.

A special appreciation goes out to Jeff Mitchell and Annabel Youens for their technical support and cover design.

CONTENTS

PREFACE

PART ONE

PART TWO

PART THREE

Preface

In recent years the modern media has been shinning a light on our public courtrooms. Sensational stories of greed and betrayal, murder and mystery captivate us as we are constantly taken on inquisitive voyages through the legal process. We have seen how individual wealth can be a great equalizer against any publicly funded judicial system. We have watched defense attorneys and prosecutors clamor for attention and notoriety on a number of cases. And while some may disagree with the public display their legal system is subject to, the unbridled scrutiny of the process has enhanced the level of fairness brought to these particular cases. To that extent, we should applaud the television pundits who regularly keep us abreast with checks and balances.

The fact is, what society is watching, and sometimes engaging in during these debates, is justice, just as it is administered in our criminal and civil courtrooms every day. Desensitization of the public, achieved through dehumanization and degradation of an accused or accuser, is a common strategy that is routinely practiced throughout our judicial process.

Whenever I find myself watching these intriguing debates, I always hear someone talk about due process. But when I found myself entangled in the justice system, absent any public scrutiny and without any means to pay for a defense, I discovered due process was not always present. And when it was not present, it was only replaced with one thing, 'undue process, or what I call poor man's justice.

Poor Man's Justice is a true story that takes the reader behind the closed doors of Canada's justice system. Unlike most true crime stories, this story is not about guilt or innocence. Instead, it shows the aftermath of sentencing, when a man who admitted guilt to the crime for which he is in jail, must struggle with a court, correctional, and parole process that punishes him for crimes he never committed, manipulating him emotionally and giving him no opportunity to confront his accusers and clear his name.

Poor Man's Justice raises a multitude of questions: What should happen when the justice system crosses the line into abusive behavior? Where does the responsibility for this abuse rest?

Why is there a lack of accountability in our courts, the Correctional Service of Canada and the parole process?

The strength and stature of a society are heightened when that society demonstrates a willingness to protect all of its citizens. To achieve this, it needs a judicial process that will look after victims' rights, while ensuring that the legal and civil rights of accused and incarcerated citizens are maintained.

So when a justice system abandons the fairness that should accompany due process, and instead tilts towards a better-safe-than-sorry philosophy, society quickly finds itself debating the meaning of the word "justice," which spawns a multitude of questions. What's right? What's wrong? What's fair? What's just? Who wins and who loses?

Poor Man's Justice illustrates the unfairness that has accompanied a slow and deliberate dismantling of due process in Canada's legal system. It is my hope that this book will help turn that tide and aid society as it searches for answers and directions that will protect the legal, civil, and human rights of all its citizens.

PART ONE

Chapter 1

Just a Matter of Time

Wind swept crystals of frozen snow slammed against the picture window. Muffled by long flowing drapes, a constant chatter ricocheted off the glass, a reminder of the growing storm outside. It was January 1991 and I quickly pushed aside my thoughts of worsening weather. They paled in comparison to recent knowledge of possible layoffs at the mine, and other, more personal problems. Equally tired of listening to the world's sad state of affairs, I wearily hit the off button on the remote control and methodically set about my routine of locking the front door and checking the kitchen stove.

Satisfied everything was safe and secure, I made my way down the stairs to the family room of our split-level home and loaded the airtight stove, then turned up the fan. I stood in front of the vents for a few moments, enjoying the increasing warmth before heading back to the upper floors, quietly passing our oldest son's room on the second level. Jeff was only days away from his fifteenth birthday and experiencing a growing sense of independence from the rest of his family. The solitude of the room fit in nicely.

I continued on, passed through the main living area, and climbed the last couple of steps to the top floor. After checking in on our youngest son, seven-year-old Steven, and our only daughter, thirteen-year-old Aimee, I entered the master bedroom.

I undressed and slid under the covers next to Geri, embracing her around the waist as I had done for years. But this night her body stiffened and a couple of soft sobs rose from beneath the covers.

"What's wrong?" I asked quietly.

A lengthy pause preceded her muffled response. "I can't talk about it," she said, her voice weak and barely audible.

"I don't understand what's been going on these last months," I whispered, "I wish you'd talk and tell me what's happening."

Prolonged silence filled the room, then, "It's someone else...and I can't...talk about it," said my wife, her voice cracking as she spoke.

"You mean somebody at work is giving you a rough time?" I said, trying desperately to avoid the pain I knew would come with the truth.

"No, you know what I mean...I can't talk about it," uttered Geri.

Suddenly my nakedness felt ugly and shameful to me, as if encroaching where it shouldn't be. I edged myself out from under the covers, shaking and unwilling to confront what had been months of growing suspicion. I pulled a comforter from the top shelf of the closet and glanced back at the outline of my wife, who remained buried under the blankets. Then, without saying a word I opened the bedroom door and made a hasty retreat for the living room couch.

The next morning we said little, speaking only to the kids as we prepared for the day. We dropped them off at school and continued on to the clinic where Geri worked. Silence cut the tense air as she slipped out of the van and disappeared into the medical building. When I picked her up at the end of the day there were no words spoken until I pulled the mini-van into our driveway. "I have to go back downtown for some groceries," Geri said, sliding into the driver's seat as I vacated it.

An hour later she returned, set a small bag of groceries on the living room floor and scurried up the stairs to our bedroom. I caught a glimpse of puffy redness around her eyes and hesitated, then followed, uncertain and fearful of the answers that lay ahead. I nervously opened the bedroom door, finding Geri lying face down on the covers, smothering her cries in a pillow.

I lowered myself onto the bed and reached out, placing a comforting hand on her back. My wife slowly rolled over and looked up at me with her red-stained eyes. "Hold me," she cried out, "All I want is you." We quickly wrapped our arms around each other in a tearful embrace, a picture of two long time friends and lovers, each trying desperately not to hurt the other.

I had fallen in love with Geri at first sight, and a passionate romance had lead to our marriage a year and a half later. That had been almost twenty years earlier, and as we now lay wrapped in one another's arms I recalled the torment of the past few months. She had become increasingly distant, and then there had been one terrible night when I heard her call out a name in her sleep. "Rob, Rob," she had murmured. After that our relationship had gradually deteriorated into prolonged tension and silence, that now, hopefully, had come to an end.

      * * *

A few years earlier, in 1989, my family and I had moved back to the small city of Fernie in southeastern British Columbia. We had lived in the valley from 1982 until 1986 while I worked at one of the local coal mines. After layoffs in 1986 we had moved to Vancouver Island. I acquired my real estate license, but set that aside when I was offered a survey contract with a mining company on the Island. When the contract ended in 1989 we returned to Fernie, where I quickly took a job back at the coal mine.

Two years had since passed, and now the talk of more layoffs had caught everyone by surprise. And the heads-up proved to be short in duration. In March, two-thirds of the employees lost their jobs, including me. The financial burden on the family brought back an increase in tension between Geri and I, this time helped along by strange phone calls that started interrupting our evenings at home. Geri would lift the receiver and quickly hang up, muttering something about a wrong number. Whenever I answered there was silence, followed by a deadening click. The calls became a nightly ritual and I could see the anxiety grow in my wife's face.

I tried desperately to hang on to what we once had, and arranged a weekend trip out of town for the two of us, but nothing seemed to help. Near the end of May it all came to an end when she told me she could no longer live a lie. I was devastated when she took our daughter Aimee and moved into a small apartment block on the opposite side of town. Our children were also hurt and confused by the sudden separation of their family. Jeff displayed his anger by refusing to talk with his mother. Aimee withdrew into her own world, while Steven clung furiously to the belief that his parents would soon reunite.

I started studying the real estate course once again, hoping to reacquire my license, but my unemployment insurance never came close to covering the monthly bills we had, which included a mortgage and two vehicle payments. It was hard to find the funds my two sons and I needed to live on, and I quickly found myself selling material goods, such as our video camera and snow-blower in exchange for grocery money.

One afternoon, hoping we could work through our problems, I went over to my estranged wife's apartment. As I walked past her neighbor's basement-suite, someone shouted, "Fuck off!" Startled by the obscenity, I glanced down and locked eyes with a man who quickly stepped back from the basement window and disappeared from sight. When I asked Geri why the man across the hall would shout such a thing at me, a look of guilt leapt across her face and she shrugged her shoulders, remaining suspiciously silent.

Why had my presence spurned this stranger's anger? "Could this, ...yes! This must be the man?" I thought to myself. Suddenly a sickening sense of betrayal gnawed at my heart, and I left my estranged wife's apartment knowing I could no longer provide for the kids, either financially or emotionally. Overcome with guilt and shame at my apparent failure, I told Jeff and Steven they would have to stay with their mother, and I immediately moved to the neighboring community of Cranbrook, an hour's drive away.

Shortly afterwards, my worst fears were realized when I found out Geri and the man from across the hall had been seen together in public. My suspicions of an ongoing affair appeared to be confirmed when the kids told me his name was Rob, and that he was the owner and landlord of the apartment block.

I was already in thrall to depression, but now feelings of rejection, coupled with fear and anger, sent me into a panic. Although I continued to study for the upcoming real estate exam, I began to drink heavily and soon lapsed into a state of suicidal

7

despair. I went days at a time without sleep and lost forty pounds in just three months. The bank also started foreclosure proceedings on our home, and repossessed our vehicles, all of which were up for sale. Geri then wiped out our remaining family possessions in a garage sale.

Feeling lost, and overwhelmed by bouts of violent shaking that made sleep impossible, I rushed to the hospital's emergency room and received a prescription for sleeping pills. I was given a half a dozen small blue tablets to tide me over until the prescription could be filled. "Take only half a pill at a time, the depression will worsen if you over do it," said the doctor.

Sleep, however, continued to elude me. I upped my intake to one and sometimes two pills at a time, hoping to find the relief I so desperately wanted. I quickly found myself in a deadly spiral. In order to get any rest I had to take the pills, but as the doctor warned, during my waking hours I slid deeper and deeper into a state of paralyzing depression.

Several days later I came into Fernie and found the landlord and my wife talking in the hallway outside their apartment doors. When I asked Geri if I could talk to her, Rob slowly moved a few steps back, but remained within earshot, showing an interest in what I had to say.

"Not right now," Geri replied to me, as she turned and smiled seductively at the other man. Rob grinned back at her, and she cooed softly, "I've got other things to do right now."

Humiliated, I retreated outside, hastily grabbed our daughter's bike and pedaled across town to our recently vacated home. I gained entrance through an unlocked back door and spent hours sitting on the hearth, slowly crumbling under the emotional strain.

Evening eventually consumed the afternoon daylight and the world around me darkened, until finally, the blackness was interrupted only by a flickering street lamp's yellowish glow, dancing across the barren rug.

I sat shivering and shaking next to the unlit fireplace, when suddenly, a loud bang, and a soft voice, called out my name. I rose and peered cautiously out the drapeless living room window, but saw nothing. I had no sooner sat back down, when again the voice whispered, "*David, David.*"

Frightened and unable to pinpoint where the intruder was, I rushed outside, hopped on my daughter bike, and peddled furiously down the hill, focusing on the nearby hospital's lights. A doctor in the emergency room quickly admitted me, diagnosing my hallucinations as a panic attack.

I was released some days later, and my mother, who was trying to help financially, sent me enough money to buy a used car. My excursions into Fernie now became more frequent, and the confrontations with the other man became harsher and more violent with each trip.

My emotions continued to grow out of control until one night I found myself outside Rob's apartment block wearing a ski mask. My hand shook viciously as I emptied a bottle of solvent all over his pickup and rushed back to Cranbrook.

Then one evening I got a call from the police, telling me I had phoned my wife's apartment and spoken in a threatening manner. I had no recollection of the call, but my son Jeff, who had apparently answered the phone, later told me I had threatened to do serious harm to the landlord.

It was frightening to learn I had made a call I couldn't remember, and I was equally alarmed by a growing sense that I was no longer able to account for my waking hours, which most often were spent in a fog of medicated drunkeness.

Trying desperately to straighten up, I set aside the sleeping pills and went on prescribed anti-depressants, which I now took along with a daily dose of Gravol pills. On the surface, things appeared to get better, I curbed my drinking and managed to find the strength to write the real estate exam.

Believing I had everything under control, I returned to Fernie and prepared to go to work in the real estate industry. It was

9

the first of October 1991, and Jeff, who had been spending most of his time at a friend's place, moved into a new apartment with me and we tried to carry on.

By this time, Rob had helped move Geri upstairs into one of the larger apartments in his building. With Geri helping paint the bottom suites, I was convinced they were planning to share the larger apartment, which would open up their two smaller ones for rent. That thought was reinforced a few days before Thanksgiving. I invited Aimee and Steven over for turkey dinner, but my daughter sadly informed me that her mother had invited the landlord up from his basement suite to share in their own family dinner.

Geri and I had some verbal confrontations over the next couple of days as my emotions again got the better of me. The exchanges only managed to increase the growing queasiness in the pit of my stomach, and I quickly increased my intake of Gravol pills, upped my daily dosage of anti-depressants and rushed back for more counseling. I told Charles Bertholf, a government mental health worker, about the emotional roller coaster I was on. We talked about my fear of suicide and discussed the repeated thoughts I was having about hurting this man who had stepped into my family's life.

As I battled my demons night after night, the confrontations with the landlord continued. Geri and Rob took Steven out of town one morning, only hours before he was to come over and spend the day with me. It was late in the evening when they returned home. I was furious and warned Rob to stay away from my son. A few days later he threatened me with a steel pipe. I retaliated by smashing out his car window with a baseball bat. A few days later he harassed me with his pickup while I was driving through town. He repeatedly roared up behind my car and slammed on his brakes, then smiled, flipped me the bird and sped away.

Each retaliation produced yet another, then early in the morning hours of October 18, 1991, the sound of breaking glass shattered our family's already splintered world.

Chapter 2

Waking Up to a Nightmare

I gasped for air, opened the apartment door and stumbled forward, leaning against the hall wall for support. Was I in the middle of a nightmare? Another hallucination?

"Dad! Dad! What happened? You're all covered in blood!"

Struggling to keep myself upright, I reached out and placed my hands on my son's shoulders.

"Dad!" Jeff yelled again. "What's happened?...What's happened?...Dad, talk to me!"

Images of flailing hands, pounding fists, a body on the floor raced through my head, jumbled and unclear. Were they real? Had I dreamed them?

But Jeff was talking to me. He was real. I was awake.

"I hurt him," I whispered, suddenly trembling and frightened by the thought.

"Dad, you have to go to the police," Jeff said, as my eyelids closed like weary shutters.

"Yes, I'll go now," I answered, steadying myself on his shoulders.

I staggered back out the door, exited the apartment block, and walked down the street to the police station, located just a minute away. I rang the buzzer and waited. There was no response. I stepped around the corner and pounded on the side door. Still there was no answer. Exhausted, I leaned against the brick wall and slowly slide to the ground.

When I next focused in on my surrounding, a police officer and a nurse were hovering above my hospital bed. Eventually the hospital's fluorescent lights gave way to the morning's, softer natural daylight and I was escorted back to a cell at the police station. Much later in the day, while curled up on the steel cot, another officer walked up to the steel bars.

"Do you remember what happened?" she asked sadly.

"I'm not too sure," I replied. "I think I hurt him?"

"You attacked your wife's landlord with a knife last night and beat on him pretty good. He'll be alright, but he needed several stitches and will have to spend a couple of days in the hospital."

"I'm glad he's going to be alright," I said, still trying to put together the blurred events of the previous night.

My legal-aid family court lawyer, Dan Sliva, came down to the station and asked me not to talk to anyone until he could find out what was happening. A few days later, with a charge of attempted murder hanging over my head, I was brought before a judge, who ordered that I undergo a psychiatric assessment.

Two sheriffs escorted me aboard a commercial flight to Vancouver, British Columbia, where the court order was to be carried out. When we landed, a light rain blanketed the airport, and the steady drizzle continued as they drove me to the outer edges of the city. The sheriff's van finally stopped in front of an aging forensic institute in Port Coquitlam. I was taken up to the second floor where the sheriffs removed my handcuffs and turned me over to a waiting staff member.

I was told to bathe and slip into institutional pajamas, after which I was taken down to a main ward that had a dorm wing branching off each side. Prisoners -- or patients, depending on the terminology one used -- were wandering aimlessly back and forth through the common area. Many appeared detached from reality as they scurried about. I noticed one lost soul plucking cigarette butts from an ashtray and sharing his good fortune with an invisible friend standing next to him. I listened as another jabbered furiously, engaging in an animated argument with a family member who had long since moved on and forgotten him.

For several days my own demons came visiting late at night, haunting me as I hid in denial of my sudden life change. While I fought to make sense of the insanity that had crept into my world, the law firm looking after my estranged wife's interests in family court, took on another client -- the bank that was foreclosing on our home. The Fernie law firm of Majic Purdy took the bank's foreclosure to the Supreme Court despite the fact that Geri's signature was also attached to the mortgage. [A few years later, the sting of this questionable legal conduct (A law firm representing both competing parties to an action) hit me hard when I ended up paying for the entire shortfall in our mortgage after a quick sale of our home during my incarceration.]

Meanwhile, back at the forensic institute, an even more devastating bit of deception was in the works, something that would change my life forever. I was summoned into one of the ward's interview rooms, where a pleasant and extremely friendly social worker greeted me.

"Hello, Mr. Mitchell. My name is Marc Leblanc and I have been asked to help you during your stay here."

The man's voice was hypnotically soothing, and I eagerly grasped his extended hand and shook it firmly. I still felt lost and very much alone and his friendly demeanor helped put me at ease. It was reassuring and comforting to have someone reach out and help me understand what was happening.

"Mr. Mitchell, I am going to set up your spending account immediately. You'll be able to buy cigarettes, chocolate bars, and anything else you need from the canteen," he said cheerfully.

"Thank you," I replied gratefully and eased my grip on his hand as we took our seats.

"That's my job. This is not a prison. It's a hospital and we try to make it as comfortable as possible," replied Leblanc, and he flashed me another warm smile. "It looks like you've got yourself in a bit of a jam," he continued, leaning back in his chair.

"Yes, I assaulted a man who was involved with my wife."

"Well, these things happen. It will probably help if you talk about it."

"I'm supposed to start talking to a doctor any day now."

"Well, you can talk to me if you want. I'm here to help, and we all work here as a team."

"I'll have to talk to my lawyer. He told me to call him if I was asked to speak to anyone other than a doctor. But I'd like to help and I'll call him today."

"Good," Leblanc responded. "Do I also have your permission to talk with your family and friends, and get some more information for the doctor?"

"Yes, that's fine," I answered.

"Great," he beamed. "We'll talk some more in a day or two."

The next day I had my first session with Dr. Dilli, one of the institution's psychiatrists. He was a pleasant man and I immediately took a liking to him. But soon after our session began, I realized I had virtually no recollection of what had gone on inside the victim's apartment during the assault. Dr. Dilli suggested I had blocked it out due to the severe stress and trauma surrounding the incident.

Over the next couple of days I went through several different tests, answering questions and interpreting pictures given to me by a psychologist who's name eluded me. "Write everything down while you're here, everything you're feeling. It will help," he said as we tried to discuss my thoughts that remained jumbled and mashed.

I also had a few more sessions with Dr. Dilli during the week, then social worker, Marc Leblanc returned.

"Did you talk with your lawyer?"

14

"Yes," I replied, "he said it was okay to answer some of your questions."

"I'm pleased to see you cooperate and willing to get this mess all straightened out. I'm going to take a few notes so I can relay them to the doctor, okay?"

"I'm just glad to have someone help."

"Tell me about your assault on this man."

"I don't remember much about it. I talked with the psychiatrist about it the other day and he said it's not unusual for someone to block out such an event."

"That's understandable," Leblanc replied. "Do you believe your wife and this man were involved in a relationship before she left you?"

"Yes. I had a fear there was someone else. There was a night around Christmas when she was talking in her sleep and called out this man's name. Then early in the New Year she told me about it, or I should say, tried to tell me about it, but I didn't want to believe it." I looked at the social worker and took a breath, recalling how my wife had put her arms around me the following day. "I thought we had put it behind us," I said, reflecting back on that more pleasant moment.

He flipped a page on his pad. "So you suspected she was having an affair with this man?"

"No," I answered. "I felt certain she was seeing someone, but I didn't know it was him at that point. I realized it when he told me to fuck off one time when I came over to see her at the apartment. After that, I saw the guilt in my wife's face. Then I found out she was seeing him in public and I fell completely apart after that."

"So as usually happens in these cases, you began drinking and having some confrontations with this guy, right?"

"Yes, we had some confrontations," I replied. "He would swear at me when I came over to the apartment. One time he took a steel pipe from the back of his pickup and threatened to kill me." I took another deep breath, recalling the escalating confrontations between us. "A few days after the pipe incident I waited for him outside his apartment and when he pulled into the parking lot I broke the window of his car with a baseball bat. After that he harassed me with his pickup, stopping just short of ramming my car. It was a few days later when I assaulted him and wound up in this trouble."

"I can understand how you felt...What do you think is going to happen in court?" Leblanc asked.

"I don't know," I answered. "I know what I did was wrong. Some people have said, that due to the circumstances I will probably get some kind of probation. I don't know. I just hope people will understand."

"Well, circumstances are important in these cases. I'm sure people will understand," he said reassuringly, then asked, "Have you ever been in trouble with the police before?"

"Not any trouble like this. I had an impaired driving charge back in 1979 and had my driver's license suspended for three months."

I caught a brief look of disappointment on the social worker's face, but Leblanc quickly replaced it with an air of affable conspiracy. "Anything else? When we're growing up in our teens we all have some problems or encounters with the police, out partying or something. What about when you were younger?"

"Once as a teenager, while I was walking home, I was stopped by the police about two blocks from my parents' house. One of the officers, who was a teammate of mine on the local hockey team, wanted to take me down to the station. I tried to walk away but they took me down and put handcuffs on me. I spent the night in jail before I was released the next morning. But I was never charged with anything. ...I'm not Jack the Ripper or John Dillinger if that's what you're looking for," I said, trying to lighten the moment and release some of the tension I felt building up.

"How about your work history? Supported your family pretty well over the years, have you?"

"Yes," I answered, "I worked at the mines in the Kootenays and also had my own mine survey business."

"Sounds like you did alright. What about men's night out? Ever have a guy's night out, drinking and gambling?"

"When I was younger I used to play cards with some friends once in awhile, but I haven't done that for years." Then, recalling the out-of-town weekend Geri and I had taken a few months earlier, I added, "Just before the separation we made an overnight trip to Montana. I wanted to take my wife out of town, just the two of us. The casinos in Eureka were advertising the Holyfield-Foreman fight, so we went down. I gave her $300 for the slot machines. I didn't gamble at all, and Geri joined me in front of the big screen and we watched the fight together."

"Sounds like a nice trip," replied Leblanc. "Kind of like a second honeymoon."

"Well, it wasn't a lot," I concluded, "but that was the idea."

"Trips like that produce a lot of points for us guys. They make up for some of the bad times, like arguments or confrontations with our better halves." Leblanc smiled and leaned forward in his chair. "There must have been a few of those in seventeen years of marriage. That's a long time and guys tend to get a little physical once in a while?"

"It wasn't a violent marriage. There were two slaps early in the marriage, one by each of us. After a short separation we got back together and things had gone pretty well for the last ten years. Up until this."

"She says that you pushed her once while she was pregnant with your daughter?"

"That would have been...fifteen years ago? If I did, I'm sorry," I replied, trying to think back.

17

"Well I wouldn't be concerned about it. A push and slap throughout a lengthy marriage like yours, hardly portrays you as a violent husband." He settled back into his chair. "You were separated from your wife ten years ago and hospitalized for depression at that time, is that correct?"

"Yes, that's right," I answered.

"Were you hospitalized during this present separation?"

"Yes. One day I came back to town and everything in the house was gone. The new wood-stove was missing from the basement. And the fridge and stove upstairs were gone. Even the deep freeze and washer and dryer had been sold." I slumped forward in my chair, recalling that fearful night, that now had me speaking at a quickening pace. "I was sitting in front of the fireplace, in the living room, and everything was gone. I was just sitting there. There was a loud bang inside my head...I mean it rang more inside my head than my ears. Then a voice called out my name. It wasn't loud. It was real soft. Just 'David, David.' I remember being scared. I looked out the window, but I didn't see anyone. When I sat back down by the fireplace, the voice came down the chimney behind me! I got out of there. Peddled to the hospital as fast as I could. The lady doctor asked me if I was hearing voices. I remember feeling relieved that she understood someone was after me."

I took a deep breath, which helped lower the level of anxiety that was evident in the short, quick sentences. "It turned out that I was having what they called a panic attack. That was a couple of months ago," I said more calmly.

"Have you talked to the doctor about this?" the social worker asked quietly.

"Yes," I answered. "I told the medical doctor about it when he was asking me some questions a couple of days after I arrived here."

"Good," replied Leblanc. "Well, we've had some open and honest talks and I'll pass my notes on to the psychiatrist. I'm sure they'll help, and good luck in your court case."

A few days after this meeting with Leblanc, I was wandering the ward, waiting for a scheduled session with Dr. Dilli, when a staff member approached me. "Mr. Mitchell, we've been informed that you're scheduled for a court appearance back in the Kootenays. The sheriffs will be here to pick you up shortly, so get your stuff together and be ready to leave."

I nervously gathered together my belongings, confused and uncertain why my lawyer had not informed me about any upcoming court appearance. The sheriffs arrived half an hour later, and we set off, driving to the East Kootenay community of Cranbrook. After a couple of hours of uneventful travelling, uneasy and exhausted, I closed my eyes and started to nod off.

Suddenly I jerked upright. It was as if a movie were running in my head. I looked on helplessly as I watched myself pounding wildly on a shadowy figure underneath me. I stood up and slowly stepped backwards, distancing myself from the shaded figure that lay in front of me. There was an eerie silence, until finally, the shadow, realizing I was no longer continuing the attack, stirred, rose from the floor, and started moving towards the door.

I focused on my own image, which remained ridged, uncertain, listening as locks were unlatched. The door swung open and the shadow disappeared while I stood motionless, my heart pounding like a drum. The paralysis finally wore off and I stepped toward the open doorway, exhausted, I made my way up the stairs.

"Was that Rob?" said a voice as I leaned against the building for support. I ignored the intrusion, then stepped onto the sidewalk and started moving forward again, spotting the victim standing behind his pickup. I angrily banged the hood with a thunderous blow. "You better run and keep running!" I yelled, and raised my fist and lowered it a second time. The victim moved onto the street, passed through the light of the lamp and disappeared into the night. ...I wiped a bead of sweat from my forehead and looked at the two sheriffs in the front seat. Their continuing chatter told me my unsettling flashback had gone unnoticed.

Chapter 3

The Ultimate Basket

It was late in the afternoon when we stopped at our half-way point, the Penticton police station where I was to spend the night. I immediately called my legal aid attorney, Dan Sliva, wanting to inquire about the hearing, and also tell him about the flashback I had just experienced.

"The flashback's important," Sliva replied, "and we will talk about it when you get here. But this is only a bail hearing and we won't be getting into that kind of evidence yet. The hearing is going to take place in Cranbrook and I'll come down and see you at the station before court."

Late the next morning we continued on to the East Kootenays, making a couple of stops along the way. We got to Cranbrook as night was falling. It had been a long day and I let out a sigh, thankful the trip was coming to an end.

The following morning Sliva came down to the police cells as he had mentioned he would. I sensed his uneasiness as he sat on the other side of the glass-partitioned cubicle and we spoke through a small vent. After telling me once again that the bail hearing was not a place to discuss our case, or my recollection of events, he withdrew some papers from his briefcase.

"I received the forensic report and brought it over," he said, and pressed the document up to the glass.

"It's done already?" I said in amazement. "I haven't finished talking with the doctor yet."

"I guess they figured they had enough information. I just received it myself and I want you to read it before you're brought over to the courthouse." Sliva pointed to a paragraph that indicated I was a high risk for suicide. "Scary, isn't it?" he added, speaking louder than necessary.

Our brief meeting ended and I was hastened back to my cell, where I anxiously started reading through the report. It mentioned the amount of alcohol I had consumed on the night of the assault, along with the possibility that it was mixed with strong medication. The document also indicated I had been very pleasant, fully cooperative, and had volunteered a great deal of information while at the forensic institute.

Then I read, "As the years went by, he admits that he escalated with his inebriations, leading to some incidents of acting out 'was in jail in his later teens for getting tough with cops.'"

The evidence in his files shows the incidents of his being physically abusive towards his spouse, inclusive of one occasion his dislocating her jaw. It appears that his reasons for concern about his wife's infidelity were not substantiated. Her involvement occurred well after she had left her husband...

It is pertinent to note further that collateral sources of information indicate that Mr. David Mitchell was when drunk "aggressive and angry...a night and day change. On top of his drinking problem there is regrettably also the evidence that at one time or another in the past he has been gambling.

Bewildered, I read on.

On several occasions he would physically assault her as already mentioned. He began being violent towards her during her second pregnancy. Finally, she decided to leave him as he continuously controlled her behavior and was preventing her from attending the sporting events that their daughter was competing in. As well, she realized she says that their children too were suffering because of their unhappy marriage. More than physical abuse, she believes that she has been enduring a great deal of emotional abuse.

Partly as the result of the information gathered during Mr. Mitchell's admission into F.P.I., as well as on the basis of the input from collateral sources, it is also worth noting that it seems arising from his personality\psychological problems, Mr. Mitchell has little concern about the future...

21

During our conversations, David minimized the importance of his charges and his actions. He indicated that he considers it entirely possible that he will be placed on probation if convicted, and he stated that he talked to several other patients on the ward who had been put on probation for much more serious offenses than this. He did not elaborate on what offenses were more serious than attempted murder.

Disturbed by the pattern of degradation in the report, a frightening image of Marc Leblanc flashed before my eyes, and I turned another page.

David has demonstrated a life-long pattern of resolving conflict through violence and threats of violence...He has little concern about using violent means to get his way...He admits to occasional physical assaults on his wife.

I flipped through a few more pages and read, "He also intimated during the initial interview with Dr. Zimich on October 23, 1991, that he heard 'soft voice' calling his name when depressed ten years ago...and chest pain leading to a trip to the hospital...panic attack." I was mystified by the social worker's misleading suggestion that the panic attack had taken place a decade earlier and not, as it actually did, only weeks before the assault.

I cautiously turned to the psychological testing section. It indicated I had a superior level of abstract reasoning ability, along with an above-average IQ and a high level of cognitive sophistication.

I also noticed that the psychiatrist's summary and conclusion differed significantly from the earlier statements. In this section of the report, Doctor Dilli wrote:

This is a man of superior intelligence who is currently very depressed, distraught and in a state of shock. There are no signs of a thought disorder and few indicators of antisocial personality traits...He has tended over a long time to avoid conflicts in his marriage. In the face of several very severe life events -- the loss of his job, the wife leaving him for another man, and the loss of his home and possessions, which were compounded by the unavailability of crisis support other than from his children -- he resorted to drinking and brooding which in turn served to deepen his despondency and to block the view on alternative solutions. Thus, a lack of assertiveness and of skills to adequately deal with emotional upsets, and the cumulative impact of the above mentioned life events combined with the conspicuousness of his wife's new alliance lead to the alleged assault.

The latter should therefore be seen as an act of desperation more than one of malevolence. If at that time he was as much under the influence of alcohol as he claims, it is arguable that he was not in control of himself.

Numbed by what I had read, when the sheriffs brought me over to the courthouse an hour later, I frantically showed Sliva the contradictions between the early part of the document and Dr. Dilli's summary and conclusion. I also pointed out the suspicious absence of any mention of the two-way confrontations between the other man and myself, and then exclaimed, "The social worker has also misrepresented the facts surrounding the panic attack!"

Sliva told me not to worry about it, and five minutes later I was escorted into the courtroom and quickly placed in the prisoner's box, no more than twenty feet from Geri and Rob.

The prosecutor immediately referred to the forensic report, highlighting some of the more unflattering elements in the document. Without showing much emotion, Judge Don Carlgren indicated he had looked at it.

Sliva requested bail be set for my release, but the judge expeditiously denied this, saying I should be sent to a place where I could receive immediate psychological help.

The hearing ended abruptly and the sheriff took me down to the court registry, where Sliva handed me a document. "If you sign it, it will show good faith on your part and help our case," he said confidently.

Without hesitating I signed the form, agreeing not to have any contact with the victim. I was then taken on an 8 hour trip to the Kamloops Regional Correctional Center (KRCC), a provincial remand prison, where I was put on suicide watch. A full week passed before I talked with one of the institution's psychologists. He told me my feelings of depression and anger were normal under the circumstances and would disappear in time.

A week later I sat quietly and patiently in front of one of the prison's psychiatrists while he read the forensic report. After twenty minutes he set it down on his desk and rose to his feet. "I'll make an appointment to see you next week," he said, then shuffled around his desk and showed me the door.

Weeks came and weeks went without any sign of the doctor returning. My constant cries for help continued to be swept aside, and a multitude of emotions threatened to drown me in a world of depression. It was only the kindness of the prison's chaplain that kept me from falling into total despair. Reverend Ray's ability to share his faith and trust helped me stay in touch with my children, and a world that was rapidly pulling away.

I reached out with my new faith and slowly grew accustomed to my new surroundings. There was an elderly Native on the cell-block who was fond of calling me, "Old-timer." I responded in kind by referring to him as "Uncle." Uncle was a talented artist and brought his Native heritage to life in his art. He was in prison for murder, but denied any knowledge of the crime, remaining steadfast in his innocence, even after his conviction. There was an appeal underway, and I often saw him pacing back and forth on the cell-block, lost deep in thought.

One day I was lying in my cell, feeling rather down and depressed when the unit guard called out, "Yard or lockup!" Opting for some quiet time, I rose from my cot to close the cell door. But before I could be sealed in, a familiar voice rang out, "Old-timer, get your shoes on and come for a walk."

I stepped out of my cell and peered down at Uncle, who was standing below me on the bottom tier. The irritated guard looked up and yelled, "If you're coming, get your shoes on and close your door. I haven't got all day."

I quickly reached into my cell and grabbed my footwear, then obediently pulled the door shut as ordered.

Once outside, Uncle and I slowly walked around the perimeter of the concrete compound. Most of the prisoners paired off in discussions along the outer fringes, while a young Native lad, about twenty years old, played with a basketball, repeatedly throwing it from one end of the courtyard to the other, trying to make that heroic buzzer ending shot. Each miss brought on a burst of laughter from the other inmates.

For the first forty-five minutes, Uncle talked to me about his grandchildren while I shared with him some of my own children's history. With only fifteen minutes remaining in our yard time, Uncle approached the subject I suspected was on his mind when he first asked me to join him.

"You're close with Reverend Ray and have a lot of faith in God," said Uncle, looking straight ahead, as if speaking to himself. "I wonder if he listens to everyone's prayers?"

Conscious of his Native heritage, I replied, "Yes, you don't have to be sitting in a church to talk to God. He can hear you anywhere, anytime."

We passed underneath the basketball net and the ball boomed off the backboard. Loud jeers and raucous laughter once again acknowledged the missed shot.

Paying little heed, Uncle and I headed back up the courtyard. "He hears all prayers, but sometimes he answers in ways we don't understand. We must have faith in him and leave it in his hands," I said, momentarily reflecting on my own situation.

When we reached the far end of the compound I instinctively reached out and latched onto the basketball that bounced at my feet. I looked up at the young man, who quickly let me know he had deliberately passed me the ball. "See if you can make it," he mocked.

I looked at the distant basket and bounced the ball back to the lad. "If I make it, they'll get on you more than they are now," I replied, looking about the compound at the other inmates.

"Just one, o-okay?" he stammered, hurling the ball back to me.

It was clear the lad was looking for someone else to miss the shot, undoubtedly hoping to ease his injured pride by having someone else bear the burden of the laughter that was raining down on him. I dribbled the ball a couple of times and took the standard stance, but realized I had no chance of reaching the basket with any kind of jump shot. I raised the ball in my right hand, thinking a baseball toss would be more effective, but a painful cramp brought my arm back down.

I was about to bounce the ball back to the young man when a sudden whisper stopped me cold. "*David, throw the ball!*" I shook my head, startled by the inner voice. Then I heard it again. "*Throw the ball underhand, David.*" I looked at Uncle and somehow understood, the shot I was being asked to take was clearly for the benefit of my companion.

I looked to the far end of the court and with a strange confidence focused my eyes on the distant net. I rolled the ball in my hands, took a wide stance, and lowered it between my legs. Then without hesitation I flung the ball skyward and watched with amazement as it arced high above the compound.

With purpose and ease it dropped, *swish*, through the hoop, without touching the rim or disturbing the strings. It bounced off the concrete, echoing a profound, *thump*, across the courtyard, truly the ultimate basket, carried by blind faith alone.

There was a split reaction from the other inmates. I suspected those who remained quiet were considering what kind of response they should display, or simply had not been paying attention. The others yelled and jeered the wide-eyed lad more than they cheered the basket.

Uncle and I continued our walk in silence. As we closed in on the backboard, I noticed my companion look up at the net, lost deep thought.

"Time's up," the guard yelled as he rose from a bench and closed his pocketbook. "Let's go back in."

Back on the cell-block, the young Native lad walked up to me. "Lucky shot!" he whispered.

I smiled and replied, "No, that's what faith will do for you." Over his shoulder I noticed Uncle sitting at one of the tables, talking to Reverend Ray. I looked back at the young man, excused myself, and headed for the sanctuary of my cell.

Chapter 4

Lawyers, Lies, and Legal Aid

On February 4, 1992, I was back in Fernie for my preliminary hearing, according to my lawyer, a proceeding meant only to determine whether there should be a trial. "This is the prosecution's time to put on its case, and our defense will take place at the actual trial -- if there is one!" said Sliva boldly. "When the judge asks if you have anything to say, you tell him that on the advice of your lawyer you will not speak at this time."

One by one, the prosecution's witnesses were called to the stand. First Constable Magnus gave her evidence of finding me huddled at the back door of the police station shortly after the assault. "He did not respond to questions, he appeared dozy and spoke in a very monotone voice," she said. "He was smelling of alcohol and said he wanted to sleep." The constable told the court that she believed I had either overdosed on drugs or consumed an enormous amount of alcohol, and for that reason she took me to the hospital. In cross-examination, my lawyer did not ask her about the remorse I had expressed the following day when she came back to my cell.

Next came a witness who had been standing by the doorway when I staggered out of the apartment that night. He lived upstairs and had heard the noise coming from the victim's downstairs apartment. "Mitchell looked tired and groggy," he stated. "He looked drunk." The witness also testified that everything became quiet for three to five minutes before the victim came out of the apartment and left the building. He informed the court that he then saw me come out of the apartment, moving slowly from one side of the stairs to the other, using the railing and the wall to hold me up. His evidence about the quiet time, supported what I had told my lawyer about stopping the assault and moving away from the victim, letting him go. It also proved that I had not come out on the heels of the victim, a sure indication that I had not chased after him as he left the apartment.

Geri took the stand and said she had called the police from her apartment that night. She testified she had been in Rob's apartment earlier that evening, and was still awake when she heard a commotion. After getting out of bed, she stated she saw me running in front of the apartment block for a few seconds.

When Sliva cross-examined her, he did not ask her to disclose the truth about her affair and did almost nothing to discredit the allegations of abuse that were included in the forensic report. I asked him why he had not questioned her in detail on the matters I had discussed with him; he quietly shushed me, stating he was saving our evidence for the trial.

Rob was the last to take the stand. He told the court he had not met my wife prior to her moving into his apartment block. He did not deny the affair, but testified that it had only started a couple of weeks before he was assaulted. The prosecution then portrayed him as someone who was not involved in any mitigating circumstances or provocation surrounding the case. Rob claimed there was no quiet time during the assault, instead, suggesting he had escaped from my grasp and fled. Despite the fact that his testimony contradicted the prosecution's earlier witness, once again my lawyer did not pursue a vigorous cross-examination.

"The reason you got away was he let you up," Sliva said.

"No! He didn't let me up," Rob shouted nervously. "I was covered in blood. I was soaked. Nobody could've held on to me."

"Yeah," replied Sliva. I shifted uncomfortably at my lawyer's apparent willingness to agree with the witness's interpretation. "But he was on top of you and you were underneath. He had the upper hand. If he wanted to continue, he could have."

"He didn't let me go," Rob shouted back, "I slipped away from him, and..."

Sliva cut in, "At the time you slipped away, he had stopped assaulting you. He was just on you, and you took the brief moment to slip away, and that's what really happened."

I felt uneasy about the fact that Sliva had not made it clear to the court that I had moved away from the victim when I let him go. I also believed he should have pointed out the blatant contradiction between what the victim had just said, and the earlier witness's testimony, which indicated there had been at least a couple of minutes of quiet time before the victim emerged from the apartment.

Sliva once again reassured me that if there were a trial that would be the time to produce our evidence and expose the falsehoods in the victim's testimony.

After all the witnesses had been heard, I followed Sliva's instructions and told the court that, on the advice of my lawyer, I had nothing to say. The judge rose from his chair and adjourned the hearing for ten minutes. When he returned, he ruled there was sufficient evidence to go to trial on the three counts I had been charged with: attempted murder, aggravated assault, and break and enter. He then picked up his gavel, quietly tapped his bench, and dismissed the court.

I was ushered into a witness room for a brief visit with my eight-year-old son, Steven. He jumped into my outstretched arms and squeezed my neck tightly. "Dad, I want you to stay," he murmured sadly. "I want you to stay."

"I have to go away, son," I said sorrowfully, "but when I come back we'll spend a lot of time together, I promise."

Following the tearful farewell, Sliva told me that the doctor who had saw me at the hospital after the assault was willing to go on the record with details concerning my emotional and physical state that night. I was then lead out the back door of the courthouse and returned to KRCC.

On February 14, 1992, Sliva sent a letter to prosecutor, Ron Webb, indicating what the admitting doctor's testimony would be: "At the time of admission he was semi-conscious and lapsing into unconsciousness." Sliva also went on to say that my family doctor had given me a prescription for Temazepam just days before the assault, describing the common side effects of this medication as dizziness, lethargy, drowsiness, confusion, staggering, and falling. Quoting the admitting doctor once again, the letter went on to say that the symptoms described by the witnesses were consistent with the effects of the combination of alcohol and Temazepam on the body.

A few days later I called Sliva from my unit at KRCC. He told me the prosecutor was offering a deal that would see the Crown drop the charges of attempted murder and break and enter, if I pled guilty to aggravated assault. Sliva added that he and Webb had discussed asking the court for a sentence of two years less a day on the assault charge if I accepted the deal.

"George Majic has lots of experience in these matters, and he told me, you should be elated with the offer," Sliva said determinedly.

However, despite this intruding endorsement from my estranged wife's attorney, my frustration over the forensic report determined my response. "Before I agree to anything, I want the false statements in the forensic report stricken from the record," I said.

A week later we talked again. This time Sliva said my demands involving the forensic report were holding up an agreement to the plea bargain, "It's putting to much pressure on me to get that done, and get an agreement as well. I thought it would be better if you could talk with a lawyer who could come up to the prison and see you personally. I've made arrangements with a lawyer in Kamloops, who will be taking over your criminal case. He will be up to see you in a day or two."

With a second bail hearing only a few weeks away, I was stunned by Sliva's quick decision to hand the case over to another lawyer.

"I'll stay on as your family court lawyer and look after your matters here at home," he added, breaking the silence.

The attorney's untimely decision left me with a heightening sense of betrayal and uneasiness. Considering the small-town relationship between Sliva and Geri's family court lawyer, George Majic, I wondered if the latter, the more experienced lawyer in the community, might be trying to influence proceedings in my criminal case, hoping to protect my estranged wife from a more through cross-examination at a trial. In that setting, she would have to answer questions surrounding her affair and explain her allegations of spousal abuse, which were now featured in government documents.

"Never mind. I'll get the new lawyer from Kamloops to look after my family court matters as well," I replied in frustration.

A few days later, my new legal-aid lawyer, Mike Vannier, showed up at the prison. I told him I wanted the false and demeaning allegations in the forensic report exposed and also insisted that he cross-examine the witnesses from the preliminary hearing.

"The other lawyer told me that he and the prosecutor were discussing a sentence of two years less a day on a charge of aggravated assault," I said. "I want you to know, that I will not accept any deal that leaves the impression that I was a wife abuser. I want the forensic report cleared up and I want this man and my wife questioned about what they said on the stand."

Vannier took some notes and quietly responded, "I'll check with the Crown about it, and get a copy of the transcript."

"Check with the psychiatrist at the forensic institute in Port Coquitlam," I replied. "Inquire about the false and misleading statements and the conflicting character portrayal in the report. I'm certain most of the report was written by the social worker and not the psychiatrist at all. And I also need a lawyer for my family court matters. Can you or someone from your firm take that on?"

"I'll check and see what we can do," Vannier answered. "I understand you also have a bail hearing coming up. I will make a request to postpone it until I can get on top of things."

"No!" I shot back sharply. "I don't want it postponed! I want that forensic report questioned and exposed for what it is." I gave the lawyer a determined look and added, "I have the report and we can go over it before the bail hearing."

"All right," he replied, "I will set up a time to come back and discuss it. Hang in there and I'll see you in a few days."

Even though I was still receiving no formal institutional help for my depression, regular talks with Reverend Ray helped lower my level of anxiety at KRCC. I was also careful not to choose sides in disputes amongst other inmates at the prison.

One afternoon, as I was watching television, a group of inmates ushered a frightened prisoner into the enclosed area. They pinned his arms behind his back and one of them quickly ripped into the man's midsection with a thunderous uppercut. Seconds later a sudden overhand right snapped the gagging prisoner's head back. The flock of men then swiftly circled the wounded prisoner, hiding his stooped body while supporting him back to his cell.

32

A few moments later one of the inmates returned. "The guy ran out on a drug deal on the outside. He was being reminded to pay his debts," he said, eyeing me cautiously.

"Tough to get money out of him if he's dead," I replied.

"They won't kill him. He'll just get a few reminders until he lets some people know where they can pick up their money."

"I appreciate the vote of confidence," I said, "but next time ask me to leave...I don't need to see it."

"Okay. Everything's cool then?"

"Everything's cool," I said, covering my tingling nerves with a feigned calmness.

After lockup that night the injured man screamed and begged for his life, even asking the guards for protection. Eventually his wails grew dimmer and I drifted off to sleep. His appeals however, were apparently successful, for the next morning he was gone, and I never saw him again.

Considering the close quarters shared by so many men in prison, it's a wonder there weren't more confrontations taking place on a daily basis. But there was one situation that arose, that quickly showed me how the prison population would join together to condemn another inmate. An elderly man, probably in his sixties, came onto our tier under a cloud of suspicion that he had molested his grandchildren. He was pushed, sworn at, and punched when out on the unit floor. He quickly withdrew, spending most of his time locked in his cell, coming out only for the odd meal. It was obvious that a free society held no monopoly on hatred for this kind of criminal. The general prison population considered sex offenders the scum of the earth and referred to them as "skin-hounds."

I had not made much headway with my new lawyer by the time my appeal for bail began at the end of March. It all began with me being summoned to the prison's admission and discharge area one day, where I was told to stand up against the wall. While only partially concealed from male and female prison staff, I was ordered to drop my pants and lower my underwear to my ankles. The ritual was repeated for the next three days by the sheriffs, who escorted me to the courthouse for the hearing. A stand-in prosecutor, presumably from Kamloops, insisted a trial date could not be arranged before the fall of 1992, and was adamant that I remain in custody until that time.

The thought of spending another six months in prison was a hopeless one, so I was receptive when, on the third day of the bail hearing, my lawyer greeted me outside the prisoner's door on the opposite side of the courtroom.

"The prosecution wants to make a deal," he said enthusiastically.

"What's that?" I asked.

"If you plead guilty to aggravated assault," he replied, "they will drop the other two charges [attempted murder and break and enter]. They will ask for a sentence of two years less a day in exchange for the guilty plea. And they will ask the court to take into consideration time already spent in custody, which is taken into consideration at double time. Sometimes they even consider giving you credit at triple time. If you accept this deal, you will only have to spend a couple more months in custody before you're free on early release. I recommend that you take the deal and get this behind you."

It appeared the prosecution wanted to go ahead with the deal it had been discussing with my first lawyer.

"What about my bail?" I asked.

"If you accept the deal, bail is unlikely because the hearing will be set quickly, probably within a month. But that will give you six and a half months at double time or maybe even triple time. Then there's your early release. You will be out and getting on with your life by the summer at the latest. On top of that they have agreed to edit most of the FPI [Forensic Psychiatric Institute] report as you requested."

The chance to regain my freedom in the near future brought on a predictable response. "Okay, I'm tired of it all," I replied wearily. "Let's get it over with."

When we entered the courtroom, Vannier nodded at the prosecutor, who responded instantly with a slight bobbing of his head.

I stood silently in the prisoner's dock and the clerk summoned the judge, who was informed that I would be pleading guilty to aggravated assault. A sentencing date was set for May 1, 1992, a month away. And as my lawyer had said, bail was denied.

April crept by, until finally, the day before sentencing I was escorted to Cranbrook. Not wanting to put my children through the hurtful process of having their father sentenced in their home town, I had agreed to have the sentencing take place in this larger community that lay sixty miles southwest of Fernie.

However, A growing sense of uneasiness crept through me when I was denied the opportunity to sit at the counsel table with my attorney the following day. The isolation of the prisoner's box, located behind the lawyers, increased my apprehension and shame, but I quickly consoled myself with the thought that I would be getting on with my life soon, maybe even this very day.

Everyone stood as Justice Provanzano entered the courtroom and strode to a huge high-backed chair behind the bench. The Supreme Court justice was adorned in a black robe with a dazzling red sash that made him look regal, yet sinister. I immediately felt like I was about to be sentenced in Darth Vader's private chambers.

The proceedings began and Mike Vannier told the judge that I was pleading guilty to the charge of aggravated assault. Prosecutor, Webb, announced that no witnesses were going to be called. I sat patiently but nervously, waiting for the judge to hand down the agreed upon sentence of two years less a day with added consideration for time served.

Ron Webb addressed the court and immediately went into the prosecution's spin on the case, using the preliminary hearing transcript. I stared at my lawyer's back, unsure what was happening.

The prosecutor submitted photographs of the victim into evidence, along with shots from the crime scene, while highlighting the victim's testimony from the transcript that suggested he had escaped from my grasp that night.

My legal-aid lawyer sat silently while the prosecutor then implied there was no relationship between the victim and my wife, prior to the separation in the marriage.

35

Justice Provanzano then asked Webb if he wanted to deal with the forensic report.

"We can do it now or after my friend has responded to the circumstances," replied the prosecutor.

"Well, we are awfully close to the morning break, and you say you only need about another five minutes," said the judge. "I would suggest this, if you're agreeable. If not, tell me. We'll take our break now, you attend to completing your chore with respect to that report. When you've got it complete -- should I read it sometime before? Should I read it during the break?"

"That would be of some assistance," responded Vanier.

"Would be of some assistance?" Justice Provanzano replied, pausing to eye my lawyer with a look of dumbfoundedness. ..."All right. Give it to the clerk or sheriff and they'll bring it to my chambers, and then give me an opportunity to read it, and then we'll come back in."

After a suspiciously brief break, in which the judge supposedly went over the fifteen page report, court was called back to order. "Yes, I've read the forensic report as edited," said the judge."

"My Lord, I have some responses with respect to circumstances," said Vannier "I can make those now, or just wait until my friend closes his submissions, and then I can just carry through with everything?"

"I understood, at least, perhaps incorrectly, I assumed you were through," said Justice Provanzano, as he glanced back at the prosecutor, "or do you have more?"

"Just as to sentence, your Honour, briefly," answered Ron Webb. "I can advise your Lordship that the Crown is seeking a sentence in the area of four to five years in addition to the time served. That's, in the Crown's submission, on the upper end of an aggravated assault conviction. However, the Crown's position is that the upper end is appropriate given the number of factors in this matter which I will discuss briefly."

I quickly looked toward my lawyer, but Vannier neither stirred nor spoke out about the plea bargain that had been agreed to. I listened in anguish and horror as the prosecutor suggested I had planned and premeditated the assault. And he once again used the preliminary hearing transcripts and the forensic report to portray me as a violent and dangerous human being.

I recalled my first lawyer's words from the earlier preliminary hearing, "*We will hit them hard with the facts at the trial.*" But now there was no way to cross-examine the victim or question him on the prior circumstances, including his harassment of me with his pickup, just a day or two before the assault.

After suggesting I had premeditated the assault, Webb made reference to the FPI report, which highlighted allegations of ongoing assaults against my wife. I stood in stunned silence, waiting for my legal-aid lawyer to defend me. But when the prosecutor finished, Vannier made no attempt to expose the deceitfulness in the forensic report, nor did he go into the depth of my severely depressed emotional state, which was evident at the time of the assault.

I relaxed slightly when he brought to the court's attention my children's statements, telling the court, that they had never seen their father physically touch or harm their mother in any way. But Justice Provanzano's comeback left little doubt about the damning effect the forensic report had left on the case, "Kids are never in the bedroom, though, when he does these things," he snapped back angrily.

My attorney appeared to wilt, hastily agreeing with the court's position that there had been no provocation in the case. He also supported the judge's suggestion that the only mitigating circumstances were the harsh words spoken on the street between Geri and me.

At the end of my so-called defense, Mike Vannier misrepresented another fact by leaving the impression that the victim's threat to use a steel pipe on me, came in response to my breaking out the window of his vehicle. The fact was, it had been the other way around. I nervously spoke out from the prisoner's box, hoping to correct the misleading impression I felt was being created. Webb turned around and looked into the gallery, then turned back and told the judge that Rob and Geri had just shook their heads. His not so subtle inference that I was lying, was all to clear.

Vannier sat silently as Justice Provanzano glared me into silence, while saying he had heard enough.

Disregarding the psychiatrist's conclusion that the assault should be seen as an act of desperation more than an act of malevolence, he gave final support to the deceit and dishonesty that the government prosecutor had brought to the case. "Because of the time of day I will be very brief. I do not intend to recap what I consider to be the factual situation behind this charge of aggravated assault. Counsel have referred to the circumstances sufficiently," he said.

"Let me briefly say the purpose of sentencing in crimes of this nature are to deter the accused and others from committing the same offense, and to serve a useful purpose towards the rehabilitation of the accused, who has been convicted, and for the protection of society. In this particular case, a crime of violence is of the type of crime that indeed society must be protected from. I think that a long term of incarceration is necessary so that he can receive the benefit of psychological and psychiatric help that will be afforded to him in the place where he will be."
[Lisa Hobbs Birnie, a former member of the National Parole Board, wrote in her book *A Rock and a Hard Place (1990):* "With time I came to consider statements, such as 'I am sentencing you to five years in prison where you will receive the psychiatric or psychological counseling that you require,'to be among the most self-deluding words in the English language.]

Justice Provanzano then concluded the sentencing hearing. "So in considering all the circumstances that a sentencing ought to be for, the deterrence of the accused and others, to show the distaste that society has for acts of violence such as this, which shows, in my opinion, a disrespect for human life. The courts ought to do what little they can to bring to your attention – and I think that you are capable as a young man to be able to appreciate the seriousness of your offense and the effect it has, not only on the victim but others closely connected to you -- and to use the sentence for the purpose of rehabilitation for you.

So therefore, I conclude that you be imprisoned for a term of three years and six months. I recommend strongly that you receive all the psychological and psychiatric counseling, and assistance that is available for you in the institution."

The judge stared down from his bench. "Is that everything, gentlemen?"

"Yes, thank you, my lord," replied Vannier.

"Yes," Webb quickly added.

I was led from the courtroom, shocked and shaking at the thought that I would not see my children for the next three and a half years.

That evening I had a phone brought to my cell and made the painful call to my kids. Jeff answered, "Hi Dad! What happened?" he exclaimed with hopeful anticipation upon hearing my voice.

Realizing his mother had not told him what had happened in court, with a heavy heart I told my son that I had been sentenced to three and a half years. There was silence, then tears, "I love you son," I whispered. "Tell Aimee and Steven I love them too." My voice cracked and my fragile emotions kept me from finding calming words of comfort for my son. "Good-bye, Jeff, I'm going to hang up the phone now," I said, breaking down, unable to continue.

"Good-bye, Dad, I love you," Jeff whispered back.

When I was returned to the remand center in Kamloops, an officer at the admission and discharge counter pushed a couple of forms towards me, placing one in front of the other.

"This is a waiver of your right to appeal," he said. "If you sign it we can get you started on your way through this mess."

"But I will be appealing my length of sentence," I replied dejectedly, signing the second document, giving the court such notice.

The officer irritably swooped up the forms. "G and H units are full. You're being assigned to 'A Unit for now," he said stiffly.

'A Unit, better known as "the Hole," is a lockdown unit for unruly prisoners. Three long days passed before I was released from that secure unit and put back in the general prison population. I immediately called Mike Vannier. "When can you come up to the prison and go over what happened?" I said angrily. "I want to appeal my sentence."

"I usually don't do appeals on cases I've lost," replied the lawyer. "I suggest you seek alternative counsel for that, ...Good luck." A sudden click told me I was hanging onto a dead phone.

PART TWO

Chapter 5

Induction into Corrections

Abandoned by my legal-aid attorney, I frantically called legal services, but was shocked to discover they were under no obligation to provide counsel for an appeal. Despite my growing distrust for the justice system, I clung to hope, still believing it would eventually give me legal representation if I showed I was prepared to move forward on my own.

A week later, while I was still making inquiries about setting a court date, a woman from the federal parole service (A segment of the justice system connected to Corrections Canada, and not the National Parole Board) showed up at the prison.

"Have a seat Mr. Mitchell," she said, eyeing me coldly. "I've been reading your file. ...Tell me, when was the first time you beat your wife?"

"I did not beat my wife!" I replied, conveying my disgust at the comment.

"That's not what I read here, Mr. Mitchell. You'll find that things will go much easier for you in this system if you're honest." The lady abruptly closed the file and rose to her feet, "You will be transferred to the Matsqui Penitentiary on the West Coast and go through an induction assessment to determine your security risk and appropriate prison placement. We'll let you know when that will happen. That's all. You can go now!"

A couple of days later, Reverend Ray offered to talk with some of the unit guards and see if he could gather support for any upcoming parole or appeal.

Another three weeks passed before I was loaded onto a bus with several other inmates, all bound for the Lower Mainland. Handcuffed, I sat and tried to picture the place I was headed for, wondering what the next three and a half years held for me.

Feverish whispering and movement interrupted my thoughts. About three seats in front of me an inmate was squatted in the aisle, his pants lowered to his ankles. Not sure what was happening and not wanting to get involved, I quickly turned away and focused on the passing scenery. But it was impossible to shut out the grunting sounds, and a minute later, when a small cheer erupted, I instinctively, and somewhat curiously glanced forward.

The prisoner was back in his seat, unraveling a tightly bound ball of clear plastic. Inside was a substantial amount of tobacco along with a number of cigarette papers and a couple of loose penny matches. He rolled himself a smoke and then passed the pouch to several other inmates who had gathered around. One of them looked in my direction and offered the pouch without saying a word. I hesitated, but only briefly, before stepping forward and taking the bag with a thankful nod. Eagerly, I rolled myself a smoke while putting aside the graphic image of the tobacco's arrival. (I learned a little bit about prison terminology during my imprisonment. This particular means of transporting contraband was known as "hooping it.")

Three hours passed before we rolled out of the Coast Range Mountains and glided into the open fields of the Fraser Valley. Forty-five minutes later my earlier thoughts leaped to life as the Matsqui Institution came into view. Two high fences crowned with razor wire surrounded the perimeter. The large compound had a massive concrete structure towering in the background. Guard towers projecting out from the fence corners caught my eye, as did the pickup trucks patrolling the outskirts.

We pulled up to the outer gate which rolled open immediately, giving us just enough room to lurch forward before the bus came to an abrupt stop in front of a second barrier. I looked back over my shoulder and watched the break in the high fence quickly disappear. Guards completed an exterior check of the bus, then the inner gate slid along the second fence line. The bus lurched forward again, this time passing a recreational yard filled with prisoners. A raucous chant, "Fresh meat!

Fresh meat!" erupted. A mixed reaction of fear and laughter swept through the bus as it turned around and pulled to a stop, next to the unnerving chatter.

We filed into the Mastqui Induction Center, showered, and put on the institution's freshly pressed coveralls. A couple of guards quickly led us up a flight of stairs and onto a dimly lit cellblock. The small slots located in the middle of the massive solid steel doors highlighted the reality of my dismal situation.

"Move it!" hollered one of the guards. I stepped into a cell on the heels of another inmate and the heavy metal door slammed shut.

As a new inductee of the Correctional Service of Canada, I spent my first week and a half at Matsqui, confined to a cell, twenty-three hours a day. The next month was consumed by spending twenty-one hours in lockdown, with the other three hours split between tier time, showers, and yard exercise.

Desperate to get my appeal underway, I made another call to legal services, but I was once again denied counsel.

After six weeks in the cramped quarters, all of it spent double bunked, I was moved downstairs where I was housed with a younger inmate, Ian*, who had gone through the process before me. He asked what I was in prison for, and wanting to assure him that he was not sharing a cell with a sex offender, I briefly told him about my assault.

A few days later I entered the cell to find my cellmate stretched out on his lower bunk, wearing just his briefs. "I made your bed," he said politely.

I glanced up at my top bunk and noticed everything neatly in place. "Thanks," I replied.

"I guess that means you owe me."

I pointed to my tobacco pouch on the desk, "Help yourself."

"I'm not talking about cigarettes," Ian replied as he uncrossed his legs and started rubbing himself through his shorts.

I glanced at my tobacco pouch and then glared back at the hopeful inmate, wishing to make my point clear, "You BETTER be talking about cigarettes!" I shot back harshly.

A look of disappointment and uncertainty leapt onto Ian's face. "Yeah! Yeah!" he whispered meekly.

I later learned that my cellmate had committed a sexual assault, so my earlier concern, that had me being upfront with him about my own situation, had obviously been misplaced.

Ten months had passed since the night of the assault, and my frayed nerves remained on edge. Then late in the afternoon, Friday, August 7, 1992, just after lockup had been called, one of the guards shouted, "Mitchell, come to the barrier!"

I nervously walked up to the locked gate on the cellblock, where I was handed a letter. The return address on the corner of the envelope indicated it was from Geri's lawyer.

I returned to my cell, listening to the sound of cell doors slamming shut, indicating the day's activities had come to an end. I nervously lifted the tab on the already unsealed envelope, flinching at the sound of my own cell-door being locked. My disgust at the prison for illegally opening my legal mail was quickly replaced by horror as I read the document, which said my wife was seeking full custody of our children. It also stated I had twenty days to respond to the order or it would be carried out in my absence. The date on the letter showed it had been written exactly twenty days earlier!

Terrified at the thought of losing some kind of legal bond to my children, I punched the button on the cell intercom and asked the guard if I could make a call to my family.

"The record shows that you have used up your calls. Besides, it's too late," replied the guard.

"I need to call my family so they can get in touch with a lawyer or I'll lose my children," I begged.

"You'll have to wait until Monday. There's a shift change on right now and the administration staff have already gone for the weekend."

The intercom went silent. I was cut off!

Terrified and lost in an increasing world of despair, for the next hour my mind wandered back over the events of the last year, until finally, I hollered out, releasing months of frustration. I picked up the lone chair in the cell and slammed it against the steel door, then pounded the intercom button once more, screaming, "You better get someone down here now or I'll rip this cell apart! All I want is one phone call to my family so they can make sure my rights are looked after!"

My frightened cellmate curled up in the corner of his bunk and an eerie silence swept across the cellblock. Then I heard a distant rumble of boots on metal and concrete, growing louder with every step.

"Move away from the door!" one of the guards barked. I did as ordered and the steel door popped open, slamming angrily against its metal stopper. "Step to the front with your arms above your head!"

I exited the cell, instinctively cushioning a blow from a baton. Six guards decked out in full riot gear pushed me up against the wall and searched vigorously for a weapon. I was then shackled and led back to the upper tier where a nurse eventually greeted me in the interrogation room. Her compassion lowered my anxiety, which included her assurance that I would be allowed to make the call I had asked for. She also made the point that I should place it to one of my brothers, realizing a call in my present state would upset my mother.

"All I have wanted is to have some doctor, or someone to talk with about all this," I said, finally breaking down. "When are they going to give me someone to talk to?"

"A psychiatrist will be in to see you in the morning," the nurse replied.

"Let's go!" hollered one of the guards.

I moved to the door where I was nudged across the hall into an isolation cell known as the Hole. A few minutes later a phone was passed through the food slot and I called my brother, Donald, in Northern Alberta. I informed him about the letter and asked him to get in touch with a family court lawyer who could help.

After the call I slowly lowered myself onto a mattress that lay atop a piece of plywood, only fractionally raised off the concrete floor. Emotionally drained, I drew my knees up to my chin and hugged my legs, pulling them tight against my chest. A short while later my tobacco pouch was gratefully passed through the slot.

That night I teetered on the edge of insanity. Inhaling one cigarette after another, I found myself crying uncontrollably one moment and laughing hysterically the next. When the breakfast cart arrived in the morning, I asked for a coffee, rolled another cigarette, and continued to wait patiently for the doctor. The morning passed and the day moved into the late afternoon, until finally, a guard peered through the slot in my cell door.

"Mitchell, you want to go to the yard?" he asked. Unable to raise a sound loud enough to speak, I responded with a gentle nod.

Two guards paraded me onto the roof of the prison -- not exactly the yard I had expected. I shielded my eyes from the bright sunlight and stared at three cages that were invisible from below, hidden by the prison walls that rose a dozen feet above the roof compound.

"Straight ahead," said one of the guards.

I shuffled into the cage in front of me and the gate slammed shut. Like a trained animal, I stood waiting for the crack of a whip, but none came. I tilted my head upward and squinted at some sauntering white clouds that floated lazily across an otherwise bright blue sky. Overhead, heavy wire mesh sealed me in.

I leaned against the concrete wall and slid to the floor, closed my eyes, and searched desperately for that kinder, gentler world I had once known. But try as I did, it eluded me; instead a thousand eyes pierced my soul, a thousand more stared through the wire, waiting for me to perform.

"BOOOOM...BOOOOMMMM!!"

The ear shattering sound rumbled across the concrete floor, shaking it violently. Exhausted, I surrendered and curled into a fetal position, succumbing to the dismal world of graying shadows.

I continued to drift, lost in time and space, until a woman's voice screamed out, pulling me back to the present, "We have to get him back inside, NOW!"

Moments later I felt myself shuffling across the prison roof, leaning heavily on guards who were supporting me under each arm. The words of the psychologist at the Forensic Institute broke through the fading light overhead. "Write everything down, everything you feel, everything you're thinking." The distant words from the past halted my frightening tumble into darkness, and I whispered hoarsely, "I need a pen and some paper!" The following day I wrote my first diary notes.

> Sunday, August 9th, 1992. I have spent the last couple of days in a cell, alone. I have had this time alone to hurt, to be angry, to laugh and to cry. A lot of it I don't understand. But tonight I have come to the conclusion that what I am angry about the most is that my story has not been told. It seems that along the way, for one reason or another, this side of the story has been one that no one wants to deal with.

I was transferred back to the lower cell-block after a few days, where a man in civilian clothes, whom I later recognized as a guard, called me into a meeting. He sternly admonished me for what he saw as my lack of strength, while telling me that the system was going to break me down and make a brand new man out of me.

Later that day I was out in the yard, thinking about my earlier and somewhat confusing meeting, when suddenly, a familiar roar broke through the peaceful sky overhead. I looked up, recalling the frightening sound I had heard just a few days before. Fighter jets from the Blue Angels streaked low over the institution, performing their maneuvers for the Abbotsford International Air Show.

> Thursday, Aug. 13, 1992. I have just gotten out of bed to write down what I know to be the truth about the way I feel. For a long time now since the assault I have been scared and confused as to why. I still don't seem to have the answer yet but I'm sure that in my talks with the doctors or others who are going to help me, that we will figure it out.

During my stay at Matsqui I kept up my diary, usually writing in the dark, late at night. I was eventually interviewed by a psychologist, and I informed him that I was writing down my thoughts. He replied, "I don't need to read them. It's to easy for someone to write down what they want others to believe. We'll just talk."

I met with Dr. Lawson two or three times during the four months I spent at Matsqui. Each interview lasted about half an hour and turned out to be nothing more than interrogation and assessment sessions, designed to gain support for the justice system's portrayal of their criminal case.

It was during one of these meetings that I first heard the word "victim" used to identify my wife. Dr. Lawson appeared to be fixated on getting me to go along with his interpretation that Geri had been severely traumatized and victimized by my assault on Rob. I told the doctor that my entire family, and hers, had been traumatized by everything that had happened, but at the same time I made it clear she had not been victimized in the manner suggested by the forensic report.

Sun Evening Aug. 16 / 92. I was forty years old when all this started and already so much time has gone by. Why can't I talk to someone and get everything OK and get started again. This is my life I am fighting for, not someone else's. I don't think the system really cares. When we are ready and able, we will get to you. In the meantime my life slips farther away. I am beginning to believe my appeal is my only hope. I hope my family can get a date set soon.

I am beginning to believe that the system or the establishment is more corrupt than the rest of society. The deceit, manipulation and dishonesty they have shown is as bad as I have ever seen. Maybe honesty, compassion and straight forwardness is not a part of society anymore, but sneakiness, underhandedness and deceit is what it's all about.

Friday Aug. 21 / 92. It is now lock up in the afternoon and it appears like I will be seeing no one to talk to this week. This has got me down a bit again, it is frustrating to have my life seem so unimportant to these people who are supposed to be helping. Something is wrong with a system that has someone wasting a year of their life because no one can or has the time to help.

Wed Aug. 26 / 92 (My 42nd birthday). I must be patient and understand that no matter when I get the chance to start again, that I will get that chance. I am sorry and regret what happened on that night in Oct. I cannot turn back the clock and must continue to focus on what's ahead and work towards the goals that I set for myself.

My last entry at the induction center was on September 5, 1992.

I feel like I am being led wherever these doctors and caseworkers want to lead me. I feel like they steer and manipulate me into saying what they want me to say. This is confusing and hard to understand.

Shortly after this last entry, one of the inmates I'd known at KRCC, came to my cell. "Did you hear what happened in the appellant court with Uncle?" he asked excitedly.

"No," I answered. "What happened?"

"He's free! His lawyers found a deathbed confession signed by some other guy. It had been buried in government files and the prosecution had withheld it, using the excuse that the guy was now dead and could not be questioned. ...So, the court overturned Uncle's conviction and set him free!"

I smiled and quietly thanked God for a basket from heaven!

Chapter 6

Minimum Security, Maximum Abuse

On September 8, 1992, I was approved for placement at a minimum-security camp. "You can leave today, but that means there won't be time to go over the assessment," said Karen*, one of three correctional officers assigned to my case. "If you want to stay and go through it with everyone, including the psychiatrist, it'll take about two weeks. ...But, you might want to consider the possibility; if you stay, and the discussion does not go well, you could lose your placement and your level of security could be raised."

"I've heard people talk about Ferndale," I said, excited and seeing no reason to suspect a problem. "It seems to be the place where most people want to go."

"It's only a step away from early release. And the institution has a golf course, and tennis courts. And you'll also receive day passes into the community!"

Without hesitation, I accepted the offer and gathered my belongings together. Two hours later I was called off the cell-block. "Mr. Mitchell, I have your report," Karen* offered pleasantly, "We've sealed it and the guard will leave it with case management at Ferndale."

"That's fine," I answered impatiently.

"Okay!" Karen* said, showing me a widening smile, "Follow me."

"Ferndale, eh?" said the waiting guard as we stepped outside. "I don't see any need for restraints. Jump in!"

I climbed into the passenger side of the pickup and a half-hour later we made a sharp turn up an open driveway, entering an area that looked more like a municipal park than a prison. My eyes darted back and forth from the golf course that lay on one side of the narrow roadway, to the treed picnic area and tennis courts on the other. I stared curiously at the simple chain-link fence surrounding the grounds and wondered if we were in the right place.

The guard pulled to a stop, adjacent to the first building. "We're here. Bring your stuff into the duty office and I'll hand over your papers."

Spellbound, I followed my escort into the building, where a man behind the counter handed me a key. "Your room's in the first trailer across the road."

After spending almost a year behind solid steel doors, it was not easy to grasp the idea of being able to come and go as I pleased. But I was not about to question this turn of events, which also included unrestricted access to several phones.

I immediately contacted the court registry for information about my appeal date, and was surprised, but not shocked to learn that the courts had made the request that I now be given a lawyer. An unsolicited recommendation from another inmate resulted in my calling Philip Derksen, a lawyer from the nearby community of Abbotsford. He readily agreed to handle my case and indicated he would come out to the prison and talk with me in a week or two.

The next day I was summoned to the administration building.

"Take a seat, Mr. Mitchell. I am Deputy Warden Glen Cross, and I would like to introduce you to some of the people who will be involved with you during your stay at Ferndale."

I nervously seated myself in the vacant chair at the end of the large conference table and eyed the dozen or so prison staff who stared back curiously. After the first few introductions, the deputy warden's voice suddenly became more determined, "Next is Carter Alexander. Carter is your case manager, and will be setting up an appointment to see you in a few days."

I focused on the man sitting a few chairs away. Our eyes locked onto one another, but as quickly as his hard forced smile appeared, it vanished, and the case manager avoided further eye contact.

The last man introduced was in charge of the works program. I was told to report to him the following morning for my work assignment. It didn't appear that I'd be dealing with any of the other staff members on a regular basis.

"Do you have any questions at this time?" Glen Cross concluded.

"No," I answered politely.

"Good, you're free to leave," he replied briskly.

A few days after I had settled into a daily work routine at the institution, doing grounds maintenance, my name rang out over the loudspeaker. "Mitchell, report to the case management building."

Carter Alexander greeted me with a cold chill that shook me as we headed down the hall to his office. "Have a seat," he said, and handed me the Matsqui Induction Center's assessment report.

Almost immediately I realized I was holding yet another degrading and dehumanizing document that portrayed me as a violent psychological misfit and someone who was living in denial of his bad character.

"I've been reading your file and it doesn't look good," said Carter. It shows a lifelong history of violence, including assaults on your wife, ...so, before you have any chance at parole, you will have to complete some courses." The case manager, who had been averting my stare, now looked directly at me. "Due to your relatively short sentence you are eligible for a parole hearing in November, but I think you should postpone the hearing for a few months, at least until you finish these programs."

The idea of putting off my release did not appeal to me, but I remained quiet, sensing Carter had more to say. "Unfortunately for you," he continued, "...one course you need to take, has already been in progress for two weeks, and won't be available for another four months. I also see that you're appealing your length of sentence, and I don't see any point in you entering other programs at the institution until that is settled. However, there is one I have recommended, and want you to start right away, a family violence program that you would attend outside the institution."

"I never assaulted my wife throughout our marriage," I replied, showing my frustration.

"You will have to sign a form that shows you have asked to take the program, and we will begin that after your appeal," said Carter, ignoring my intrusion. "Of course, that's only if your appeal is unsuccessful and you're still here."

Tired of being pushed aside, I leaned forward and closed the distance between us, "I don't believe the family violence program is necessary. It was almost a twenty-year relationship between the children's mother and myself, and there was only one slap by each of us during that entire period. I want you to know I don't agree with a lot of what's been written in these reports, and most of the forensic report was supposed to've been edited out at the sentencing hearing. And for me to sign something that indicates I asked to take that course would give some validity to what these people have written, and I won't do that. I assaulted the man she was involved with, not her!" I said more emphatically.

"Well as long as you're appealing your length of sentence, there will be no other programs you can take, or that you can complete, either before your appeal or before your first parole hearing." Carter closed the file. "That's all. I'll call you when we need to talk again."

"I just want you to understand that I am willing to take any course you want me too, but I will not sign anything that could be used to support what these people said."

"Well, you have to sign the forms that say you are asking for the program. That's the way the system works!" Carter said angrily, rising from his chair. "I've got other work to do now, so I'll make arrangements for your CO2 [assistant correctional officer] to see you in a few days. That'll be all. You can leave!"

It was now clear to me why the assessment team at Matsqui had shuffled me out of the institution without going over the report.

A few days later, Virginia Deardon summoned me to the duty office and introduced herself as my CO2. She suggested that I apply for escorted day passes that would allow me to leave the institution. "These passes look good in the eyes of the National Parole Board," Virginia offered helpfully.

I signed the application and handed it back to her. "It would be nice if we could have a chat and get to know each other a little better," she said pleasantly, then invited me into a nearby office. After some initial pleasantries, she opened a folder on her desk and informed me she had been reading my file.

"I notice in here, that it shows you have a past history of inflicting physical and emotional abuse on your wife. Do you want to tell me about it?"

I sighed. "There was one slap and a push early in the marriage."

"Well your file indicates there was much more to it than that!" she retorted. "But I want to know about the emotional abuse. Did you ever have arguments with her?"

"I'm not sure what you mean," I replied. "If you're asking me if we ever argued or had disagreements, the answer is yes. We had those times like any other couple. Not a lot, and when we did it was most often about finances. But they were not violent arguments."

I cursed my lawyer and the Crown prosecutor under my breath, and then added, "We might not have been the *Leave it to Beaver* family, but I don't believe there are many families that don't have some arguments along the way."

Virginia popped out of her chair and angrily straightened her arms, supporting herself on the desk. "That's abuse, Mr. Mitchell! Arguing is ABUSE! ARGUING with your wife is ABUSIVE BEHAVIOR! It's called SPOUSAL ABUSE, Mr. Mitchell. You just admitted you yelled at her! Why don't you just own up to the ABUSE!" she screamed.

Her outburst caught me off guard and my sudden surprise quickly turned to anger. "I never said I yelled at her. You indicated that!" I shot back. "And if you look at what the psychiatrist from the forensic institute said, you'll see that I avoided as much conflict in my marriage as possible. I don't know where you're coming from," I said, now bolting out of my chair as well. "I was told you people were going to listen, and help me get some of these things straightened out, but I don't see that happening."

I opened the office door and headed for the main exit. "What's the matter, Mr. Mitchell?" hollered Virginia as I moved through the outer office. "Can't stand the conflict, so you're walking away again, as always?" Ignoring her comment, I opened the main door and stepped outside.

A week later my request for an escorted pass was denied. Carter summoned me to his office, where he showed me a monthly progress summary report he had written. It indicated I had been physically and emotionally abusive towards my wife over a number of years.

"That's garbage!" I shouted.

Carter smiled. "Well, your pass was not granted because you've refused to sign up for any courses that will reduce your threat to the public. On top of that, you've shown a bad attitude by refusing to talk with your case management team. You walked out of a meeting with Virginia the other day." Carter's smirk widened into a grin. "Is there anything else you want to talk to me about, Mr. Mitchell?" he asked suggestively.

I sensed Carter wanted to talk about signing forms -- specifically, one that would show I had put in a request to take the family violence program. I ignored his implied suggestion and answered, "I have not refused to talk to either you or Virginia. I will gladly talk anytime you ask me to."

"Good-day, Mr. Mitchell," said Carter dryly.

Frustrated and disillusioned, I abandoned further attempts to call upon my case management team for help, instead seeking comfort with thoughts of my appeal.

I understood the prosecution had used the less-than-honest character assassination in the forensic report to support their case. And I was convinced Marc Leblanc had written most of that report. The problem was, the psychiatrist's signature gave it some authority.

I looked through the phone book and came up with an office number for Dr. Dilli. I hastily dialed the number and asked to speak with the doctor. A few seconds later a familiar voice came across the line, "Yes, can I help you?"

"Hello," I replied. "Doctor, this is David Mitchell calling. If you remember, I saw you about a year ago over at the forensic institute."

"Ah, yes, yes, I remember," Dr. Dilli responded. "How are you doing?"

"Well, not so well right now. I'm at the Ferndale Institution."

"Oh," said the doctor quietly.

"I am calling about the forensic report that was done on me while I was in Port Coquitlam. The report has your signature on it, but it appears that someone else wrote it."

"Did you read the summary and conclusion?" asked Dr. Dilli firmly.

"Yes, I have no problem with it. In fact, I believe you were pretty much right on," I replied. "It is the rest of the report I'm having some trouble with."

"I did not write the rest of the report. It was done by the social worker. I will only take responsibility for the summary and conclusion of that report," hastily replied the doctor. I caught my breath as Dilli continued, "Did you hear what I said? If you want to discuss the rest of the report you will have to talk to the social worker."

"I understand," I said, regaining my voice. "Did any of my legal-aid lawyers, the courts, or anyone ever contact you about the report?"

"No, no one, I've never talked to anyone. No one called me."

With my suspicions confirmed, I thanked the doctor and hung up the phone.

It was now near the end of September, and Philip Derksen, my new legal-aid lawyer, came out to the institution. After I gave him a brief outline of the case, he told me he would arrange for a court date at which time an appeal date would be established.

Because of my growing distrust of the government's legal-aid program, I informed him I wanted to be present during the application. He agreed, and a couple of days later his office called to let me know the hearing was scheduled for the next morning, and that I should be prepared to be escorted to court.

The next morning, dressed up in my best clothes, I waited in the duty office for the sheriffs to arrive. After an hour had passed, with no one in sight, I called the lawyer's office and was told he had already left.

I waited another hour before reluctantly retreating to my room, unsure what problem had arisen. Late that afternoon I called the lawyer again, hoping to catch him in his office at the end of the day. His secretary put me through, and Derksen immediately told me how surprised he was that I had not been brought to the courthouse. He then told me the court had turned down my request to attend the appeal.

"On what grounds?" I asked in dismay.

"Well, they didn't say specifically," he replied. "But it's common practice that the appellant is not present under these circumstances."

Uttering my disgust, I hung up the phone and early the next morning called the court registry. I asked why I had not been brought into court, and demanded to know why my request to be present at my appeal had been denied. The clerk was non-committal, avoiding any direct response, adding only, that the date of the appeal had been set for late October. I immediately called Derksen's office and dismissed him, then called the legal-aid office and demanded new counsel.

"We're not obligated to give you any further legal representation because you took it upon yourself to dismiss a lawyer who had already agreed to represent you," responded the legal aid worker, somewhat curtly.

Suspicions about my legal assistance, or lack of, continued to grow, as did my determination. I quickly set about preparing my own case. I contacted Reverend Ray at KRCC, who told me one of the unit guards had written a letter of support for my appeal. Ray said he had mailed it to me, along with a letter of his own, that he had sent to the National Parole Board.

Wanting yet more support, I thought an honest medical diagnosis would help offset the less than flattering innuendo that had started accumulating in the government file. I went to Carter and informed him that I wanted to speak with a psychologist.

"I can't do that as long as you have an appeal before the courts," snapped Carter. "Besides, the psychologists are booked solid with inmates, who we know will be around long enough to benefit from their help." After a deliberate pause the case manager continued, "And you should know, I've also gone back over your file. I'm recommending that you be enrolled in the living without violence program." Carter flashed me another one of his wide challenging grins.

"Well," I replied, "I've already told you, I will not refuse to take any program you put me in."

"I've got the form right here," replied Carter. "If you sign it today, you can have it completed in time for your parole hearing."

"I told you before that I will not sign any forms that'll support what these people have put on the record in my case. If you want me to take the program, enter me into it!"

"I told you, that's not how it works, ...Good-day!" shouted an infuriated Carter Alexander.

A few days later I was called to the duty office and a staff member handed me another one of Carter's progress summary reports, telling me it needed my signature. The report again portrayed me as a violent, anti-social misfit. I slashed across the report with a pen, crossing out many of the demeaning statements, while inserting remarks, questioning the report's integrity.

"You can't do that!" the duty officer screamed.

"I just did! It's garbage. And he knows it," I replied angrily, pushing the document back across the counter without signing it.

On October 6 I was once again standing in the duty office, when a notice on the bulletin board caught my attention. New Directions, a vocational testing and counseling service was conducting a session at the prison, and the notice indicated that it was just about to start. I hurried over to the classroom, where an enthusiastic young woman, Yvonne Hopp, introduced herself, and then set a lengthy multiple-choice questionnaire on top of my desk. When I was finished, she said she would get back to me with the results in a week or two.

60

The following day I realized some time had passed since I had talked to Reverend Ray, so I asked Carter about the mail I was expecting.

"Yes, we got a letter from Kamloops, that was mailed to case management. I have it on file," said Carter.

"I want the letter," I replied, trying to hold back my anger. "It's mine. I know it was addressed to me, and for you people to hold it is wrong."

"It's case management's letter and we will keep it in our files!" yelled Carter. "Maybe there were two letters and yours got lost."

I walked over to the administration building, and without mentioning my conversation with Carter, I asked the secretary in the front office if she had received a letter from Kamloops, which had been addressed to me. She innocently informed me that there had been one letter taken by case management, that had my name on it. I went back and confronted Carter, who had remained outside, puffing on a cigarette. "I just talked with administration and they said there was only one letter, and it had my name on it!"

"I believe the letter was intended for case management," snapped Carter.

"Can I see it?" I asked.

Carter hesitated, then replied, "I'll go get it and bring it out for you to look at, but you can't have it."

A few minutes later the case manager reappeared, clinging tightly to the letter while holding it up for me to read, "To Whom It May Concern." offered an open invitation at the top. Underneath, the author quickly made the point that he did not perceive me as a threat to anyone, suggesting that further incarceration beyond the time I had already served would be unnecessary. The letter was signed by one of the unit officers from the Kamloops Regional Correctional Center.

Carter folded up the letter, smiled, and disappeared back into the case management building without saying a word.

I immediately called Reverend Ray, who confirmed that he had mailed the letter to me, with "C/O DAVID MITCHELL" clearly written on the envelope.

The following day I confronted Marilyn McNeil, the woman who headed the Ferndale case management group. "Case management has a letter of mine and I would like it back," I demanded.

"The letter was addressed, 'To whom it may concern," she said in defense of the theft. "It concerned case management, therefore we had the right to keep it. Besides, we just sent it back to Kamloops."

My frustration at the correctional service hit new heights, and I promptly contacted Prison Legal Services, a government-funded society with a mandate to help inmates with legal problems. After telling me there was nothing they could do, it was suggested that I get in touch with the correctional investigator's office. I did so, and two women from that Government funded office came into the prison a few days later.

I was called into a meeting with one of the investigators and hastily went over the recent events.

"There really is nothing I can do," she responded, "because the institution will just deny it."

"I know if you just ask them about it, they will deny it! You're an investigator -- let's go and investigate," I said irritably. "Let's start with the letter from Kamloops. I will go with you over to the case management building. We can talk to Carter and the head of case management. Then we can go over to the administration building and talk with the secretary who told me they took the letter. Then we can call Reverend Ray in Kamloops."

The woman's face turned red. "DON'T TELL ME HOW TO DO MY JOB! YOU HAVE NO PROOF, IT'S YOUR WORD AGAINST THEIRS!"

My anger and frustration quickly surfaced. "I must have watched the wrong movies. I always thought the investigator went out and investigated to find proof," I said with deliberate sarcasm

62

"That will be all, Mr. Mitchell! If we need to talk to you again, we know where to find you."

"With those skills, only if they don't transfer me," I mumbled, heading for the door, leaving the open-mouthed investigator gasping.

The next day I was summoned to the administration building and the secretary directed me to the warden's office. I knocked, and a quiet voice on the other side invited me in. I opened the door and almost stepped into a desk that was far too large for the small room. Behind it sat Warden Dillon, who appeared to be quiet and reserved. He maintained a low profile at the institution, going about his administrative duties while leaving the more hands-on job of running the prison to his assistant, Glen Cross. Warden Dillon motioned to a chair.

I had just gotten settled, when a cursory light tap on the warden's door preceded it's opening, curiously, without any response from the warden.

I looked up uncertainly as Glen Cross and Carter Alexander stepped into the crowded office. They both smiled and pulled up chairs, seating themselves next to me.

"I assume you know what this meeting is all about, Mr. Mitchell," said Warden Dillon calmly.

"I assumed it was about the opening and theft of my mail," I replied hesitantly, "and the correctional investigators who were here the other day?"

I looked curiously at the other two men. Carter Alexander glared at me, "I believe the letter was meant for case management. And besides, I don't believe the letter reflects your bad attitude at this institution," he blurted.

Deputy Warden Cross then made his presence felt. "Mr. Mitchell has written all over some of Mr. Alexander's progress summary reports and also refuses to sign them."

Cross gave me a sinister glance, and then looked back at Warden Dillon. "Mr. Mitchell is becoming a very difficult inmate and we believe a transfer to higher security should be considered."

Before anymore could be said, Dillon took back control of the meeting. "I don't see anything that would warrant a transfer to higher security...at this time," he said as he looked at me. "Now, let's get back to this mail issue. Mr. Mitchell, I like to have these kinds of disputes settled within the institution." He frowned and leaned forward in his chair. "As far as this letter from Kamloops goes, I have not had the opportunity to speak to the head of case management yet. She is away from the institution for a few days and I will speak to her when she returns. We are all sympathetic to your case Mr. Mitchell, and want to see you get out of these institutions and on with your life. I suggest that you attempt to work more closely with your case management team in the future and gain their support for your parole. That's all. You can go now."

As I feared, the visit by the correctional investigator's office had no effect on the conduct of case management. My mail continued to be opened and read, including some legal correspondence from the courts. But none of it mattered to these people. They were the law. They made the laws. They owned the law! Whenever they wanted something changed, they could easily change the law. They wrote the rules and regulations and applied them as they wished. And when there were no rules or regulations, they simply made them up.

Frustrated and losing hope, I filed for a change in case management.

On October 20, Len Fox, an MLA I knew personally, and had been someone whom I had earlier contacted for help, kept his word and wrote a letter of support that I could take to my parole hearing. After I informed Carter about the letter, he summoned me to the duty office, and to my surprise, showed some compassion. He left me with the impression that he never believed what he had written in the progress summary reports, stating he had to stand by his words, only because he had not had time to get to know me better.

"Then why all the garbage Carter?" I asked, "Why has this system felt the need to label me as it has?" Carter sighed in resignation, but in the end, his offer was the same. Carter asked me to drop my appeal and postpone the parole hearing. Once again I declined.

The following day, Yvonne Hopp, the woman from New Directions, returned with my evaluation, telling me she had also given a copy to case management. I thanked her and went back to my room to read the evaluation and her recommendations.

The report indicated I had a variety of career possibilities, including counseling, where my strong social and service-oriented interest patterns would be useful. The assessment portrayed me as sensitive, insightful, and understanding, someone who held a warm attitude towards the work place, while having a strong ability to engage in verbal and written communication.

The second half of the assessment showed an average score on the self-control scale and indicated I was cautious, responsible, and demonstrated care and commitment to others.

The report ended with a recommendation that I pursue a career in counseling, concentrating on working with youth, social services clients, or drug and alcohol clients.

I thought the idea of pursuing a career in counseling was interesting. I knew I would enjoy the challenge, and the work, but how could I pursue such a goal under my present circumstances?

As I mulled over the assessment, Carter's angry voice exploded through the prison speakers. "MITCHELL, report to the case management building IMMEDIATELY!"

"Sit down," he growled as I stepped into his office. "I have received an assessment report from New Directions. Who told you to take that assessment? I never gave you instructions to take that! Don't ever do anything like that again unless I give you permission."

"I'm sorry," I said. "I saw the notice on the bulletin board and assumed it was for anyone who wanted to take it. I thought it'd show what programs I should, or should not be taking."

"It doesn't help anything!" Carter shouted. "It's of no use at all, and don't do it again! That's all. You can leave now."

"What you're angry about is the fact that this assessment contradicts what you people have written," I said defiantly, leaving Carter mumbling under his breath.

A couple of hours after leaving Carter's office and the case management building behind, I was summoned to the duty office. "You're being transferred back to Kamloops," said Bill Kinnar, one of Ferndale's chief administrators. He peered mischievously at me over the rims of his bifocals. "You're to be a witness in a murder trial."

"I don't know anything about any murder," I said, horrified at the suggestion that I knew anything about such a matter.

"Well, you'll have to take that up with the people who summoned you to court. The sheriffs will escort you tomorrow morning."

I edged out of Bill Kinnar's office, leaned against the wall, and slowly bent over at the waist, numbed by this latest turn of events. A psychiatric nurse, a women by the name of Heather, noticed my uncomfortable state and stopped to ask what was wrong. Still trying to get my breath and unable to answer, Heather directed me into an open office across the hall.

The turmoil of the last year, combined with a growing confusion over the conduct of my justice system had pushed me to the edge. I was on the verge of snapping, and Heather sensed it. She kept her distance, giving me room to breathe and release some of the tension. I let out a sigh, and just as I was about to suck in a breath of air, my ears picked up a scuffing sound behind me.

I looked at the nurse. "Someone's listening outside the door," I said quietly.

"Just a minute," Heather said as she quickly moved towards the door.

Realizing he had been discovered, our eavesdropper began a hasty retreat, but he was too late. Heather stepped into the hall. "Carter, I want to talk to you!" she hollered.

They disappeared out of earshot and five minutes passed before the nurse stepped back into the office and closed the door. Heather then informed me that I had been summoned by a defense attorney, to testify about whether or not I had seen his client talk with one particular inmate while I was at KRCC, something I could not testify to conclusively, one way or the other.

I walked the grounds that evening, brooding about what was going to take place over the next couple of days. As I was moving doggedly along the wood-chip path, I noticed another employee from New Directions pulling into the institution's parking lot. Elizabeth Gavin had talked with me about post-secondary schooling shortly after I had arrived at Ferndale. This evening she called me into a meeting, and asked if I would be willing to take another evaluation.

"Why?" I asked in bewilderment, recalling Carter's reaction to the last New Directions report.

Elizabeth glanced over my shoulder at the closed door. I sensed some fear in her voice as she hesitantly responded, not answering my question, but hinting that more was going on than I realized. "David, I'm very concerned about what is going on. These people play for real and they are not happy with you. I'm afraid for you, and this trip to Kamloops scares me." Elizabeth leaned closer, this time speaking just above a whisper. "I'm afraid something is going to happen to you and you will not be coming back!"

An icy chill shook me violently. "I don't understand. Are you saying my life is in danger?"

"I don't know," she answered. "I'm just very afraid something's going to happen."

Without another word I walked outside and stared aimlessly at the multitude of stars that brightened the clear night sky. I buttoned up my light summer jacket, only to realize it was not the evening air that had me shivering.

It was the last week of October 1992. A full year had passed since the assault. I stepped into a nearby phone booth and called my oldest brother, Tom, in New York State, desperate to hear a voice I could trust.

As ordered, I was waiting at the duty office the next morning when the sheriffs arrived. I was handcuffed and loaded into the front cage of the van, joining three inmates from other institutions. I pushed up against a steel mesh barrier that separated us from two juvenile offenders in the back.

The first hour of the trip was relatively quiet. I had just started to relax as best I could, when one of the youths hollered, "I know who you are!"

We all turned and looked in the direction of the sudden outburst. The young lad was pointing his finger at me. "You're the guy who molested your children. Skin-hound! Skin-hound!" he yelled.

I sat frozen in horror, my heartbeat accelerating as I glanced at the other four inmates, whose eyes were fixed coldly on mine. I knew I had to defuse the situation quickly. Even if nothing were to happen in the van, there certainly would be trouble on the unit once we got to KRCC.

I turned to the young offender. "You had better get your facts straight before you make those kind of statements!" I hollered. "If you need to know, I assaulted a man who was involved in an affair with my wife."

"That's not what I was told," the lad replied.

I stared at the youth in disbelief, and then astonishment, as another thought rushed through my mind: Setup!

"Who told you that?" I blurted out angrily. A look of uncertainty and fear leapt across the young man's face, and he pulled back from the barrier without saying another word. Beneath us, the steady drone of tires on pavement highlighted the unnerving silence that now filled the van.

About a half-hour out of Kamloops the van stopped at a highway pullout, and waiting sheriffs whisked the two youths away to a nearby provincial prison camp.

I now understood Elizabeth's fear, and her warning that these people played for real. It was as clear, and paralyzing as the cold mountain air outside.

After the admission procedures at KRCC were taken care of, we were sent to our assigned cell-blocks. Fortunately, I was housed on one of the units where I had spent some of my time prior to sentencing. I talked to a couple of inmates who had knowledge of my case, and they helped set the record straight with the new prisoners from the van, who had also come onto the cell-block with me.

Reverend Ray got word that I was back in the institution and we talked about the letter he had mailed me. Ray said he would try to find out what had happened to it, adding that he was not aware of its return to KRCC.

My trips to the courthouse as a witness started almost immediately, as did my humiliation. Every morning for the next week, sheriffs ordered me to lower my pants and underwear, often in view of correctional staff, both male and female. After some degrading probing and spreading, I was handcuffed and driven downtown, where I was locked in a holding cell in the basement of the Kamloops courthouse.

I spent ten or twelve hours in isolation every day without speaking to, or seeing anyone, including the lawyer who had summoned me to court. The routine never changed. For lunch, a hot meat pie would be slid under the bars, and in the evenings I would be handed a small lunch bag before being taken back up the hill to spend the night at KRCC.

At the end of the week I called the defense attorney, who told me he no longer planned to call me as a witness. He then said he had relayed that information to the sheriff's office a few days earlier. I immediately confronted the prison officials, and my daily trips to the courthouse stopped. However, I remained in lockdown at the provincial prison for another two weeks, given one excuse after another as to why I wasn't being returned to Ferndale.

I then received notice that my appeal had been postponed. Suspiciously, this news was followed with another notice, stating I would be escorted back to the coast the following day.

The message was loud and clear: PLAY THE GAME, MR. MITCHELL, OR WE WILL MAKE YOUR LIFE HELL AND THERE IS NOTHING YOU CAN DO ABOUT IT.

I arrived back at Ferndale in the evening, and despite the late hour, my case management team greeted me in the duty office. Carter and Virginia suggested I cancel the appeal and delay my parole hearing as well. "It'll give you time to complete the family violence program," Virginia said, flicking me a sadistic a smile.

I let her remark slide and focused my attention on Carter. "Tell me, who told those kids that were on that trip to Kamloops, that I had molested my children?"

Carter smiled. "I don't know what you're talking about. We have no record of you molesting your kids."

I rose from my chair. "Carter, I will not ask for a postponement of my parole hearing, nor will I cancel my appeal! ...And by the way," I said, "I received confirmation that the letter from Kamloops was mailed specifically to me!"

Carter stiffened but did not reply as I stepped through the open doorway and disappeared.

The following morning I was summoned back to the duty office. This time I sensed a troubled man sitting in the chair in front of me. Carter's speech was slow and his tone subdued. "David," he began, "we...we want you to get through this. If you drop your appeal and postpone your parole hearing for...for just a couple of months, you will be able to get out of here...back with your kids and on with your life."

"Carter," I replied, "I have a right to my appeal and I have a right to my parole hearing, without the correctional service interfering with it in a manner that forces me to postpone it. These people lied to me, they lied about me! What about my rights, Carter?" I said. "Who stood up for David Mitchell? Who gave these people the right to strip me of my citizenship? Who gave them the right to coerce and manipulate the court process?"

"I've told you before. No one believes what's been written," responded Carter as he stared out the window. It was then that I noticed a tear slowly edging its way down the side of his cheek. "It's all under seal. No one will ever see it."

Carter's words did little to ease my mind about what people might believe if they ever did read the reports.

"What you did was wrong," Carter said, continuing with his apologetic tone. "It doesn't matter about the circumstances. You are here now and you have to do whatever you can to get out of here on parole. Trust me, that's the way it works!"

Carter turned away from the window and looked directly at me. "I think you're a decent person and I don't want to see you ruin your life fighting this system. If you try, you'll lose. This system has more power than you. Change your attitude, go along with what you're told, and get out of here!"

"I know what I did was wrong and I can't turn back the clock. But what this system is doing is wrong!" I said, still unable to get past the mass deception I had been subjected too.

"David, you have to understand that most of the counseling for your feelings will come only after you're out in the community. This system has to deal with the public's feelings and its emotions. You're taking this too personally and that's what I've been trying to tell you. You've been smart enough to understand what's been happening. Nothing has happened just by chance. If you want to call it 'playing the game,' then play the game! Get out in the community and back with your kids. We'll pay for a counselor to help you on the outside."

Carter took a breath and then pleaded once more, "Postpone the parole hearing and drop the appeal. In a couple of months you will get out on day parole and you can get this dealt with."

I sensed Carter felt trapped, and had been as honest with me as he believed he could be. The question was, how far would his compassion let him go?

I picked my words carefully, making my position as clear as I could. "A couple of days before I was sent to Kamloops, I had a talk with someone about a Christian counselor. Someone who is willing to come into the institution and speak with me. I am going to do whatever I can to get some answers, whether you help me or not."

"What counselor?" snapped Carter. "No one can come in here and give you counseling unless we approve it! You will have to give me his name if you want me to give him clearance into the institution."

"His name is Doug Hampson," I answered.

"I'll look into it," Carter said defensively, "but he can't come in until I approve it."

I slowly rose from my chair, sensing I was trapped in a dangerous world of power and deception. Justice Provanzano had said I was being sentenced for reasons of rehabilitation, and for the protection of society. I'd been sent to a place where the public had been told I would get help for what the court had called, my deep emotional problems. I had now arrived at that place, only to be told that no one believed what had been written. On top of that I was being asked to play a deceptive parole game that was designed to show some rehabilitation had taken place.

Filled with uncertainty, I left Carter behind and considered my future. A future that was to be determined at a parole hearing on November 24, only days away.

Jim Wilson, a kind and compassionate man from Abbotsford, who worked tirelessly, putting prison inmates in touch with people from the community, brought Doug Hampson in to see me. Because Doug had not been approved as my counselor, he visited as a guest only. We talked for about an hour out on the grounds and I found his insight into the workings of corrections extremely helpful. His experience also validated my personal feelings. Doug brought two special gifts with him into the institution that day: a warm and caring friendship, and a valuable book. As our visit came to an end, he handed me a large textbook, *Psychology and Life* by Philip G. Zimbardo.

"David," he said, "I would like you to read this book. It will give you a lot of the answers you are looking for. It will also help you understand what you're going through in prison, and what's happening to you as you react to these people and they react to you."

(Shortly after this unofficial visit, Doug was given permission to begin a life skills and anger management course at the prison, and I became a student in his class. However, Doug was never assigned to me as a counselor, and I received no official private sessions with him, although I went out of my way to make contact with him whenever the situation arose.)

I studied the textbook religiously and pondered over every chapter. My actions on that fateful night over a year earlier had frightened me, as they had a lot of other people. I understood that we all deserved honest answers, and I was determined to find them.

And as hard as it was to admit, until I could find some of those answers for myself, I lived with my own doubts about returning home. Unfortunately, as my bitter feelings towards Geri and the other man had subsided over the past year, my anger at the justice system had not, it instead, had been growing day by day. The manipulation and dishonesty of the legal and correctional process had disillusioned me, and the slowness of the process, which no doubt hurt my chances at parole, had only made matters worse. I now had to learn how to deal with these new emotions that were choking the life out of me.

It was late in the afternoon on November 23, when Carter summoned me to his office. "I have just looked at the hearing list for tomorrow," he said, "and I see you're not on it. It's too late in the day to call the National Parole Board office so I will have to wait until the morning to find out what happened."

I remained silent, sensing my case manager was not finished.

"It may be just as well, seeing as your case management team is not supporting you for early release at this time. It really would be in your best interest to postpone the hearing, for at least another month anyway."

"Carter, I'll be showing up for my hearing tomorrow, and if I'm not heard, I'll call the media and Prison Legal Services," I said, leaving my case manager to ponder his next move.

When I entered the duty office the following morning it was bustling with all the activity that accompanies any hearing day. There were inmates standing up against the counter and several staff milling about the room on the other side.

Out of the milieu stepped Carter. "I have an assessment here that you need to look at before you go into the hearing," he said.

I looked at the document and realized I was reading a community assessment completed by a halfway house in Vernon, BC. With all the turmoil and infighting between case management and myself, I had completely forgotten about the halfway house applications I had discussed with Carter. I had in fact made a final decision to apply to houses in Victoria, where my children were planning to go to university. Carter had insisted that I keep my options open and was adamant I apply to the house in Vernon. So it came as no great surprise, then, that this community assessment was non-supportive and filled with disparaging innuendo and condemnation. The assessment highlighted the point that I had not taken certain institutional programs. It also suggested I should be considered as someone who would be at a high risk to re-offend if returned to society. Needless to say, the halfway house staff from Vernon concluded that I was unfit for residency at their home. Suspiciously, there was no assessment from the Victoria halfway house.

I angrily handed the paper back to Carter and rushed back to my room, picked up the material I had prepared for the hearing and stepped back outside. I paced up and down the long driveway in a frenzy, muttering to myself, "I'll talk to the board," I told myself encouragingly, "I'll tell them what these people are doing. I'll straighten it all out!"

Chapter 7

Boards and Courts

I entered the hearing room, which had been set up in the prison chapel, and seated myself across the table from two well-dressed gentlemen. One took charge, introducing himself as Mike Young.

Carter and Virginia positioned themselves to my right, and the National Parole Board hearing began.

"I have here, an assessment done by a halfway house in Vernon. Have you seen that?" Mr. Young asked.

"I was shown that only about an hour or two ago," I answered.

"You're entitled to have time to reflect on any of these documents. You're entitled to fifteen days. If you wish for the time, you can postpone the hearing."

I recoiled from the parole board's attempt to succeed where the correctional service had failed. "No," I answered, "I do not wish to postpone it, but I do wish to comment on the report."

My response caught Mike Young off guard and he struggled to regain his composure. "Oh, yes...you can make comments, but first of all I have to assure you that you are given the...the opportunity to consider them and...to react to them in a considered way. And you're entitled to fifteen days, especially where in fact the report's sensitivity does not accept you. So it does make a difference to your release plan."

"Well I want to get on and get my side of things told," I responded, "and I've been sitting here and nobody's been working with me, and I think it's time something happened."

"But, uh, I recognize you may feel that way. What I'm pointing out to you is," he said, as he pointed at the community assessment, "have you seen that?"

"I've seen it, and I'll comment on it." I answered irritably, upset at what I saw as another attempt to push back my parole.

"Okay," replied Mike Young with resignation, "we'll deal with that later."

Without further delay, the board member began dwelling on the institution's unflattering progress summary reports, and Carter's recommendation that parole be denied. He then asked about my appeal, which was now set for December 3, less than two weeks away. I let it be known that I was seeking a reduction in sentence while expecting a decision to be handed down that same day.

Young's demeanor suddenly changed, and a more emotional character filled the suit across from me, "If YOU don't think you have a problem with violence, YOU HAVE A PROBLEM!" he shouted, suggesting that my continued incarceration was warranted. "You are quite an angry person."

"I'm trying to get through this thing," I answered out loud, "and these people are doing what they can to interfere in my attempts to do so!"

Carter Alexander eased himself into the conversation. "Well I...I think that, uh, that I'm still...My major opinions are...are expressed in the report. Um... I believe that Mr. Mitchell, um, still requires extensive psychological treatment and, uh...unfortunately that has...that has just started. And, uh, and I think that he...he needs to have fairly extensive treatment before he stops being a risk."

"Who am I a risk to, Carter?" I asked, cutting in on my case manager's stuttering explanation.

Carter ignored my intrusion, "I also think that...uh, that there are multiple issues that need to be treated in, uh, different areas, like anger management. In regards to his release plans to Victoria, he talked to me about that after the major documentation was done for this hearing, and what with the negative recommendation and the short time frame I never asked for another community assessment."

I looked across the table at Mr. Young. Not about to give up, I laid my notes on the table and addressed the Board. "These are from my diary notes dated Thursday, October 22, 9:45 p.m.," I said, then looked at Carter and asked if he recalled our talk that day.

The case manager grunted in unison with a slight nodding of his head.

I turned back to my diary and started reading, "I have been thinking about my talk with Carter this morning. We talked for approximately one hour in the duty office. I told Carter about my talk with the doctor, and how he confirmed what I believed all along, that it was the social worker that wrote the FPI report. Most of our conversation was about that report and the others done on me.

...I told Carter that all the people involved in the deception of these reports, and in the opening and stealing of my mail had to understand it was wrong. All I ever wanted was to understand that night and what happened to me."

My voice quivered as I read what Carter's response had been that day, "Carter said, 'My report is based on a very short time in knowing you and reading your files. I have not had enough time to get to know you, but I believe you are a good person and have worked hard throughout most of your life to always improve yourself, and have been a good, loving, and caring father."

I set the diary notes down and collapsed back into my chair, nervously distancing myself from the Board.

"Okay, if there's nothing further," said Mike Young, "I will ask you to leave and we will call you back in five or ten minutes."

My heart pounded and my hands trembled as I gathered my documents off the table. The sound made by the rustling paper cut into the deafening silence, then helplessly, the papers slipped from my fingers, scattering about the floor.

"Sorry for the mess," I said apologetically, collapsing to my knees. I jammed the papers into my binder and sheepishly rose to take refuge in the only other room the building had to offer.

A few seconds later Virginia appeared in the open doorway. "Tough hearing, eh?" she said, flashing me a pleasing grin before stepping outside with Carter.

I moved to the far side of the room and stared out the huge window. A tear came to rest on the edge of my lip, and I gently closed my eyes and reached back in time. The warm vision of my children roaring down Snow Valley in front of me brought on more tears. I squeezed my eyes tighter, and watched Jeff and Steven skate up and down the ice during one of their Saturday afternoon hockey games. Then I stood and cheered Aimee, as she powered her way around the rink in an exciting game of ringette.

"It's time," Virginia said. "They're ready for us!"

I sadly withdrew from my daydream and followed Carter and Virginia back to the waiting parole board.

"Mr. Mitchell, we are going to deny day parole," said Mike Young, "The board considers that you have many unresolved deep emotional problems and an ongoing problem with anger. You provide the distinct impression that you, yourself, are a victim and you show minimal insight into the nature of your problems. We feel you need intensive treatment, and until you have successfully participated in such treatment and counseling, you remain a risk in any form of conditional release."

I staggered to my feet and headed for the door in silence, leaving everyone behind. I exited the chapel, realizing it was not the high fences, topped with razor wire, or the low chain-link mesh of this minimum-security institution that imprisoned me. It was the paper, the power of the pen, the monitor on the computer screen and the printer that rested beside it. It was unrestricted power that flowed through the minds and fingers of those who controlled the keyboard. It was power, real power, absolute power!

"Tomorrow," I whispered, "I'll call the kids tomorrow."

With my appeal only a week away, I had little time to waste wallowing in self-pity, something case management unwittingly helped me with by keeping my mind occupied as I moved forward with that process as well.

Carter summoned me to his office. "I just received this disturbing report that indicates the police had to attend at your family residence on several occasions to break up domestic disputes."

"That's absolutely false, and nothing but more of this system's garbage," I replied angrily. I reached for the paper on Carter's desk. "I'd like to read it!"

"It's classified and protected information. If you want to see it, you will have to write to the privacy commission."

Carter's reluctance to show me the alleged report, left me suspecting he had no such statement in front of him, at least not one that was authentic.

Carter then mocked my appeal, saying I should drop it and get on with doing what had to be done to achieve parole.

I ignored case management's attempts to intimidate me throughout the week, and with more determination than ever, I prepared my court presentation.

I had received a letter from Crown prosecutor Carol Baird, which outlined how she expected and hoped the hearing would proceed. She suggested that if I followed the friendly format she had outlined, I could, and probably would receive a favorable ruling. The prosecutor had gone so far as to suggest the points I should raise, and how I should present them to the judges.

Her letter also contained a subtle threat that did not go unnoticed. It suggested that if I were to deviate from the suggested path and become antagonistic, attacking the earlier court proceeding, it could put a positive outcome in jeopardy.

However, I felt I had a strong case. Evidence had been suppressed and misrepresented. Important circumstances surrounding the assault had been withheld, including the full extent of my emotional state. I had also let the victim go, and when the evidence was properly considered, that point became clear. On top of all that, I now had the psychiatrist, Dr. Dilli, telling me that he would not accept responsibility for anything in the forensic report other than his summary and conclusion.

On December 3, 1992, believing I was prepared the best I could, the sheriffs escorted me to the upper floors of the stylish glass courthouse in downtown Vancouver.

The elevator door opened and I followed another young sheriff along a narrow unpainted corridor, filled with several twists and turns. I wrinkled my nose at the dank smell of concrete and mortar, until finally, we stopped in front of a door to our right. "There's a hearing going on right now. Pay attention to the lawyer and how he addresses the bench," the sheriff advised.

He turned the knob and quietly pushed the door open. I nervously stepped forward, easing onto a plush carpet that reflected the undeniable richness inside the room.

The lawyer, who had been addressing the bench, stopped his monologue and followed the gaze of the three judges whose attention had been diverted by our entrance. Their intense and somewhat inquisitive stares quickly had me looking for a place to hide.

"Take a seat at the other counsel table Mr. Mitchell. We're almost through," said one of the judges. His welcome indicated my appearance was expected. I seated myself in an elegant oak chair and glanced over at the attorney, who looked annoyed by the interruption. The chief justice then asked the lawyer to finish up.

I listened closely for the next five minutes and noted that the lawyer referred to the two gentlemen on the bench as 'My Lords" and the lone woman as 'My Lady." After another ten minutes he concluded addressing the bench and the appellant court set his case down for the day.

When he vacated his position behind the counsel table, a woman quickly filled his slot and pulled a handful of documents out of her briefcase, laying them quietly on the table.

The court reporter stood and announced, "Regina vs. David Howard Mitchell, on appeal."

Carol Baird, the government attorney, continued to stand, facing the bench in silence. I quickly rose from my chair and faced the three justices in a show of respect.

Ms Baird gave a brief outline of the case and then turned the proceedings over to me. I nervously started reading a statement to the court, referring to the dishonest forensic report that had been used to influence the judge at the sentencing hearing. I relayed to the court my belief, that the report had not been edited to the degree I had been lead to believe it was going to be. I gave the bench examples of some of the innuendo and suspicion that filled the document, highlighting those that suggested spousal abuse. At this, Madam Justice Southin asked for the evidence bag. The prosecutor was obviously not pleased as she realized I had not followed her advice. She fumbled with her briefcase and finally pulled out a sealed package that she had failed to lay on the table with her other papers.

Madam Justice Southin emptied the evidence bag and flipped through the documents. "Where is the forensic report the sentencing judge looked at?" she asked. "It's not here. If it was used as evidence in this case it should be in the bag."

The judge continued, breaking an uneasy silence in the room. "What would you say, counsel, if I suggested to you that the report was not edited at all, but instead, had been highlighted?" said Madam Justice Southin, showing her irritation.

Baird's search for a reply was cut short when the three judges took a break to discuss matters. Fifteen minutes later they reappeared and asked if I would be willing to adjourn the hearing to a later date and come back with counsel.

I was leery of getting another legal-aid lawyer involved, so I hesitated. However, one of the judges gave me some confidence when he told me they could proceed with the case now, but if I were successful it would still be a few months before I could be released with a reduced sentence. He then confidently stated that if I came back with a lawyer in a couple of months, everything could be wrapped up in a proper manner.

I hastily informed the three judges that legal-aid had refused me further counsel. With that, the bench made it clear that they would get me a lawyer, even if it had to be paid for by the attorney general's office.

I was skeptical about the court appointing me a lawyer, and asked if I could pick anyone I wanted. The judge who appeared to be controlling the panel was taken aback, saying, that if he granted that request, I would go out and get the best lawyer in the country, at a very high cost no doubt! He then asked me if I had a lawyer in mind. I gave the name of a lawyer, who also happened to be a former team-mate on a hockey team I had played for. The bench quickly approved him. With that settled, the court set the hearing over for a future date, while ordering government counsel to find and forward the missing forensic report onto the court.

I was returned to Ferndale, and immediately called the law office of lawyer, Dave Jenkins, in Prince George BC. He was not available to take the case, but his office gave me the name and phone number of a lawyer in Victoria. I made the call and Adrian Brooks agreed to act as my new counsel.

Meanwhile, my troubles with Ferndale case management continued to heat up. I put in a request to work on the outside grounds crew, which would raise my level of pay to twenty dollars a day, a significant increase from the five dollars a day I was getting working inside the institution. Carter, unrelenting, sabotaged my efforts with more of his condemning reports which I angrily disputed with deputy warden, Glen Cross, while demanding a change in case management.

A few days later, Carter's loud and angry voice boomed through the camp loudspeakers. "MITCHELL, REPORT TO THE DUTY OFFICE IMMEDIATELY!"

Carter's confrontational tone indicated our meeting was not going to be filled with a lot of civility. When I was still about a hundred feet from the duty office, the speakers exploded to life once more, this time leaving no doubt. "MITCHELL, TO THE DUTY OFFICE ON THE DOUBLE!!"

The loud shrill sent fear percolating through my veins, but that was quickly replaced by a swell of anger and disdain towards those who were controlling my life.

Seconds later I entered the duty office, and fear quickly set in once again. Behind the counter, stood Carter, his face bright red and his pupils glazed. Thinning white hair hung in scattered strands about his head, highlighting aging beyond his years.

With only four feet between us, his voice was ear-splitting. "DON'T YOU EVER QUESTION ANY OF MY REPORTS AGAIN! AND WHEN I CALL YOU, YOU OBEY, IMMEDIATELY!!!"

I knew there was something wrong with Carter, but I couldn't put my finger on it. Nor did I want a confrontation with him in this open setting. I fought a desire to raise my own voice, with only moderate success. "Carter, I do not appreciate the tone you used, and I will be dammed if I will allow you to demean and degrade me in front of the whole institution. I don't have to accept that!"

Carter stared over my shoulder, as if gazing into the distance at some ghostly shadow moving behind me. "Just remember what I said," he replied. "You can go now."

That was the last time I saw Carter for several months. A couple of days later, word spread throughout the camp that he had been admitted to a drug and alcohol treatment center.

After Carter's absence, and my request that Virginia be taken off my case, I was assigned a new caseworker, Marjorie. She was more of an assistant than a full-fledged case manager, but she basically handled both roles. We got along pretty well and my battle with case management appeared to be over.

It was now the holiday season and missing a second Christmas with the kids was as difficult as the first. The mild climate of the West Coast took a holiday as well. The institution took on a winter wonderland appearance when an unusual cold snap kept a heavy snowfall around for a couple of weeks.

In January 1993 my new lawyer, Adrian Brooks, came to Ferndale, and we briefly went over the case, and the forensic report. When I told him about the supportive letter from the guard at KRCC, he said there was no point in pursuing the stolen letter, because the appellant court never heard new evidence anyway.

I told Brooks what the judges had said during my appearance in December, telling him that I believed my release was assured, and that I expected to be present at the new hearing. Brooks told me these things were never a done deal, and added that it was unlikely I would be allowed to attend the hearing.

I informed him I had agreed to come back with a lawyer, not send one in my place. He said he would look into it and do what he could to make sure I was present.

While I was waiting for him to get back to me, I went before the Prison Work Board with another request for assignment on the outside work crew, which was once again denied.

The next day I walked in on two correctional officers who were rummaging through the lone dresser in my room.

"Security asked us to search your room," one of them said sheepishly, then without any further explanation they left.

The next day I was called into the Glen Cross's office and lectured on my attitude. The deputy warden let me know that as long as I continued to fight the system, my progress summary reports would never get any better. He then mentioned my children and told me I should be thinking about them. "You should pay heed to your case management team and get out of the institution," he barked, then rose and guided me down the hall to the front desk, all the while making it clear that I should seriously consider what he had just said.

"How can this system justify using reports written by someone who is now in a drug and alcohol treatment center?" I replied bitterly. "Someone who was obviously unfit to be writing the reports in the first place?"

Cross's face flushed with anger, "You better watch what you say, mister!" he bellowed, whirling on his heels, "Come back to the office! Now!"

"Who told you that?" he snapped as he lowered himself into the chair he had just vacated.

"I heard it around the institution," I answered calmly.

"Well, it's not serious. It's only a little problem, and we're getting it straightened out." Cross looked directly at me. "You better not go around talking about it," he said in a much lower tone.

I thought that remark amusing, as all the inmates seemed to know where Carter was. But I let the remark slide, instead making my position clear to the deputy warden. "Well maybe this institution should consider what it's writing," I said, "and what it's saying about me!"

Chapter 8

The Midnight Run

Adrian Brooks' initial visit to Ferndale, also turned out to be his last. My repeated requests that he come back to the institution and go over the case with me proved fruitless.

However, I was told I could attend my appeal, and on February 25, 1993, I was escorted back to the courthouse in Vancouver. Brooks came down from the upper floors to see me in the basement cells. His refusal to come back to Ferndale and go over the case with me was a bitter pill to swallow. But he had said everything was under control, and I felt I had to bite my tongue and hope for the best.

"It appears Crown counsel doesn't want you in the courtroom and has asked the bench to bar you from the hearing," Brooks said.

"What?" I hollered.

"The court is considering the request," he cautioned, "but I have spoken to the matter and they will allow you up if you promise not to speak. If you interrupt, they will have the sheriff bring you back down to the cells."

"I thought I had already been granted the right to attend my hearing?"

"Well, yes, and you're here. That's something. Almost no prisoner is allowed at these hearings. In fact, most have to remain at their institutions during the proceedings." Brooks shuffled nervously, "So, although you're here, the prosecution has requested that you not be allowed into the courtroom. ...But what I'm saying is, if I can go back up and promise the bench that you will not speak or disrupt the proceedings, they will allow you to sit in on the hearing, based on the fact that you represented yourself earlier."

The lack of any in-depth discussion with this man had me worried. However, I saw no practical alternative but to give into the court's demand. Besides, if I fired him and went up there alone, I would be doing so without any prepared presentation.

"Okay," I said reluctantly, "it looks like I have no choice."

"I'll go up and let the court know we talked, and the sheriff will be down to get you shortly."

Fifteen minutes later I made the familiar elevator trip to the top floors. But this time, instead of going directly into the courtroom, the sheriff placed me in small holding cell, saying my lawyer wanted to speak to me first. Five minutes later Adrian Brooks showed up with a photocopy of the forensic report and asked if I could read the blacked-out sections. I looked at the copy carefully and realized that although the copier had darkened the supposedly edited portions of the document, it had only made them more difficult, but not impossible, to read.

I read aloud a number of sentences that were still legible, and then told Brooks that I should be looking at the original copy that the sentencing judge had studied. I was stunned when he informed me there was no original available, and that the sentencing judge, Provanzano, might have looked at a photocopy similar to this one.

"They will bring you into the courtroom in a few minutes," he concluded, and stepped back out the door, taking the photocopied forensic report with him.

Minutes later I was escorted into the hearing and seated next to Adrian Brooks. I looked up at the bench and immediately realized, Madam Justice Southin was not present. Instead, three serious-looking men glared down at me, none of whom I recognized from the first hearing.

Court was called to order and government counsel, Carol Baird, launched into an aggressive attack. She opened by challenging my character, then produced a less-than-favorable report from Corrections Canada, a.k.a. Ferndale.

Adrian Brooks handed me a copy of the case management summary document, and told me to stay calm as I looked through it. I recognized the standard labeling I had become accustomed to seeing and quickly turned my attention back to the proceedings. I listened with a growing sense of discomfort and anger as Baird continued to degrade and dehumanize me. Then fear crept in when she concluded her presentation with a request that my sentence be increased to a term of five years.

Keeping in mind the court's demand that I not speak, I sat silently as Adrian Brooks read from a lengthy statement that was filled with a lot of rhetoric, and little substance. Not once did I hear him attack the prosecuting attorney from the sentencing hearing, nor did he mention my legal-aid lawyers' unethical manipulation concerning the plea-bargain. There was no address or challenge to the forensic report. Nor did Brooks shine any light on the comments made to me by Dr. Dilli during my earlier phone conversation, when the doctor identified Marc Leblanc as the involved author of the forensic document.

When Brooks finished his presentation, Baird, once again addressed the bench, this time arguing that my actions were a clear indication that I had little respect for human life.

With that comment, one judge spoke up, suggesting that provocation should be considered in this case if I had reasonably assumed there was a pre-existing affair between the victim and my wife. The judge then rebuffed Baird for her suggestion that the violence in my case should be looked upon in the same light as a random act of violence.

"You have to admit this violence is different," said the judge.

"We consider violence to be violence," Carol Baird replied.

There was a lack of assurance in her comment, and the judge's raised eyebrow indicated he was not about to give it any additional weight.

"The court is going to reserve its decision in this case," said one of the other Supreme Court Justices, who then stood and led the other two back to their chambers.

When the last judge had disappeared, the sheriff reached out and firmly grasped my arm. "Let's go," he said. I planted my feet in protest and turned to my lawyer, "Why are they reserving judgment? I thought I was going to be released with a reduced sentence?" Brooks paid no heed to my inquiries, saying only that I would be sent a copy of the ruling when the decision was handed down.

The sheriff gave another tug, this time leading me to the prisoner's door. I stepped into the narrow concrete hallway, listening as muffled laughter echoed from behind me. The words, "It's done!" pierced my ears, then the door slammed shut. With my head slumped forward in defeat and dismay, the musty smell of concrete once again filtered through my nostrils.

This time, instead of a quick trip back to Ferndale, two sheriffs escorted me to the Vancouver City police cells. Six hours later they returned, this time, not only did they handcuff me, but, I was shackled with a set of waist and leg irons, restraints I had never experienced before. I was loaded into the van, and after hours of picking up and dropping off prisoners throughout the Lower Mainland, we finally pulled into the Ferndale Institution. It was midnight.

The van pulled to a stop next to the duty office and a sheriff helped me out of the cage, giving me a gentle prod as my feet hit the ground. Without saying a word I shuffled forward, hobbled by the leg irons that had been gnawing at my ankles for hours.

"Long day, eh?" grinned the duty officer as one of the sheriffs removed my restraints. Too tired and sore to respond, I accepted my room key in silence and awkwardly stumbled over to my trailer.
****

In March, while I was waiting for the appeal decision, Ron Bentley, a lawyer connected to the legal-aid program back in Fernie, got in touch with me. He told me that Geri's lawyer had come to him, asking who they should contact about my family court matters. Bentley appeared anxious to take on the job, and convinced me to apply for a divorce.

But after mulling it over for a few days, I had some nervous second thoughts, and called him back with instructions to withdraw the application until I could be present. My change of heart appeared to upset the lawyer, and he told me Geri could proceed in my absence on the grounds that we had already been separated for over a year.

"That's fine," I said. "If she does, you tell the court that I will not oppose the divorce. But that's all you're to do until I can be present for any hearing that deals with the division of assets and custody."

A few weeks later I received the expected notice that Geri was proceeding with her own application. I accepted the fact that our marriage was over, but I also felt a deep sadness at the way it had ended. Through the good times and the bad, I had always thought of Geri as my best friend.

88

On April 6, 1993, I received another notice, a letter from the court of appeal. My application for a reduction in sentence had been denied.

Chapter 9

Learning the Parole Game

After the court decision, Marjorie told me I would have an opportunity to apply for parole once again, sometime early in the summer. She suggested I contact the Manchester House in Victoria, the same halfway house I had asked Carter to contact several months earlier. I did so and was encouraged by the staff's positive response to my application for residency. With my opportunity for release through the courts gone, and a successful parole looking like a possibility, I lowered my guard and settled into a regular routine at Ferndale. I was buoyed by Marjorie's support, and the calmer atmosphere at the institution. I was no longer subjected to the degrading and dehumanizing progress summary reports. I was also allowed into the community on escorted day passes, and my request to work on the outside grounds crew was finally approved.

I was convinced the quick turnaround was linked to my loss in the Appellant Court. That decision now gave case management the sole power to determine my date of release through the parole process.

A warming trend in the month of April was a clear indication that summer and my possible freedom were just around the corner. One day as I was enjoying the spring weather, Cliff, a correctional employee I had seen around the institution, asked me if I would be interested in taking part in a new program, titled, 'Leisure Education. He described it as a class that was designed to help inmates understand the positive aspects of getting involved in recreational activities upon their release into the community.

"It will look good at your next parole hearing to have this course under your belt," Cliff said, while telling me he was going to instruct the class. "The course is scheduled to run two days a week for six weeks. And they won't start until after your work crew has returned for the day, so that won't be a problem."

"I've been involved in positive recreational activities all my life," I replied, not convinced the program was necessary, "and not only in team and individual sports, but I have participated in my children's sports as well."

"With that background, your participation would help those who have not been as fortunate," Cliff replied.

A play on my vanity did the trick. I was no different that most prisoners, who when incarcerated are invariably dehumanized, which leads, after just a short period of time, to a sense of helplessness and worthlessness. Prisoners quickly crave any scrap of positive reinforcement, and I fit the bill perfectly. Delighted to feel needed again, I agreed to participate in the course and filled out a written questionnaire as a precursor.

Around the same time, another correctional officer joined the Ferndale staff. Virginia Deardon called me into a meeting to introduce me to a man, who looked to be in his mid-30s.

"David, my name is Julian Methot," he said pleasantly. "I understand that the cog-skills program is probably not something you're in need of, but I have taught the program before and I know it well. I will be teaching the course, starting in a couple of weeks, and I was hoping you would consider participating in the class. It'll give us a chance to get to know one another better."

Although it wasn't stated so, it appeared Julian was to become a fill-in member of my Case Management team. And the course, 'Cog-skills, is a cognitive living skills program that is highly touted by Corrections Canada. It is designed to teach people how to promote themselves in a positive manner when they rejoin society. I considered it debatable whether such a course, taught by individuals who routinely abused others, would be helpful at all.

Julian nonchalantly pushed some papers across his desk, and I glanced at the top page of a questionnaire that required written responses.

"Am I going to be given the questionnaire to determine if I need to take the course?" I asked.

A grin crossed Julian's face. "I can't give it to you now. You just looked at the answers!" I glanced back down at the form and Julian quickly exposed more papers that had been hidden underneath. He read what was allegedly one of the answers, then pulled the questionnaire back and immediately engaged me in a friendly discussion about the institution.

I shrugged off his somewhat strange behavior and informed him that things had gone rather smoothly over the last couple of months. Eventually, Julian moved the conversation towards my anger at the justice system.

"I will deal with the lawyers and the social worker from forensics, in court, when I get out," I said.

"Well, the system can be dishonest, there is no doubt about that," replied Julian. "Listen, like I said, I don't think you need to take the cog-skills program, but I'd like you to come to class anyway. It should be over by your parole date, and in any event, there will be no need for you to finish it."

Julian eased back in his chair, and once again my esteem was targeted. "I think it would be helpful for the other inmates to have someone in the class who's lived his whole life on the outside."

"I don't know," I responded. "I'm working outside the institution during the day. I'm also set to start another course, and I'm working on my release plan with a halfway house in Victoria."

"That's okay," Julian replied. "We can work around that."

"If I came to the class, there may be times when I'll be late or have to leave early to call the halfway house. They've asked me to make any calls to them at 3 o'clock," I said, trying politely to turn down the offer, but leaving open a compromise. "The leisure education program is also scheduled to begin late in the afternoon...but those classes are only twice a week...so during the other three days I suppose I could attend."

"That's fine! Don't worry about it, we'll work around it somehow. I do have a couple of multiple-choice questionnaires that I will need you to fill out though. Ottawa needs a record that will show the cog-skills program was not required...Here," Julian said, pulling them from the pile on his desk. "You can check them off in the room across the hall if you want."

I did as requested and left the duty office, satisfied that I was not going to be harnessed into taking any more institutional programs.

Over the next couple of weeks I attended the leisure education course I had committed myself to. At the same time I maintained close contact with the Manchester House, who informed me they were waiting for a progress summary report from Ferndale so they could go ahead with a community assessment. While we all waited on Ferndale case management, one thing became clear; I wasn't going to be getting any credit for the leisure education program which started to fall apart immediately. One inmate left after the first week, calling the course nothing more than an institutional mind game. Although I agreed, I kept my thoughts about the course to myself, entering them only into my diary, making note that the program was designed to "re-label and compartmentalize" the participants, something I had studied in the text given to me by Doug Hampson.

Leisure Education, in fact, did not introduce inmates to recreational activities at all! Instead, with a camera up and running, each session had quickly turned into a personal attack on the inmates. The underlying theme was: "You are in prison today and engage in antisocial behavior because of your lack of social skills." Participants were defined as dysfunctional human beings, who were in need of institutional programming before they could be safely returned to society. The class, feeling dehumanized and degraded, revolted, putting the instructor under fire almost every day. He quickly began denying all responsibility, telling everyone it was a new course and that he had not designed the format. Needless to say, the class never made it past the second week. Coincidence or not, the cog-skills program was about to start and I was suddenly free to attend that course on a regular basis.

It was now near the end of April, and Marilyn McNeil, head of case management at Ferndale, called me into a meeting. When I arrived at her office I was shocked to see Carter Alexander sitting calmly off to one side.

"I just wanted to let you know that Carter is back at the institution," Marilyn said pleasantly. "He will not be resuming his previous duties as your case manager, however, he will work with your case management team due to the fact that he knows more about your case than anyone else."

Then, in what I saw as a friendly gesture, Marilyn and Carter both acknowledged that mistakes had been made, including an admission that case management had been less than fair with me. They also expressed hope that things would go more smoothly from this point on.

However, the first Sunday after Carter's return, I was given reason to suspect things had not changed all that much. I was dressed and prepared to spend a day out in the community with Richard and Ruby Engle, a couple from Abbotsford, who gave freely of their time to escort prisoners on day passes. (Jim Wilson had put me in touch with Richard, just as he had Doug Hampson). This particular morning when I arrived at the duty office I was told there was no pass, and I would not be allowed to leave the institution.

Throughout the following week I made inquiries, but no one came up with any explanation. The next Friday I made the point of going over to the administration building just before quitting time. I asked if my Sunday pass was approved and the office assistant looked through the papers on her desk. "Yes," she said, "it's here, I'm just about to leave. I'll be dropping them off on my way out."

A half-hour later I made an inquiry at the duty office. The Sunday pass was confirmed.

The next day, Saturday, I was out on the par three golf course when I noticed Virginia Deardon's pickup rolling up the prison driveway. Although it was not a regular workday for her, I gave her appearance no further thought and continued on with my round of golf.

On Sunday morning, about 15 minutes before Richard and Ruby were to arrive, I walked over to the duty office.

"You going somewhere?" asked the duty officer. "I never saw a pass for you."

"I know it's there," I replied. "I checked on Friday afternoon. Look again!"

The guard flipped through the papers on the clipboard. "No, there's nothing here."

A vivid image of Virginia's pickup suddenly flashed through my mind. While I was thinking about her probable involvement in the disappearance of my pass, Richard and Ruby pulled into the parking lot.

After informing my friends that the pass had gone missing again, with a special kindness I had come to cherish, they offered to stay and visit. However, I was not about to let the correctional service's abusive nature take away a day of church activities that I knew they looked forward to. As much as I would have enjoyed their company, I insisted they go ahead without me, and enjoy themselves.

I dejectedly walked back to my room, recalling what the warden had said to me: "I suggest you attempt to work more closely with your case management team in the future and gain their support for your parole."

"How?...How?" I quietly asked myself, "How do I play the game?"

Two days later Carter Alexander summoned me to the case management building. "I just received this message from Marilyn McNeil. It indicates you have not been in contact with the Manchester House in Victoria, so I'm going to have them move your C.A. [community assessment] back to May 20, until I find out what's going on."

"That's not true! I've been directly in touch with those people!" I said, hoping to avoid another confrontation with my former case manager.

"I've also been shown your latest case management report, and it rates your behavior at Ferndale as poor! You might not qualify or be ready for a placement at a halfway house," said Carter sternly.

Upset at what appeared to be Carter's direct re-involvement in my case, I went back to my trailer and called the Manchester House in Victoria. Kathy Roy informed me that Judy Chouinard, the woman I had talked with earlier, was now gone for the month, and that she, Kathy, was taking over my application for residency. I gave her the same information I had given Judy, and asked her to call Carter and let him know that I had been in touch with the house.

I hung up the phone, walked back to the case management building and promptly informed Carter about my conversation with Kathy. Then added, "And I want to know why, all of a sudden, there is a report that suggests I might be an unsuitable candidate for a halfway house?"

"I told you before, don't question reports and case management memorandum!" yelled Carter.

Convinced he was purposely trying to scuttle my parole, I dismissed any thoughts of backing down, and reminded Carter about the earlier unfairness he and Marilyn McNeil had admitted to.

Carter quickly denied ever suggesting such a thing.

With his denial of the conversation that had taken place only a few days earlier, my anger rose to new heights, as did my voice. "CARTER, LOOK AT ME. LOOK ME IN THE EYE WHEN YOU'RE TALKING TO ME!" I shouted.

Carter slid his chair back from his desk and bolted to his feet. I followed suit and stood my ground. With only a few feet between us, Carter's voice suddenly exploded. "I'LL LOOK YOU IN THE EYE THEN, MR. MITCHELL!!! IF THAT'S THE WAY YOU WANT IT, FINE! THIS MEETING IS OVER!!" He hastily stepped to the door and opened it without saying another word.

"Are you terminating the meeting, Carter?" I asked, wanting to make it clear that I was not walking out on a meeting, an accusation he had made months earlier. "Do you want me to leave?" I asked sarcastically.

"It's four o'clock, and I have to go!" Carter replied in frustration.

It was nine the next morning when I was called back to his office. I made an entry in my diary.

> Thursday, May 13th, 1993, 9:40 a.m. I have just came back from a meeting with Carter Alexander. He informed me that he was not going to support me for either Full Parole or Day Parole. He felt my frustration at the system was inappropriate and that my anger at the system would send me into a relapse and start me drinking again.

The meeting left no doubt in my mind that Carter had resumed his duties as my case manager.

As my parole date loomed closer, I began to panic, knowing the NPB would be looking at my application through the eyes of case management. I made repeated requests to meet with anyone, but all my attempts were futile. At one point I was even denied entry into the case management building. Without the staff's help or support, I desperately worked alone to put together my release plan for the National Parole Board, making sure I attended the cog-skills program on a regular basis, while staying in regular contact with the halfway house in Victoria.

During one of my calls to the house, Kathy told me they were still waiting for the progress summary report from Ferndale. Without it, the screening committee could not make a decision on my application for residency.

I quickly contacted MLA Len Fox's office in Victoria. Claire Vessey, his office assistant, sent the Manchester House a letter signed by Len. It indicated I had been a productive member of society, adding that the MLA's office was supportive of my residency in Victoria.

I then went back to Carter and reminded him of his responsibility to provide the house with a progress summary report.

"I haven't had time to finish it yet!" snapped Carter. "I'll get to it when I can!"

But when he realized the MLA's office had already contacted the Manchester House, Carter quickly produced a supportive report and faxed it off to Victoria. I sensed his displeasure when he told me I had wasted too much time on my release plan. His remark left me a little baffled and concerned. Was he telling me there had been no need for me to spend time on it because a supportive progress summary report would take care of everything, or was he saying, it did not matter because parole was out of the question?

I tried not to dwell on Carter's negativity and took comfort in the fact that I had everything in place. On June 10, Kathy Roy informed me that the screening had gone well, and that I had been approved for residency. Claire Culhane, a well-known and respected prisoner's rights activist also agreed to speak on my behalf at the parole hearing, which was set for June 23, 1993.

I continued to attend the cog-skills class on a regular basis, although I did not care for the direction the course had taken. Day in and day out, Julian routinely promoted the correctional service as a necessary evil that inmates should not take personally.

I also started to notice a negative change in Julian's attitude towards me. Then on June 16, after becoming irritated when class members took time off to pick up their camp pay, even though he had accepted this break in class on earlier occasions, he turned to me, and said he was also concerned about the times I had shown up late.

With my parole hearing just around the corner and my anxiety rising, the last thing I needed was for Julian to start getting on my case.

I went to bed that evening and found myself reflecting on my two years of incarceration. I thought about the courts and the lawyers, and my rights of "due process." I considered all the psychological reports, concluding that no one -- not even Christ himself -- could survive the justice system's psychological assessment program. In an attempt to ease my mind, I opened the textbook I often read at night, Psychology and Life.

One particular passage I had reflected on earlier, was located in a chapter dealing with personality issues and theories, where the author, Philip G Zimbardo, wrote, "Our first impressions bias us strongly, and subsequent evaluations are reinterpreted so as to fit in with the original 'true' view. Once established, a belief needs little evidence to support it, but much to refute it."

I considered how Mark Leblanc's forensic report certainly proved Zimbardo correct. It had been a group-think mentality within the justice system that had taken a manipulative forensic report, and run with it.

Sensing a connection to Corrections Canada, I turned the pages to Zimbardo's description of 'group-think and its eight major characteristics. The first described was an illusion of invulnerability within the group, while the second was the collective rationalization of the group's actions, which allows it to discount any evidence that is contrary to any decision it makes.

The third characteristic Zimbardo talked about was "An unquestioned belief in the group's inherent morality, which leads the group to ignore the ethical or moral consequences of the decision."

The next four characteristics of 'group-think involved stereotyped views and other references to conformity and illusions of unanimity.

People with "good" intentions often perform "evil" acts through blind obedience to authority, or through group-think, in which persons in highly cohesive groups become so preoccupied with seeking and maintaining unanimity of thought that their critical thinking is rendered ineffective.

I felt like I was staring straight into the heart of Corrections Canada when I looked at the eighth and final characteristic. It summed up my thoughts. "The emergence of self-appointed mind guards--group members who suppress inconsistent information and reproach anyone who deviates from the group consensus." There could be no doubt that the theft of my mail was directly linked to this insidious characteristic. Marilyn McNeil's words had certainly put an exclamation mark on that point, "It was addressed to whom it may concern, and it concerned us!" had been her words.

I lay the textbook across my chest and pondered the concept of parole. The recent weeks of abusive behavior by case management could no longer be considered a coincidence. As was the case leading up to my first parole hearing, threats and intimidating remarks were once again becoming constant reminders that I could be denied my freedom. I closed my eyes and envisioned an experiment described in the text. It involved a mock prison setting, where Zimbardo made reference to students from Stanford who had been randomly selected to play the role of either a prisoner or a guard. He had described it as follows:

> In a remarkably short period of time, a perverted relationship developed between the prisoners and the guards. After an initial rebellion was crushed, the prisoners reacted passively as the guards escalated their aggression. In less than thirty-six hours, the first prisoner had to be released because of uncontrolled crying, fits of rage, disorganized thinking, and severe depression. Three more prisoners developed similar symptoms and also had to be released on successive days. A fifth prisoner was

released from the study when he developed a psychosomatic rash over his entire body, triggered by rejection of his parole appeal by the mock Parole Board. Within days the students had come to treat each other, not as peers, but as dehumanized enemies.

I looked at the passage on dehumanized relationships:

Would you ever deliberately humiliate, embarrass, or degrade another person?...These and other anti-social behaviors become possible for normal, morally upright and idealistic people to perform under conditions in which people stop perceiving others as having the same feelings, impulses, thoughts and purposes in life that they do. Such a psychological erasure of human qualities is called dehumanization.

It was now late in the night and I closed the book, convinced that the justice system was engaged in a massive game of deception. It all revolved around a ploy of psychological witch-hunts that processed and catalogued accused citizens and inmates as evil antisocial misfits, ...all done to keep the public desensitized while the system applied pressure on people to plea-bargain or play the parole game, whatever the case may be.

When all was read, said, and done, I was convinced that the justice system had built a prison industry based on a twisted definition of the word "parole." Achieving freedom through this means of early release no longer meant you had been rehabilitated, or had even earned it on merit, instead, it confirmed your dehumanization and acceptance into submission. Parole was simply the undignified reward for your compliance.

I had to find a way out of the nightmare. As Zimbardo had written, I was caught up in one of society's largest "social traps." I considered his conclusion, "As a victim in a trap it would appear that your only hope is either in removing yourself from it or working to restructure it: to change the choices it offers."

I closed my eyes, illuminating a vision of my children. I had been fighting for almost two years, trying to hang onto my dignity and sense of self-worth. Sadly, I realized this had proved to be more of a hindrance than a help when it came to achieving my freedom.

"David, you have a hearing in one week," I said to myself. "Do whatever you have to do. Play the game, play it the best you can!"

Chapter 10

Playing the Parole Game

Playing the parole game was not going to be easy. I had no experience, and time was running short. But I woke the next morning, prepared to do whatever I had to do to gain my freedom.

Julian's sudden concerns about cog-skills' class members coming late and leaving early seemed like a good place to start. And his personal jab at me for occasionally coming late had also raised a red flag.

I stopped by the duty office and Julian emerged from his back office. With the same friendly attitude he had displayed when we first met, he asked me to come back after lunch, saying he would discuss the matter then. When I returned in the afternoon, however, Julian showed me a noticeably different demeanor.

"Follow me!" he said icily as he turned and headed down the hall.

Julian's sudden hostility heightened my alertness, so when I stepped into his office and Carter Alexander greeted me with a sinister grin, my surprise was muted.

"Sit down," said the cog-skills instructor harshly. "I invited Carter to join us. I'm not going to beat around the bush. I think your coming to class late is a real problem, and I know you're doing it on purpose."

"I'm not late on purpose. I told you when you asked me to take the course there would be times when I might not arrive on time because of work. And I've been working on my parole hearing and placement at the halfway house as well, which I also talked to you about."

"You could've come and seen me in the mornings about that!" snapped Carter.

"Carter," I replied calmly, focusing my attention on the case manager, "you have refused to talk with me when I've come over to the case management building. And as far as the mornings go, our work crew leaves the institution before you're even here!"

Julian quickly jumped back into the conversation. "So you're saying your work is more important than the class!"

"That's not what I'm saying," I answered, turning back to my new adversary. "You asked me to come to the class, and I did. You know I'm working on the outside grounds crew, but if you feel the class should take precedence, then I'm willing to discuss it."

Carter leaned forward in his chair and planted his face inches from mine. "The program is important to you!!" he screamed. "And you have not, and are not, doing the program properly!!"

Julian and Carter now started firing their condemnations simultaneously.

"You're blaming the system...," Julian began.

"You better get...," shrilled Carter.

"...for everything!"

"Why don't you..."

"Get your act together..."

"...take your own responsibility..."

"...and stop blaming case management."

"...if you want to get out of here!"

Julian's voice suddenly faded and Carter's heightened anger ricocheted off the walls. "AND STOP QUESTIONING REPORTS! I HAVE A LOT OF CONCERNS ABOUT YOU!"

I calmly looked at Carter, avoiding any angry comeback. "Carter, I would like to discuss any concerns you have. I think it would help clear things up."

"I DON'T HAVE TIME FOR YOU NOW!!" Carter hollered. "AND YOU...ARE...NOT...A...REFORMER...IN...HERE!!!"

Julian was more hesitant. "You're just playing games," he said accusingly, "and you're still blaming the system for everything."

"I'm not playing any games," I said, keeping a level tone. "I requested this meeting to address the concerns you had expressed the other day, and I think the direction of this meeting is inappropriate."

"We will discuss your lateness and come to a decision," snapped Julian. "You can leave now!"

I pushed myself out of my chair and stepped past Carter, apprehensively, but satisfied with the thought that I had projected a calming presence.

When I entered Julian's cog-skills class that afternoon, I was still thinking about the heated meeting earlier in the day. But the class worked out a solution for picking up camp pay, and in an effort to ease tensions, I let Julian know that my release plan was now in place, and that would no longer interfere with the class.

Six Days to Parole Hearing:
It was late afternoon on Thursday, June 17, and staff members were slowly making their exit for the day when Julian's voice crackled over the camp speakers. "Mitchell to the duty office."

I complied immediately and Julian greeted me with a clipboard in one hand and a pen in the other. "I just need you to sign this," he said.

"What is it?" I asked as I steadied the clipboard and reached for his pen.

"That's not important," said Julian. "Just sign it."

I tightened my grip on the clipboard. "I would like to read it first," I replied defensively, wanting to comply, but leery of his matter of fact tone.

"Why do you want to read it? You don't need to read it!" Julian shot back impatiently.

"I need to know what I'm signing, Julian," I said, growing frustrated by his much-too-eager and unusual request.

"It's just the questionnaire that I've got to send to Ottawa," he said, pulling the clipboard out of my grasp. Julian quickly flipped through the pages and I recognized the multiple-choice questionnaire I had completed when I agreed to take his course. Then I realized the section requiring written responses had also been completed.

"I never answered that written part of the questionnaire," I said.

Julian held out the clipboard again. "Sure you did. The answers are all here."

"That's not my writing, Julian. And those, I imagine, are not my answers. I think we should discuss this."

"I see what you're doing!" barked Julian.

"I'm not doing anything. I didn't answer any written part of that questionnaire!"

I had no sooner snatched the clipboard out of Julian's grasp when the cog-skills instructor grabbed it back, this time holding it tight against his chest. "YOU GOT A PROBLEM???" he screamed.

"YES, I'VE GOT A PROBLEM," I yelled back. "I didn't give those answers!"

"You're being aggressive!" said Julian, this time more quietly, but with a taunting grin.

"Whose handwriting is that?" I asked, certain I already knew the answer.

"Its mine," the cog-skills instructor answered. "I asked the questions, you gave the answers, and I wrote them down. Simple, eh?"

"You never asked me the questions, and I never gave you any answers," I replied in disgust.

"It's your word against mine," Julian whispered, then raised his voice and ended the confrontation. "I see what you're doing. I don't have time for this -- and DON'T come back to my class tomorrow."

Dejected and frustrated, I left the duty office, convinced that Julian and Carter were attempting to sabotage my parole. I called Claire Culhane, the prisoner's rights advocate who was going to attend my hearing. She told me she had seen this type of intimidation just prior to a parole hearing before, adding that if I did not sign the questionnaire, I need not worry.

> Five Days To Parole Hearing:
> June, 18th/93, 8:01 a.m. I hope we can get things straightened out today. When I asked Julian yesterday to sit down and discuss this questionnaire and he refused and told me not to come back to his class today, he left me in a situation where I have to miss another day of work.
> Today I am going to try and find out why I was told not to come back to his class. As far as the questionnaire goes, Julian said that it is his word against mine, but as Claire said, I did not sign it.

I closed my diary and thought about the parole hearing that was only a few days away. Even with Claire's help, how could I expect the National Parole Board to believe me over case management? As Julian had said, it was my word against theirs. The more I thought about it, the more convinced I became that I had to find a way around Julian and Carter's manipulation and intimidation.

"Yes," I said to myself. "If I'm going to play the game, I have to show them I'm on board. I have to convince them I'm ready to do whatever they want!"

I had to make my first move a convincing one. No matter what shots they took at me, I had to maintain the same calmness I had shown a few days earlier. I went for a walk in the area of the duty office, certain that Carter or Julian were looking for an opportunity to check out my reaction to being kicked out of the cog-skills program just days before my parole hearing.

My intuition was dead on!

"Let's go for a walk," Carter said calmly, as he stepped out of the duty office.

"Okay," I answered agreeably. As we strolled over to a picnic table on the other side of the parking lot, I showed Carter my quiet concern. "I don't know if you heard. Julian said I can't come back to his class. He won't give me an explanation and I was hoping you would speak with him and find out why."

"David, I believe you're a responsible adult and therefore have to take responsibility for your actions and be prepared to suffer the consequences."

I nodded, and again responded submissively. "I understand."

Carter then made what I believed was a subtle inquiry about the depth of my commitment to play the game. "Sometimes retreat is the better part of valor," he coached.

I raised my head and peered into the distance, letting Carter take in my thoughtful nod before he continued, "It's not my place to talk to Julian about this, it's yours," he advised.

"I tried, but he wouldn't."

"Well, it's possible that he was just frustrated at the time, and didn't feel like talking."

Carter rose from the bench and I did likewise. Together we walked back to the duty office. Just as we reached the front steps, Julian stepped through the doorway and looked down at us from the top landing.

"Julian," I said, pinning him down quickly, "I would like to talk and get an explanation on why you don't want me back in class."

"I think it's clear, and I don't want to waste my time with you," he growled.

"I'm not clear on the reason at all?"

"Don't waste my time!" the cog-skills instructor said while stepping back inside.

"It looks like he won't discuss it," I said, turning to Carter, "I'll come over to your office later and find out if he has given you an explanation?"

It was one o'clock when I went over to Carter's office, hoping to find out if my new submissive attitude had brought about any change.

"I just received this memo from Julian," Carter said. "It states that you have been dismissed from the class because you are constantly coming late and have been using aggressive and intimidating behavior."

Carter lowered the memo and leaned on his desk. "I'm going to ask for a postponement of your hearing and send a copy of this memo to the National Parole Board."

It appeared my willingness to play the game had failed. But still convinced it was a game of intimidation, I called Carter's bluff. "I won't postpone the hearing, Carter, and Claire Culhane told me you couldn't present anything new to the board less than 14 days before the hearing."

"I'm sending it anyway!"

Holding my growing anger in check, I left Carter's office and wrote up our meeting in my diary, mulling over the deception that had accompanied my entry into the cog-skills program. It appeared I had been duped into taking the program so case management could hold it over my head. Now, if I did not fall into line and surrender, they could use my removal from the program as a weapon to scuttle my parole.

I looked at my watch and realized the cog-skills class was about to begin. With my future at stake, I grabbed my notes and headed out the door.

As I made my way up the sidewalk towards the classroom, Julian stepped onto the small landing above the steps. Blocking my entrance, he said, "You can't come in."

"Listen, Julian," I replied. "I'm not looking for any confrontation. Carter just showed me your memo, and I don't believe I have been either aggressive or intimidating with you."

"You called me a liar!"

"I did not call you a liar."

"You implied it the other day in the duty office."

As I suspected, it was about the questionnaire. "Well, Julian, if you want to give me a copy of the questionnaire, I'm willing to look at it," I said, deliberately softening my tone. "If you don't want me to look at it, that's fine too. I won't even ask you for a copy of it." I stayed relaxed, trying to present an image of someone looking for calmer ground. "I'm willing to drop it, and we can agree to disagree and let it go."

Julian hesitated, and I sensed my opening. "I haven't done anything wrong, Julian," I added quickly. "You asked me to take this course and I agreed to do it, and I would like to finish it."

Alerted to the possibility that I may be ready to let things slide, Julian responded warily. "Well, you can come in. But sit in the corner and don't say a word!"

Two Days To Parole Hearing:
During the cog-skills class on Monday I had no problems with Julian. In fact, he appeared more relaxed than ever.

One Day To Parole Hearing:
On Tuesday, June 22, 1993, I was summoned to the duty office and Virginia Deardon, who was no longer a member of my case management team, showed me a community assessment report. "The Manchester House is supportive of your day parole!" she proudly announced.

She turned a couple of pages and then read a section of the document out loud. "Regarding psychological counseling, the Vancouver Island district office has a staff psychologist, Dr. M. Beattie, who is available for one-to-one counseling and group sessions as practicable. Psychological interventions include sex offender therapy."

Virginia grinned as she pointed to the paragraph. Meanwhile, two other inmates, who had been standing at the counter, glanced at me and then left without saying a word.

"What you just did was crap, Virginia. You people are sick as hell!" I blurted out angrily. "What's this about seeing someone who deals with sex offenses?"

A short burst of laughter escaped from Virginia, then she responded, "She deals with cases that involve either violence or sex offenses. This is just referring to her area of practice. In your case she'll be dealing with anger."

My former case worker then picked up the document and ended our encounter, telling me Carter would call me over to his office later in the day. In the afternoon, Carter greeted me, displaying a surprisingly pleasant demeanor.

"David," he said, calmly smiling, "case management is going to support your day parole application tomorrow."

Chapter 11

A View in a Crystal Ball

I was showered and dressed by six a.m. on Wednesday, June 23, 1993. I gobbled down a hearty breakfast, filled my coffee mug and positioned myself next to a window in the visitor's trailer overlooking the parking lot.

At eight o'clock Carter arrived and entered the duty office. Just before nine, Harry DeJong, an MLA who shared an office with Len Fox, drove into the institution. I quickly stepped outside to thank him for coming to the hearing in place of Len, who had prior commitments.

As we were walking back to the visitor's trailer, Carter approached us, asking if I was ready.

"Yes, we're all set," I replied.

"Good," said Carter as he enthusiastically reached for the hand of the politician. "Hello, I'm David's case manager, Carter Alexander. We have worked hard with David, and the hearing should go well!" he boasted.

My case manager then engaged in more rhetoric with the politician, and I excused myself to greet Richard Engle who had just pulled into the parking lot. When we returned to the group that was gathering by the duty office, I realized I had missed Claire Culhane's arrival. The prisoner's rights advocate approached me, "They're here." I followed her gaze and zeroed in on another car that had just pulled into the institution.

A small group emerged from the vehicle, walked across the parking lot and headed towards the hearing room. Hoping to hide my nervous energy, I quickly engaged in several conversations with everyone around me. Richard patted me on the back. "You'll do fine, David. God's watching over this hearing."

No sooner had Richard's reassuring voice relaxed me, when Carter yelled out "It's time! They're ready!" His blast sent me into a panic.

I dashed off to my room and picked up a prepared statement and other documents I had put together for the hearing.

When I rejoined the group on the sidewalk, Carter whispered in my ear, "Just relax, don't say too much, let me handle it, and we'll get you out of here."

My friends, supporters, and case management team took their seats and the two-person panel, Terry Elliot and Vivian Reed, introduced themselves. The hearing began and Mr. Elliot asked if I had seen the progress summary reports he had just laid on the table.

"As far as I can recall. I've had to look at so many I can't be sure..." My comeback appeared to break the ice, and Terry Elliot's snicker helped lower the tension in the room.

After acknowledging what had been almost two years of imprisonment, he asked me about the assault, and I gave a brief summary. As the hearing progressed, Vivian Reed appeared more intent on portraying me as a deviant individual, and both members sought my support for institutional programming. When I tried to read my prepared statement, the two-member panel responded angrily.

"I would like to hear from YOU!" interrupted Mr. Elliot.

"I would really PREFER it if you would actually answer the questions," said Ms. Reed, "rather than reading statements by psychiatrists."

"I want to read my own statement," I replied defensively.

"Oh...okay," said Ms. Reed. "But it's...you know, it's," she stammered, "if...if you really do have an understanding of...of...of why...why you don't think you will do it again..."

Mr. Elliot quickly cut in. "According to our information you do have a record of aggressive and assaultive behavior."

"I dispute a great deal of that."

"I've looked at the writing on the copy of the progress summary that you wrote all over, disagreeing with everything. It, uh,...it indicated a certain amount of anger coming out, the way you did that," he said hesitantly.

The board member then attempted to gain my support for the prosecution's portrayal of events leading up to the assault. "And, uh, he was sort of an innocent person in this whole affair wasn't he?" Elliot said, referring to the victim.

"Parole, David, think of your parole," I said to myself. I had to start giving these people something to hang their hats on. I swallowed hard and gave them the answer they wanted. "Yes, he was," I replied.

Mr. Elliot appeared pleased and relieved by my answer. "I mean, it wasn't his fault that you were separated. Maybe he, uh...your wife to him was just a single women and he had, uh, every right to associate with her?"

"My parole is one the line. How do I answer that?" I said to myself.

"I don't want to debate or say things involving this man and my wife," I replied quietly.

"But, it should...," Mr. Elliot stammered.

"I just simply want to state that I hold no animosity towards this man. I don't know what more I can say."

"Do you consider yourself a violent person, Mr. Mitchell?" said Ms. Reed. "Because there are a number of incidents of violence in your record that cannot be disputed."

I wondered what record and number of violent incidents she was talking about. I had already acknowledged that one push and a slap had occurred in the lengthy marriage, and I certainly had not disputed the assault on the victim. I relayed those facts to the panel once again.

"Yes, that's right," she acknowledged, "so it would appear that when you're under stress, then you, uh, you...you lash out."

"Certainly under that severe emotional strain, yes!" I said.

"So is it fair to say, when you're under stress, your behavior deteriorates?"

"In those situations, yes, that did happen," I replied.

Ms. Reed then asked me how I had dealt with any angry feelings I might have had more recently. "Give me an example of when you were angry lately and what you've done about it."

"Well, probably here recently in the institution," I began, "in regards to a problem I perceived with the cog-skills instructor here, who I felt had unfairly filled in some sort of report, saying that I gave the answers, which I did not. And I tried to settle that with that gentleman, and..."

"Let's go back a bit with that cog-skills program." Ms. Reed said, interrupting me in mid-sentence. "You were...," she started to say, then quickly cut herself short, "uh, applied for it, were accepted into it along with nine others. Um, it appears at the time that you didn't particularly always arrive on time and you left early. You didn't take it too seriously, is that correct?"

"No, that's not correct..."

"Did you arrive and did you attend every class and stay every...all...all the time?" she interjected.

"No, there were occasions, in which not only myself, but the entire class would get up and leave for canteen [camp pay] and things like that. And we discussed it with the instructor, and he was going to go to canteen and get us a different time to do it.   ... There were other occasions where I was working on my parole and towards my acceptance at the halfway house in Victoria. So I had times where I had gotten up and left to make phone calls. Which were appointed phone calls, whenever someone at the halfway house said to call at 3 p.m. I was also dealing with the MLA's office in Victoria, so there were some occasions when I had to get up, but I explained those and what I was doing and felt that it was important for me to be accepted by a halfway house."

"Uh-huh," replied Ms. Reed. "More important than taking cog-skills?

PLAY THE GAME, DAVID. PLAY THE GAME! Flashed the warning sign.

"Uh,...no," I said, then described what my response to Julian had been. "I said I would be willing to sit down and discuss it."

"Uh-huh," she said. "But he also accused you of being, uh...using aggressive and, uh, intimidating behavior."

"Well," I responded, "Julian and I sat down and agreed to disagree about it, and I continued to stay in the cog-skills program."

Ms. Reed seemed surprised to hear that I was still attending the class. "Are you in one now? So...you started it over again?"

"No," I replied, "I'm still taking the same one."

"Oh? I thought you were kicked out of the class."

Vivian Reed's comments were convincing evidence that the National Parole knew something about the events that had been going on at the institution. I concluded that it not only knew I had been manipulated into taking the class, but also knew that Julian had filled in the questionnaire. I also understood the Board would never admit to any of it, and my parole would almost assuredly go out the window if I made the accusation.

"No," I answered, "he told me not to come back."

"Right!" she said.

"I wanted some explanation as to how these answers were put on the sheet, and he just basically told me he did not have time to talk to me about it and said you're being aggressive. I said, well, I feel we should sit down and discuss it because I did not give those answers. He just said don't come back to my class. I felt I had done nothing wrong, so I showed back up. We discussed it and agreed to disagree, so to speak, and dropped it!"

"You're aware," said Mr. Elliot, "that that is a program that has been strongly recommended for you to complete and actively participate in, and it could have a very strong influence on our decision?"

115

There it was! Said loud and clear. My parole now rested on completion of the cog-skills program. The message was undeniable: Mr. Mitchell, you better admit you need it, you better finish it, and if you have to lick the shoes of your case management team to do that, YOU BETTER DO IT!!!

A heightening wave of fear rolled through me as I realized my case management team now had the power to take my parole away from me, even if it were to be granted at this hearing. Carter and Julian could simply go back to the National Parole Board and tell them I had been dismissed from the class once again. The trap was sprung and I was on the inside, looking for a way out.

"There is a great deal that is in that course that is coming up that I have already done with Doug Hampson," I blurted out.

"What benefits have you derived from that program, the cog-skills?" cut in Ms. Reed. "It's not over, is it?"

"No," I said.

"Have you found it useful?" she asked.

Parole, David, parole! The thought never left me. With nowhere left to go I gave Ms. Reed the answer she wanted, while managing to slip in the fact that I knew where the real help had come from. "Yes," I answered, "I have. In planning, problem solving...again, these are all things I did with Doug."

Mr. Elliot stepped back into the conversation, doing his best to support Corrections Canada's perceived fulfillment of the court's sentencing demand. "And beyond that, you've been following one-on-one psychological counseling." (It was a statement, not a question.) "And, uh, I realize you aren't finished the cognitive living skills."

"No," I replied, "but I don't believe that's my fault..."

"Well...But you're going to finish it," Elliot said briskly.

116

I thought about what Julian had said to me when we first met: "The program should be over before your parole hearing, and if it's not, don't worry about it, you won't have to finish it."

"If, uh, I am in the program here, and I am not on day parole, I will be finishing it...yes," I said, stumbling over my words.

Mr. Elliot left no doubt about the justice system's position. "That," he said, "may be part of the conditions of your day parole. If we do grant one, it may be one of the requirements that you finish it."

Now feeling confident that I would comply, Mr. Elliot moved on. "Anyway, now tell us how you're putting all these things together to prevent similar circumstances from happening again. Which is, after all, what we're here for -- to decide what sort of a risk you present to the public of re-offending. So just relate it to us."

It had taken them a long time to come back around to the same question they had originally asked. I reached for my notes again. "Well, I think that's what I have written here so I'll..."

"You can use your notes," said Mr. Elliot, "but don't read from somebody else's notes."

"No," I replied, "these are mine."

I laid the statement on the table and read.

"I have accepted my responsibility for the assault on the victim, and I am sorry, and I regret it. My past shows me to have been a contributing member of society, and it is my desire to once again be a contributing and productive member.

This crime, as wrong as it was, which goes against not only the values that we as a society set out, but my own personal values as well, is not a crime restricted to an individual with a criminal nature. In this case the crime was done under severe emotional stress which clouded "good reason and good judgment.""

I finished my statement by talking about the support I had in the community and then looked at Mr. Elliot.

He appeared satisfied and turned to Ms. Reed. "Okay, Vivian, I'm..."

"I have a couple of other questions," she replied. "On the night of the offense, when you went to the victim's place. What did you intend to do? Did you intend to hurt him?"

I gave the obvious answer, "Yes, I believe I did, yes."

"You took a knife," continued Ms. Reed, "so you must have intended to hurt him quite badly."

"I don't know if I can answer that," I replied. "I don't know how 'badly' I wanted to hurt this man. I know I wanted to hurt him. I was hurting inside and wanted to strike back I guess."

"Do you consider yourself quite fortunate that he didn't die?" she asked. "You weren't sure afterwards whether this man had died or not?"

Ms. Reed again seemed more intent on portraying me as a vicious criminal with little or no remorse, and not someone who had been driven by circumstances. But, I knew I had let the victim go, and that he had been alive and well enough to run off into the night. I gave Ms. Reed the only answer I could. I let her know of my concern for the man the following day when I became more aware of the incident during my talk with Constable Magnus.

"Yes I was," I answered. "Well, I was scared as to how bad he was hurt. The next day I was talking to the police officer, and she assured me that he was going to be all right, and I thanked her for that information. I didn't totally understand everything that had happened, but I knew I had hurt this man."

"My next question is quite a different one," said Ms. Reed, bringing up the fear factor that the justice system wanted to keep near the surface of my case. "Um, your current case management has recommended day parole, but there was a change in the case management team, and there were totally different recommendations. Um, the previous one, Ms. Deardon, felt that,...uh,...you, uh...She felt that you...She opposed any kind of conditional release, due to your behavior while you were on her case load..."

118

After Virginia's angry input was inserted into the fray, Claire Culhane spoke out, chastising the Correctional Service, while demanding that the National Parole Board release me.

When the prisoner's rights activist concluded, we were all asked to vacate the room. Ten minutes later we were called back in. My heart jumped when the board members announced they were granting me parole, even though they made my release conditional on finishing the cog-skills program. I reached across the table and thanked the panel members.

After a jubilant, but short gathering outside, everyone dispersed, leaving Carter and I standing alone. "Now all you have to do is finish cog-skills!" said my case manager. His satisfied grin showed a comforting assurance about my compliance.

With my freedom tied to my willingness to play the parole game, I attended the cog-skills class for the next two weeks, speaking only when spoken to. Whenever Julian addressed me directly, I tried to assure him that I was considering and understanding his point of view, that being, that the system just had a job to do. But after the parole hearing it became clear that Julian no longer held a strong commitment to the course.

On the evening of June 30, one week after the hearing, I had a quiet and reflective talk with Doug Hampson. He told me that the first and most important thing for me to do was to get myself clear of the system before I pursued any quest for answers.

On the morning of July 5, I called the halfway house in Victoria and received confirmation from Kathy Roy that they had a bed waiting for me. I quickly went over to see Carter about setting a date to leave.

After that meeting I made one of the last entries in my diary before leaving the Ferndale Institution in 1993.

> July 5/93 Monday 9:52 AM: I talked with Kathy Roy on the phone this morning to confirm if I had a room and on what days they would accept me. She told me that they have a room already for me and that they would accept me on any day of the week, including

weekends. I told her that I would get a day confirmed with case management and call her back.

I went over and talked with Carter and told him about my conversation with Kathy and he called Julian into his office and the three of us talked. I let them know that I wanted to leave for Victoria on Friday July 16th. (That was the day I expected the cog-skills' program to be completed)

Carter asked Julian if I would be finished the program then. Julian said that he would do up the certificate and other paper work on the Tuesday or Wednesday before that Friday and that he believed I was the best student since the parole hearing and then said that he didn't think I could argue about that. Carter and Julian began laughing and Julian said that "if I wanted, he could always make something up."

I felt embarrassed and humiliated at what they were saying and the arrogance they were showing. I weakly laughed with them and said, "I have no comment on that." Julian said "good, you're realizing things can't always go your way!"

What's missing from the diary, are the winks and smiles exchanged by Carter and Julian while I bit my tongue throughout the humiliating experience.

With the class in some disarray, Julian ended it on July 9, a week earlier than expected. I spent the remaining time relaxing around the institution.

A couple of days before my release, I noticed a couple of white-collar inmates walk onto the golf course. It was about noon when they teed off, and I decided to grab my putter and three golf balls and go over to the ninth hole to relax.

Later in the afternoon, when I was walking past the duty office, one of the officers came out and asked me to step inside. I followed him into one of the rooms where Bill Kinnar sat, waiting behind his desk.

"Mr. Mitchell, it has been brought to my attention that you have been on the golf course before the designated time...How do you plead?"

I tried hard to hold back my stunned amusement at this last-ditch effort to intimidate me, but managed only modest success.

"You think this is amusing, Mr. Mitchell," the administrator said as he glared over the top of his spectacles, much as he had done months before when he announced my transfer back to Kamloops as a witness for a murder trial. "You think you're something, taking on this system, hey! This is serious, Mr. Mitchell. You are in my court today!...Now, HOW DO YOU PLEAD?"

"Not guilty, your honor."

"GUILTY! GUILTY!" Kinnar screamed. "THIS COURT FINDS YOU GUILTY!!"

"Can I go now?" I asked.

"I don't want to ever see you back in my court again, Mr. Mitchell. The punishment of this court will be severe next time!" With his clenched fist he gaveled his hearing adjourned. "NOW you can go," he said sternly.

The day before I was to leave, Julian summoned me to his office and handed me my cog-skills certificate. "There, now you're qualified to rejoin society," he said smugly.

I glanced at the document that gave society confirmation of a successful rehabilitation. I looked back at the Cog-skills instructor, who had remained seated. "Julian, what are you going to do when the glitter fades on this system's crystal ball and the people on the outside start looking in? What are you going to do when you're stuck inside, with no escape, and no place to hide?"

Julian scoffed at my words, but as he looked back at me I saw the uncertainty and fear in his eyes. I knew he was wondering.

Early the next morning, on Friday, July 16, 1993, Richard and Ruby Engel came out to the institution as arranged. While we were walking across the parking lot, I stopped and rested my hand on my friend's shoulder. "Richard, you and Ruby meet me out on the street. I'm going to walk out of this place!"

Richard smiled and nodded. I turned and quickly broke into a light lope down the long driveway and dashed through the gate-less barrier to my freedom.

Chapter 12

Day Parole

Five hours after leaving Ferndale, we arrived at Manchester House in Victoria on Vancouver Island. I thanked Richard and Ruby for their support, and then we said our good-byes, promising to stay in touch. The next day I had a dozen resumes printed, and five days later I had a job at a building materials store in the city. Although I settled into work comfortably, I remained haunted by the abuse and lack of due process I'd witnessed in the justice system. In particular, I struggled emotionally with the degrading stigma that went with the label "wife beater." What would people think of me if they believed what the justice system had written?

I searched for a lawyer, hoping to find someone who would proceed with a civil suit, but quickly realized it was going to be difficult to find legal representation willing to challenge their own. After several law firms turned me down, I decided to file the necessary court papers myself.

It was mid August by the time the court registry gave me a tentative date for a hearing, telling me it would not take place before the spring of 1994.

The Manchester House reestablished Judy Chouinard as my Federal case coordinator, and the parole officer in charge of the inmates at the halfway house was Bob Locke. Bob was a middle-aged man confined to a wheelchair who showed a spirit and enthusiasm that I admired. He told me that he hoped things would go well during my day parole, and assured me that I would have the opportunity to apply for full parole in December. He also told me he had assigned a new psychologist, Bruce Monkhouse to my case. My sessions with Monkhouse centered mostly on my anger and frustration at the lawyers involved in my case, along with what I saw as the abusive nature of corrections.

Monkhouse appeared to understand the depth of my disdain for the lawyers and correctional staff who had abused my legal and civil rights. He listened intently as I described how the legal-aid lawyers involved in the case had mislead me and given me inadequate representation. And he showed no surprise when I told him how case-workers at Ferndale had engaged in manufactured documentation and mail theft. With each session, his quiet acceptance of my anger helped lower my sense of alienation from society. And my increased freedom along with Sunday evening phone calls to my children helped raise my diminished self-esteem. During one of these calls, Steven told me Rob and his mother had gotten into an argument, and that Geri and the kids had since moved out of the fiveplex.

In September I was moved to quieter quarters on the top floor of the halfway house and started to anticipate my full parole hearing in December. If full parole was granted, I would be eligible to move into the community on my own, something I was definitely looking forward to.

As the weeks went by, however, I realized how much I missed my children. I desperately wanted to spend some time with them before they grew to an age where that chance would be lost. Jeff was now in his final year of high school, and Aimee was right behind in Grade 11. Even if they did come out to Victoria in a year or two, it would be several years before Steven was ready to leave home. I decided to let Judy know that after my full parole was granted in December, I was thinking of quitting my job and going back to Fernie.

A few days later I realized she had passed on word of my intentions to Bob Locke, who suggested that I should not consider such a move because Geri would need more time to feel comfortable about my return to that community. That was a problem I felt she had to deal with. I was not about to let her feelings separate me from the children. When I remained unconvinced, Bob suggested I consider moving to Cranbrook instead, the community that was only an hour's drive from Fernie. That he said, was a move he could support. Uplifted by his promise of support for full parole, I accepted the compromise.

Shortly after making my intentions known, I received a phone call from Ron Bentley, who had earlier sat in on for me during Geri's divorce application. He now said he had received a summons on my behalf for a family court appearance, scheduled for November 2, 1993. He asked me what I wanted to do about it, while suggesting that I let him attend the hearing as my representative and get the custody and access matter settled.

After receiving little feedback on the divorce proceeding, other than knowing that I was now divorced, I was growing ever more suspicious of legal-aid, and some of the court activities that had gone on outside of my presence. I considered the possibility there might be yet more collaboration going on, this time using the family court process to cover up the manipulation that had occurred in the criminal justice system.

"I don't want anything done until I can get back for the hearing," I said.

"Well, maybe I'll just go into the hearing and see what this is all about," Bentley replied.

"No, you get it delayed until after my parole," I shot back.

My suspicions that things may not be above board grew stronger when a week later I received a copy of the summons from Ron Bentley's office. It said: "If you do not appear, the Court may make an order in your absence or may issue a warrant for your arrest."

I immediately suspected the summons was meant to frighten me into allowing the legal-aid lawyer to show up at the hearing, leaving me with a false sense of security that I was being protected while I remained in Victoria. I rushed down to Len Fox's office and faxed a letter to the court registry in Fernie, stating that under no circumstances did any solicitor or lawyer have the authority to represent me without my personal consent before the court.

I then called Ron Bentley and let him know about the fax, informing him that I wanted to be brought back for the hearing. Ron suddenly showed a change of heart, informing me that he would not be available to represent me in court on that particular day. He suggested that I look for other counsel.

A couple of days later at the parole office, Bob Locke showed me a community assessment. It had been completed by the East Kootenay parole officer who would be in charge of my case if I returned to the area. In the report, parole officer, Dennis Larose, portrayed me as a tyrant and someone whom my ex-wife needed protection from. The document strongly suggested I should not be allowed back into the community of Fernie.

However, I also felt the report made it clear that the parole board would follow the court's lead when it set its parole conditions. I read, "The issue of visitation should be revisited immediately preceding the court proceedings. We will then be able to make arrangements that are in the spirit and direction of the courts."

I was uneasy about going into a family court hearing without a lawyer. If the hearing was going to deal with access and custody, exposing the character assassination the justice system had engaged in would be important. Most of the reports had demeaned and degraded me, and would no doubt be a factor in any decision the court made. I sat down with Judy Chouinard and let her know I wanted the hearing postponed until I could get back home and obtain legal representation. Judy pointed out that the summons indicated I could be charged for failing to make an appearance. She said if that happened I could lose my chance at full parole and maybe even have my day parole reviewed. It was hard to accept the fact that I might be sent back to prison for not attending this family court hearing, where I would have to represent myself without the aid of a lawyer.

Judy, however, convinced me to attend, and try to work things out. "It will go a long way towards securing your chance at full parole," she added. "A lawyer shouldn't be necessary if you go into court and keep your cool. If you do, I'm certain you'll get just about everything you want as far as custody and access go."

"Well, I'll attend the hearing, but I'm still going to tell some of my story," I replied bitterly.

"Just keep it toned down or there may be repercussions," warned Judy.

A few days later I received a notice from the National Parole Board telling me I was to have no contact with my children until after the hearing. I felt the Board's order was unfair and told Bob Locke so, reminding him that I had not seen my children for over two years.

When I received my travel permit from the Victoria parole office on October 27, 1993, it said I was to have no contact with Geri or Rob, but made no mention of the children.

I phoned to let the kids know that I would be arriving by bus at noon on Friday, October 29. When I arrived, Jeff and Aimee greeted me with lengthy hugs and we enjoyed a light lunch. It was hard to hide my

126

disappointment when they told me Steven was staying over at a friend's place, and Geri wouldn't tell them where he was.

I spent much of the weekend with Jeff and Aimee, catching up on some of their life events over the last two years. When they realized I was nervous about running into the victim of my assault, they eased my mind by telling me they thought he had sold the apartment and moved out of the area.

On Monday I walked across town to Steven's elementary school. The secretary nervously informed me that the school had been told that I was not allowed to see my son. I brought the principal into the discussion and produced the travel pass that stipulated no contact with the children's mother and the victim of my assault. I pointed out that there was no mention of the kids. I then explained that Geri only had interim custody of our children and that I was entitled to access.

When it became clear the principal would feel more comfortable if the decision were taken out of his hands, I politely asked him to call the police and have someone come down to the school. An officer showed up five minutes later and I handed him the pass. He made a quick phone call to the Victoria parole office and after a brief discussion with someone on the other end, the officer told the principal that as far as he was concerned, there was no problem.

Steven, had celebrated his eighth birthday only a month and a half before his life had been torn apart by his family's separation. A few months later his dad had also been taken out of his life. Steven was now nearly 11, and when he stepped out of his classroom this day, some of the childish features I remembered were clearly gone. He had grown considerably and his strawberry blond hair had blossomed into a rich dark red. The glasses he wore were something new, and there was almost no resemblance to the picture that graced my wallet.

Steven now stood in the middle of the hall, frightened and motionless. The vision I had of him running into my open arms splintered and shattered when he said, "Dad, I can't see you. Mom said that you're not allowed to come here and see me."

His innocent words cut deep, and I felt my legs buckle and shake from the sudden fear that maybe I had lost my son. But when I looked into his eyes, they told me something different. I might not have seen

127

Steven for a few years, but for the first eight years of his life he had had no closer friend than his father. I realized that the fear in his eyes, was not of me, but had been planted in him by others.

"Steven, it's all right," I said. "I talked with the policeman and the principal, and they said it was okay."

A familiar tight-lipped smile of joy crossed his face, but I still sensed some uncertainty. "I don't know," he said, "Mom's lawyer said..."

Unable to wait any longer, I stepped forward, lifted Steven into my arms, and hugged him. I reassured him once again that everything would be fine and asked him if he wanted to come out to the school-yard and talk for a few moments.

His arms closed about my neck. "Yeah!" he said excitedly. We sat at a picnic table and I let my youngest son know I had already seen his brother and sister. That helped ease his mind even more. I asked Steven about his school and his friends, and he eagerly told me about his teacher and classmates. We chattered for about 15 minutes before we decided he should head back to his class.

"I'm staying at the Three Sisters Motel, so bring your trunks over after school. We're all going for a swim in the pool, okay?" I said as I hugged him one more time. "You better get back to class and I'll see you later."

"Right after school?" replied Steven quickly. "Can I come over right after school?"

"Yes," I answered, "and Jeff and Aimee. We'll all go for a swim, and then out for supper."

Right on schedule, the kids arrived at the motel shortly after 3:30. Steven never moved far from me, and his enthusiasm returned with abundance in the pool. After the swim, Jeff and Aimee told me they would be at the courthouse the next morning to lend their support.

FAMILY COURT NOVEMBER 2, 1993

128

I met Jeff and Aimee outside the courthouse at 9:30 the following morning. When we learned that the hearing would not start for another 30 to 45 minutes, we decided to spend the time at a nearby doughnut shop.

We returned half an hour later. "Hurry, hurry! They're waiting for you," the woman from the court registry hollered.

We rushed upstairs to the courtroom and I placed a statement I had prepared on the counsel table. Jeff and Aimee took seats right behind me. I turned to look at them and noticed Geri sitting in the back row of the gallery seats. Beside her sat Steven, looking scared and confused. The fear I saw in him tugged at my stomach.

I now suspected that the start of proceedings had been delayed to give her time to slip away from the courthouse and take Steven out of school. It hurt me to see my youngest son nervously sitting in an atmosphere that would have confused and terrified any 10-year-old. I glared at the man standing behind the other counsel table. George Majic, Geri's lawyer, presented a go-for-the-throat demeanor in the courtroom, backed by a win-at-all-cost reputation.

The court clerk summoned the judge and announced the proceedings. I flinched as I recognized Judge Don Carlgren. He had presided over my first bail hearing in 1991, and I recalled that he had looked at a copy of the forensic report that day.

George Majic addressed the bench, mentioning that all the children were present and that he felt it would be appropriate for all three to be seated together. "I would like them to be here so they can see what's happening," he said as he turned and motioned to Geri, who brought Steven forward.

"Mr. Mitchell, what do you think about that?" asked Judge Carlgren.

I motioned for Jeff and Aimee to join and comfort Steven who looked frightened and lost. "I would love to see my kids up here," I answered.

Jeff and Aimee moved to the far side of the courtroom and joined Steven in the jury box that was located next to the other counsel table. George Majic looked over at me and smiled, then motioned for Geri to take her seat in a strategically placed chair at the end of the table, only a few feet away from our three children. I looked on, now isolated on the other side of the courtroom. I had no doubt that this was a deliberate tactic designed to move Jeff and Aimee away from me and closer to their mother, taking away the children's visible support for their father. The look of confusion and fear on Steven's face kept my pulse racing and I thought to myself, "Is there no end to the sewers these people will crawl into!"

Geri was called to the stand and there was some discussion of financial matters and maintenance. Then her lawyer switched modes and sought support for the character assassination that had been carried out in the criminal courts, and expanded on by Corrections Canada.

"Describe for His Honour your feelings about intimidation and the fear that you have for this man," said George Majic.

"Well," said Geri, "umxxxooo!!! uh, marriage. mmmmxxxooo---second child, mmxxxxooo!!--youngest child--uhhxxxooo!!

Unable to make out what she was saying, I interjected. "Excuse me a second. Can I get her to speak up?...I can't hear."

"I couldn't hear the last comment either," the judge responded. "You said the youngest child wasn't allowed to--"

The judge's request was left hanging as Geri continued, "...I would have to leave without the first child and that's the sort of thing--," and then her voice trailed off again.

Although I found Geri's testimony hard to follow, I felt I had picked up on a couple of points that she and her lawyer were trying to put into the record. One of them was a suggestion that not only was she afraid of me, but I was also someone the children feared.

George Majic understood there was no evidence to support the contention that I had a lifelong history of violence, and most certainly not against his client. So with Geri now in position to be cross-examined, their questions and answers indicated that physical violence wasn't necessary in the marriage because the fear she felt arose out of the emotional abuse she had allegedly endured throughout the lengthy relationship.

When it was my turn to question Geri, I was visibly shaking and upset. I had hoped that the hearing would help the family heal, at least to a point where we would be able to have a degree of civility when the children's best interests were being discussed, but I had now been forced into a position of having to redeem myself. I tried to attack the innuendo and suspicions that had been used against me during my incarceration, focusing mostly on the allegations of spousal abuse, and the system's continued inference that the children's mother had been the victim of ongoing assaults and abuse throughout the marriage.

When I attempted to get clarification on the subject of abuse, Geri's responses became non-committal, and I quickly became flustered when I realized she was deliberately refusing to answer the questions directly.

Suddenly Judge Carlgren interrupted. "But the first thing you started off with was to say that you had slapped her once in 17 years of marriage, and I'm going to ask her if she agrees or disagrees with that."

The judge turned from me and addressed Geri. "Is that true or not?" he asked.

"Yes, that's true," Geri said quietly.

I was elated that the allegations of ongoing physical abuse in the marriage had now been exposed as false. I turned and smiled across the courtroom at our children, feeling a sense of jubilation at the prospect of being able to go back to the parole board with an answer that would support what I had been saying all along.

The judge and my ex-wife were still talking, and when I turned my attention back to the proceedings, I heard her say something about a push. Then she again confirmed there had only been one slap in the 17 years of marriage, while indicating it was my controlling behavior that she found abusive, and that the physical violence wasn't really necessary.

Judge Carlgren handed me back my cross-examination. "Go ahead, Mr. Mitchell," he said.

I turned to my notes, where I had written down some of the allegations I had read in documents that had materialized during my incarceration. I questioned Geri about her claim that I had prevented her from attending our daughter's sporting activities, especially those that were held outside the community. She acknowledged that was not the case, testifying that she went on several trips alone with our daughter while I stayed at home and worked.

I was also upset that the relationship between Geri and Rob had been misrepresented. I felt my emotional state at the time of the assault had not been considered because the court did not have a full understanding of the circumstances surrounding the assault. My anger over this led me to a place I immediately regretted as I brought up some of the past activities surrounding my ex-wife's history. Realizing I would hurt my children if I continued, I stopped the cross-examination. However it was clear that the few questions I had asked about her relationship with Rob, had left her upset. She had angrily declared that it had been her choice to make. In the end she left the stand in a huff, staring straight ahead, careful not to look at me.

Then I was sworn in and I described to the court the good relationship I had with my children. I admonished the justice system for the dishonesty that had taken place in the criminal courts and condemned the correctional service for its abuse, specifically mentioning the Ferndale Institution and the theft of my mail.

Over the objection of Majic, I read excerpts from the text *Psychology and Life* and also read parts of my diary, being careful not to attack or demean the children's mother during my sworn testimony. In fact, outside of quoting Dr. Dilli's summary and conclusion in the forensic report, I made no mention of Geri during my presentation. When I concluded I asked the court to grant joint custody, then started to rise and leave the witness box.

"Not so fast, Mr. Mitchell," said Geri's counsel. "I have a few questions."

The first thing Majic attacked me on was the perceived breach of the National Parole Board's order that I not see the kids until after the hearing. I suspected the animated tirade behind his counsel table had everything to do with the fact that Jeff and Aimee had shown up at the courthouse to support me. There was little doubt that the kids support contradicted the justice system's documentation, that had been meant to leave the impression my children were fearful of me.

After suggesting the perceived breach showed a lack of respect for the law, Majic tried to prove that the criminal court record in my case had been truthful when it said I was in complete control of myself on the night of the assault. I responded by referring to Dr. Dilli's summary and conclusion in the forensic report. The doctor's words clearly disputed Majic's suggestion. "It is arguable that he was not in control of himself," had been Dilli's final words.

Then Majic asked, "Are you saying it's somebody else's fault that you broke into that place with a knife?"

I again told Majic, that I believed Dr. Dilli's comments regarding my emotional state at the time were accurate. He then made the point that I had pled guilty at the sentencing hearing. When I started to explain how that came about, Majic stammered, "No, ...No," cutting me off.

The lawyer then tried to get me to agree that the children's mother should be fearful of me. I promptly dismissed that assertion as well. Majic let it go, and out of nowhere, ridiculed me for not having a financial statement prepared for the hearing. However, besides some locked-in RRSPs, I had nothing left in my life but my children, and I suspected Mr. Majic knew it.

I left the stand and returned to the counsel table, where I responded to some more questions from the bench. "I have an objection to any structure that does not give my children and me the freedom to see one another when we want," I said.

I felt reassured about my chances for equal access when Judge Carlgren responded confidently to my comment. "Given what the parole board has done to date, I would expect that they probably will permit you to return to Fernie."

I asked the judge if there was anything in the family court agreement that kept me from coming into the community to see my children and participate in their school activities or any other sporting events.

"I don't see it," replied Judge Carlgren.

That evening the kids and I went out for supper and enthusiastically discussed the long-awaited Christmas we would finally get

133

to spend together. The following day the kids showed up at the bus station and we said our good-byes with more hugs and promises that we would see one another soon, confident that the National Parole Board would make a judgment that reflected the spirit and direction of the court.

Chapter 13

A Stolen Christmas

Even though I had muted my condemnation of the justice system during the family court hearing, my exposure of even a few of the deceitful actions that had occurred during my incarceration had been too much for the system to bear. Bob Locke was reassigned, and another parole officer, Dave Paul, took over my case. He immediately went to work, repeatedly admonishing me for calling the correctional service abusive.

Frustrated and upset, I asked Bob Locke if he could get me back on his caseload. Bob told me that these kind of switches happened routinely and there was nothing he could do about it. However, he did say that I was eligible for a student loan and encouraged me to apply for funds, and for courses at the East Kootenay College in Cranbrook. I did so, but Dave Paul continued to engage in his daily sessions of intimidation, constantly threatening to withhold his support for my full parole. There had been no specific date set for the hearing, but now it didn't appear to matter as my new parole officer said it was unlikely to take place before the New Year.

In desperation I fought back. I bought two large, colored, cardboard placards and a couple of felt pens, wrote up my plea, naming the lawyers and condemning them and the correctional service for their conduct, while making the point that they were now vindictively scuttling a planned Christmas reunion between three children and their father. I attached photos of the kids to the signs and spent a day protesting in front of the courthouse. The following day I moved down the street and continued my public display in front of the solicitor-general's office, all the while slipping deeper into a paralyzing state of depression.

On December 8, strained to the point of exhaustion, my nerves finally collapsed. After hours of uncontrollable shaking at the halfway house, I was admitted to the hospital emergency room, where the nurses covered me with warm blankets. "David, these people play for real! I'm afraid for you!" The unnerving words from the past forced me under the protective cover of darkness; I slid beneath the heavy wool into unconsciousness. Just over a month had elapsed since the promising family court hearing, but the parole service's recent onslaught of psychological abuse had managed to drain me emotionally.

And they weren't finished yet. Instead, the psychological abuse recklessly intensified a few days later. Back at the half-way house, Dave Paul suggested a parole decision could still be made before Christmas. "If you agree to accept a paper decision, you could still get home by the holidays," he coaxed.

The justice system quickly had me running in circles and reaching for any carrot it dangled in front of me. Confused and desperate, I started faxing letters to the National Parole Board, agreeing to accept a paper decision that could get me home in time for a Christmas reunion with the kids. But when it became clear that my faxes from the MLA's office were creating a paper trail, one that showed I was being pressured to accept a decision without being present to state my case, the board backed down and set a hearing date.

A glint of delight crossed Dave Paul's face when he informed me the hearing would not take place until January 11, 1994. "David, you've been through this before. Hang in there," I said quietly, trying to hide my pain and disappointment at the loss of yet another Christmas with the kids.

The threats and intimidation continued to gather steam for the next two weeks, and just days before Christmas I was summoned to the parole office for another meeting.

"We've had to block out the beginning and the end of this victim impact statement we received from your ex-wife," said Dave Paul. "By law we're not supposed to show it to you, but we thought you should see what she wrote."

I reached out and took the document from his hand.

"If I were you," he added, "I would be careful what you say to the board."

The victim impact statement did all it could to dehumanize and portray me as someone bent on revenge against Geri, who claimed in the document to be deathly afraid of me.

"It doesn't look good for your parole," said Dave Paul mischievously.

"How can she write a victim impact statement and send it to you people?" I said dejectedly. "She was not the victim of my assault."

I frantically called the court transcriber and asked for a copy of the court transcripts from the November 2 family court hearing. If I could show the board that there had only been one slap in the marriage, certainly that would help. Dejectedly, I listened as the lady told there was not enough time to do the entire transcript. However, she promised to transcribe, and send Geri's testimony to me by way of the parole office.

Fearful that her sworn testimony might not arrive in time, which would support the fact there had only been one slap in the 17 years, I decided to try and involve the media. I talked with Clem Chapple, a parliamentary reporter for one of the major TV networks in the area. He believed my story was too detailed for a television news story, and said I should consider writing a book. I called the local paper, the *Times Colonist*, and columnist Jody Patterson came over to the halfway house. She also felt my story was so broad and complicated that it would be hard for her to do it justice in the paper. Jody echoed Clem Chapple's suggestion that the story could be better told in a book.

With my nerves on edge and my concentration level low, I took my leave from work a few weeks early. The halfway house administrator, who had not been involved with my case, now joined the fray. He lashed out at me for picketing against the justice system and threatened to send me back to prison for stepping away from my job before I knew whether or not I would be granted full parole.

As the New Year approached, the situation appeared hopeless, and Judy Chouinard called me into her small office on the top floor of the halfway house. I could see the pain in her eyes as she pleaded with me to back off the system, undoubtedly hoping such a move would temper the correctional service's anger at me.

The relentless pressure I was feeling had reached a critical stage. Freedom once again hinged on my willingness to play the parole game.

Fighting a sickening sense of fear, I removed my diary notes and a few other documents from my array of papers, loaded the remainder into my briefcase and headed downtown to the parliament buildings, where I had stored a couple of boxes in the MLA's office. I shredded just about everything and then went over to the courthouse and canceled my lawsuit against the justice system.

The time had come. I swallowed hard, took a deep breath, and headed for the parole office. With tears streaming down my cheeks, I begged for their support, letting Dave Dystra, the head of the local office, know I had withdrawn my legal action against the system. I opened my briefcase and started ripping up the remaining documents and notes. Dystra looked on without saying a word as the mangled and torn pieces of paper slowly filled the box he had set down in front of me.

The following day Dave Paul showed up at the halfway house, beaming with delight and bubbling with enthusiasm. He congratulated me on my change of attitude and joyfully declared that he was now supporting my application for parole.

Full Parole Hearing:

When I entered the parole office on January 11, 1994 I was handed a copy of Geri's testimony from the November 2 hearing. I quickly glanced through it, looking for her acknowledgement of only one slap in the lengthy marriage. Although I found it, I was horrified when I read other comments that I had not picked up on. I assumed most of it fit into the mumbling I had heard that day as Geri gave her testimony. Already assured of support for my full parole, I decided to hang onto the partial transcript and look into it in more detail once I got back home.

I walked into the hearing and my heart skipped a beat when I realized Mr. Young was one of the panel members. I had not forgotten the angry and antagonistic nature of this man who had denied me day parole at my first parole hearing over a year earlier.

The other man, whom I did not recognize, motioned for me to sit in a chair directly across the table from him.

"Your name is David Mitchell?" he asked.

"Yes," I answered.

"And your FPS# is 315377B?"

"Um, I'm not familiar with the numbers," I replied.

"Okay," he said, clearly displeased.

"I try not to keep track of it," I added quickly.

"Well, you'll be keeping track of it for a while yet," he said emphatically. "My name is Wilson Segg and my colleague is Michael Young, and we're the members of the board dealing with your case today."

Mr. Segg asked all the people in the room to identify themselves and then turned back to me. "You continually believe for one reason or another that you've been unfairly treated by the justice system," he began abruptly. "Why is that?"

"Those are my personal views and I don't think they should be a part of this hearing," I replied cautiously.

"But I'm asking you why!" he insisted.

In the face of his insistence, I reluctantly and briefly described what I saw as the dishonest actions of my legal-aid lawyers and the prosecutor.

"Okay...uh, there was also concerns raised regarding, uh, you contacting your children in violation of your conditional conditions when you went to Fernie prior to your court date," he said, suddenly changing the subject. "I would like to refer to the conditional conditions that were imposed by one of the voting members, my colleague Mr. Young. It states clearly, 'No contact with the victim, your former wife or your children except as expressly directed by the courts following'--the key word there is *following*--the hearing set for November 2, 1993."

Mr. Segg stopped and leaned forward. "Now there's some indication on file that you contacted your children prior to that court date."

"My children were at the bus waiting for me when I got there," I replied.

After a lengthy discussion of the conditions attached to my travel certificate, Mr. Segg asked if I had a copy of it with me.

I handed the travel certificate across the table. A look of frustration crossed his face as he read the document. "Okay, this cert doesn't include the additional condition that was imposed on October 18," he said quietly.

Mr. Young spoke up. "That would be on the travel permit, wouldn't it?" he asked as he looked at my parole officer.

"Yes," Dave Paul responded nervously.

"That is what I am trying to say," I said, "The travel permit that I got from this office stated only that I was not to have contact with my ex-wife."

With the realization that the board's condition had been left off the travel permit, Mr. Young looked at Dave Paul in disgust. "Then that was a serious mistake on the part of Victoria parole!" he said bitterly.

Mr. Young now brought up his concerns over my anger at the system, and the psychological stress that was attached to it. When he finished, Mr. Segg added, "What it does mean is that you may need some protection for yourself, and some other people may need some protection for themselves."

"I have no desire to hurt or harm anyone," I pleaded. "I think that is pretty clear."

"I don't think you had any desire to do what you did to your victim at the time either, did you?" Mr. Young said quietly.

His admission caught me off guard. "Pardon me?" I said, unsure if I had heard correctly.

"I don't think you had any desire,. . . objective desire,. . . to do what you did to your victim at the time either."

I realized that for the first time, someone from the justice system, other than a doctor or counselor, had acknowledged some understanding of my emotional state at the time of the assault. I then heard Mr. Young question my sense of being victimized, and I asked him to explain what he meant.

"In the sense that you feel you have been badly abused by the criminal justice system," Mr. Young replied, "that you feel you have been misunderstood."

"Are you saying I was not?" I asked.

"As far as I know you weren't," his voice quivered, "but you may have been."

"Do I have the right to my opinion on that?" I asked.

"You have the right to your opinion, but it is how it comes out," he replied. "There are abuses in the criminal justice system, I'm quite sure. And there are a lot of people who go through it."

I started to acknowledge his more than truthful statement, but Mr. Young cut me short. "A lot of people go through that," he said. "It's, uh, it's interesting though, to see how you have reacted to that abuse," he paused to catch himself, "that you perceive as opposed to other people."

"And how have I reacted that is wrong, in your opinion?" I asked.

"I think, I think . . . I think you're," Mr. Young stammered, "you're very frustrated and stressed to the point where it's exhibited at every turn."

Mr. Young's anger returned as he brought up my recent frustration with the condition that I have no contact with my children. "Well, I . . . I'm not too sure you didn't take advantage of the board when you went to court last time," he said, "because I think you were aware of what the board's decision was."

"That's not what we're talking about here," I responded. "We're talking about my frustration and anger..."

Mr. Young cut me short. "You were talking about not violating any conditions! You were aware of what the board's decision was!"

"That was the board's decision!" I challenged him abruptly. "I think you also understand, and I think it is quite clear, that the relationship between myself and my children is a very, very healthy one."

"That's right, and I think the board recognized that the relationship was important and the board said, 'Fair enough, you go to court, deal with it,' and the board allowed you to do it!"

Mr. Young's statement was more than a little disingenuous when you considered the facts. First of all I had not wanted to go into family court until I had legal representation with me, but the justice system had forced me to do so with its threats of re-imprisonment for disobeying a court summons. On top of that there had been talk of revoking my day parole if I did not get the family court case settled!

Both Mr. Segg and Mr. Young then exploded over the fact that I had seen my kids prior to the hearing. "...I DON'T REALLY CARE WHAT'S ON THE TRAVEL PASS!!" screamed Mr. Segg.

Their intense anger over the fact that I had seen my children before the family court hearing was out of all proportion. I suspected my earlier deduction had been correct. My children attending the hearing in support of their father was something the justice system had not wanted to see.

When the panel's anger finally subsided, Dave Paul was asked for his input.

"I would just like to add, that when David Mitchell was first released I saw a very angry, hostile, and bitter person. Uh, well to be perfectly honest, I didn't understand why he was still really angry. He felt he was unjustly persecuted by our justice system and, and things began to change in December when I took over his case on a full-time basis."

I looked at Dave Paul in astonishment as he remained focused on the panel and continued. "Um, we have had a lot of go-arounds, a lot of confrontations about his behaviors. Um, he can't just look at his point of view. He's got to be willing to look at other people's point of view, and he has to accept that. I'm not saying he's perfect, but I do believe he has begun to accept that. Yeah, there is a lot of problems on his own part."

I rolled my eyes at his dishonest account of events. Just two weeks earlier he had still been threatening to withhold his support for my full parole.

Dave Paul went a step farther and used me as an example to pat the justice system on the back, confident that with my parole hanging in the balance I would not disagree with anything he said. I played the game, sitting quietly, and angrily, accepting his self-serving statements.

Judy Chouinard then gave her presentation. I had come to understand the pressure people felt, to follow and support the paper trail laid out by this abusive bureaucracy. However, after Judy's expected support in this area, she contradicted some of the innuendo which had been put into the record, including one of Dave Paul's earlier statements. She questioned his insinuation that I didn't listen to other points of view. "He doesn't automatically dismiss you because your opinion is different," Judy said.

Mr. Segg then turned to me and asked if I had anything else to add. I asked the panel for confirmation that it had seen the letter written by my son Jeff, a supportive letter asking why I had not been allowed to come home for Christmas after the family court hearing. The panel acknowledged the letter, while also confirming the existence of a positive reference letter from my employer.

With the mention of my employer's letter, Judy spoke up once again, "I should probably add that David got the job within about four days of arriving at Manchester. He has never been so much as 30 seconds late for curfew." She then emphasized her closing comment. "There has never, ever, been a suspicion or complaint against David in any way, shape, or form against the rules of the house. A fantastic day parole in that regard!" she said boldly.

"Okay," responded Mr. Segg, "if you will all step outside for a few moments."

15 agonizing minutes passed before the board summoned us back.

"Mr. Mitchell, um, we've made a decision to grant you your full parole," announced Mr. Segg.

143

My heart jumped, and then he continued. "NOW, I want you to listen very carefully to our reasons why we've also opted to impose five additional conditions on that release. Since your release on day parole, you've made significant advancement in your dealing with anger management problems. Counseling reports indicate that you have gained significant benefit and that you will not present a risk while on full parole. You have developed an insight into your criminal behavior. However, this understanding appears to have been clouded by your...," he paused and glanced up at me, "...by your distrust for the justice system."

I listened as Mr. Segg read the first four conditions that one might expect to see on any parole document: abstain from alcohol, submit to breathalyzer, follow psychological counseling, and have no contact with the victim and, in this case, with my ex-wife as well. All of them, subject to the approval of my parole officer. "And the fifth," he said, "not to enter within a 10-mile radius of your ex-wife's residence."

There it was! After I had fought in family court for the right to engage in my children's activities, in their community, the board had taken it away with a restriction that prevented me from entering the city of Fernie.

A swell of hostility rose, but I quickly checked myself with the thought that I had just been granted full parole. Somewhat hesitantly, I addressed the panel. "Can I question that one for just a moment?"

Mr. Segg's quick, but quiet response told me he had expected my inquiry. "Yes, yes," he replied.

"What about the court hearing and the spirit of the court? What about my son's statement, and the children's wish for their father to participate in their lives?" I pleaded, "What about my son's graduation?"

"After you have lived in the neighboring community for some time," answered Mr. Segg, "and Dennis [the East Kootenay parole officer] gets to know you better and you're able to establish some credibility with him, maybe Dennis may choose to ask for terms and conditions to be altered and modifications of that condition, but in the initial release..."

"Can that be done before my son's graduation?" I pleaded.

"Don't know...Don't know," said Mr. Young.

"It may never happen," responded Mr. Segg.

"I mean it's possible, if everything goes well, as it should," I begged, "that, that, that it can be changed before Jeff's graduation," I said, faltering badly now as I choked back my disappointment and anger.

"I guess, I guess what we're saying is..." said Mr. Young, who paused before continuing more emphatically. "I want to make it perfectly clear! We believe that you will follow the requirements of your parole!"

With the stern warning still hanging in the air, Mr. Segg brought the hearing to an end with one final act of intimidation. "That's our decision for the day. Um, we hope things work out for you, but let me give you this warning. Sometimes people on full parole let their guard down a bit too much. You are still serving your sentence in the community. We suggest that you remember your FPS number. Don't try to lose it too fast," he said, raising his voice once again, "because you will be serving your sentence in the community until October of 1995. And you're under the supervision of corrections until that time. One would hope you're going to make some wiser judgments in the future than you have while on day parole!"

My disdain for the constant threats and intimidation suddenly dissolved my will to remain silent. "Well," I shot back, "I thought my day parole had gone pretty well!"

"That's our decision for today!" barked Mr. Segg, ignoring my comeback.

The following day I returned to the parole office, looking for my release papers. Dave Paul walked up to me as I was standing at the front counter. "See how easy it is!" he exclaimed proudly.

"What you did in the hearing was garbage!" I replied. "To come in at the last minute and take some kind of self-serving credit, after abusing me for weeks leading up to the hearing was disgusting!"

Dave Paul's face turned a bright crimson. "I'm going to call the board and tell them what you just said! I will tell them to cancel your parole immediately!" he shouted.

145

"Go ahead, go ahead and try!" I said, calling his bluff.

Dave Dystra approached the counter and broke up the confrontation, telling me to come back the next day and pick up the papers.

The following morning, two hours before my bus was scheduled to leave, the parole office still refused to hand over my parole documents. Dystra suggested an apology to Dave Paul might help matters. And then, on cue, the parole officer stepped into view.

"Your integrity and honesty really should be questioned," I said as I stared at Dave Paul. "You have no right to withhold my parole papers because you're angry, ..and I meant everything I said yesterday." I turned back to Dave Dystra. "If I don't get the parole papers, I'll walk over to the parliament building and have a chat with some MLAs, and then call the media. I will then get on the bus and leave for home, with or without my papers!"

"Apologize to me!" screamed Dave Paul.

"I have nothing to apologize to you for," I replied sharply as my eyes shifted to the approaching figure of Bob Locke. My former parole officer eased his wheelchair up to the counter, reached up, and without saying a word, handed me my release papers. Without uttering a word, he wheeled his chair about and disappeared around the corner.

Dave Paul muttered under his breath, then abruptly stormed off in a rage. Without hesitation, I nodded at Dave Dystra, turned, and headed for the bus station.

Chapter 14

Challenging the National Parole Board

It was noon on January 14 when the bus pulled into the city of Cranbrook. In stark contrast to the milder West Coast climate, a snowstorm was busy blanketing the Rocky Mountain community. I sheepishly snapped up my light summer jacket, grabbed my bags, and checked into a nearby motel.

After running a hot bath and lingering in the tub for a half-hour, I made a call to my new parole officer, Dennis Larose, who lived in the neighboring community of Creston. He told me he would come into Cranbrook at the end of the week and go over my parole conditions. In the evening I phoned the kids in Fernie, 60 miles to the northeast and made arrangements for them to drive my car into Cranbrook and visit me the following weekend.

I had found myself a reasonable apartment and registered at the college by the time Dennis dropped by and gave me the name, phone number, and address of a counselor I was to contact. We also spent some time discussing my parole conditions. I relayed to him what the parole board had said about the fifth condition being removed at his discretion. "I would like to see it taken off in a couple of months," I said.

"We'll talk about it at that time," replied Dennis, who then added an additional condition that restricted me from traveling more than 50 miles on the main highways leading north or south out of Cranbrook. The city of Fernie blocked the third route out of the area, and the United States boarder lay less than 50 miles south of the city. The correctional service had effectively penned me in.

The fact was, my focus wasn't on traveling any place other than family court. At the November hearing, Judge Carlgren had indicated that the court saw no reason why I would not be allowed into Fernie, suggesting the parole board would probably grant that as well. He then stated that after I had been granted parole, the matter of access could be revisited in court, along with any problems that arose.

Well I had a problem! The fifth parole condition, restricting me from entering within 10 miles of Fernie was going to severely curtail my access to my children. I had a strong suspicion that the dishonest and dehumanizing victim impact statement signed by Geri just before my parole hearing, had been initiated by the criminal justice system. Done so, in an effort to offset Judge Carlgren's comments that suggested the board would most likely follow the spirit and direction of the family court, and allow me back into the community.

I filed for a hearing and was given a date of March 9. I contacted legal-aid for help, who assigned a lawyer who lived in the city of Nelson, a community beyond the 50-mile travel limit, a distance which severely hampered my ability to go over the case.

I quietly pondered the new condition imposed by Dennis. It supported my suspicions that the justice system was manipulating the family court process in an effort to protect individuals who had been involved in unethical, and maybe even illegal conduct in my criminal case. That suspicion rose to new heights when my new legal-aid lawyer, Ley Apsassin came into Cranbrook and pleaded with me to drop my attempts to look for answers in family court.

However, I remained undeterred and mailed her some of the false documentation that the justice system had on file. She returned the papers with a letter of her own, telling me the documents added nothing to the case. A few days later her office informed me she was no longer available to proceed on my behalf. I hastily made my way back to the legal-aid office, but to my dismay, I was refused funds to pay for new legal counsel. Once again I was forced to fend for myself.

Besides the difficulties I was experiencing with my legal matters, a lack of money for living expenses, which included bus fare to Cranbrook for the kids, was also becoming a problem. I tried to get more money through the student loan program, with no luck. With my money rapidly running out, I set my schooling aside and started looking for full-time work.

I also kept up my mandatory counseling sessions with Kevin Kennedy. He acknowledged that I had a good understanding of the problems that had surfaced in my marriage, and felt that I would not likely allow them to be repeated in any future relationship. He also believed I posed no danger to my ex-wife and that a fair agreement concerning access and custody issues would end matters.

148

However, my anger and frustration with the justice system was another matter altogether. Most of our counseling sessions focused on this area, and Kevin warned me, "If you try and attack the criminal justice system in family court, it will fight hard to protect itself!" Kevin believed the enormous stress associated with challenging the justice system would drain me emotionally, and he suggested I drop my quest for answers. However, he also made it clear that the decision was mine, and mine alone to make. With our positions clear, we both agreed to postpone our next meeting until after the family court hearing. Then we would discuss the outcome of the hearing and where we would go from there.

The day before my date in family court, Dennis Larose assured me that if I got things settled in court, it would have a bearing on the removal of the restrictive condition imposed by the parole board.

So on March 9, 1994, accompanied once again by Jeff and Aimee, I addressed the family court judge in Fernie, BC. "My ex-wife sent a letter to the National Parole Board after the last hearing, which has interfered with my access. And I would like the whole thing reviewed," I said determinedly.

"Just a moment, just a moment," replied Judge Diebolt. "Just listen to me! Has this court prevented you from access to Fernie?"

"No, it has not," I answered.

"Okay!" exclaimed the judge, "The parole board has."

"Yes, they have!" I replied bitterly.

"Okay," said Judge Diebolt. "I have nothing to do with the National Parole Board. Any order I make today won't necessarily affect the National Parole Board and what they do."

"Not necessarily, but it will," I answered. "I talked with the parole officer yesterday. He was in Cranbrook to see me and he said, 'If you get that matter straightened out, yes, it will have a bearing on this.'"

Then without hesitation, I informed the court that I wanted to question the falsehoods in the victim impact statement, Geri had recently signed.

149

"Well, Your Honor," said George Majic, "I am not sure that this is the proper forum for this type of hearing. We were here to review the access and we've made a proposal. I haven't heard him say anything about it. If he has a problem with the parole board, that's between him and the parole board. I'm not prepared, Your Honor, to embark on the calling of evidence to refute what Mr. Mitchell is going to say here. Not today."

I shrugged off Majic's plea, and presented the court with a copy of the victim impact statement. After reading it, the judge addressed her counsel. "Mr. Majic, what's your position?"

"There is nothing in this letter that casts any aspersions on this man," replied George Majic, "and I am not going to allow my client to be cross-examined about this!"

Judge Diebolt quickly supported my ex-wife's counsel and ruled that no evidence would be heard that involved the National Parole Board.

I stood my ground and angrily insisted that I be allowed to question the allegations in the victim impact statement. The letter clearly stated that I had abused my wife for years, and threatened to do her harm throughout the marriage, and it suggested that I now posed a threat to her in the community.

"Mr. Mitchell, for the last time, I am going to make a statement to you," said Judge Diebolt. "You don't seem to understand or appreciate, for this hearing today, there is no allegation of abuse being made against you in this hearing! Do you understand that? Do you not understand that?"

I defiantly held my position, believing I had a right to question a process that allowed damaging innuendo and suspicions to be put into a record, without having the support of evidence. It was after all, innuendo that the National Parole Board was using to justify its restrictions.

Judge Diebolt sighed once again. "Sometimes things are said in a courtroom and then pursuing them ad nauseam gains nothing," he replied. "You are not going to structure this hearing." Judge Diebolt then adjourned the proceedings and set a new hearing date of April 12, a little over a month away, insisting that the whole matter should be reheard before Judge Carlgren, who had been the presiding judge at the November hearing.

150

The postponement meant the parole condition and the restricted access to my children would remain in place. Upset with the delay, I returned to Cranbrook, firmly set on challenging the National Parole Board. I called the kids and told them that I would be back in Fernie on Friday to file court papers, inviting them to return to Cranbrook with me and spend the weekend if they wished.

Unfortunately, as president of the student body, Jeff had obligations for the upcoming graduation ceremonies. However, Aimee received her mother's permission, and I made arrangements for her and Steven to return to Cranbrook with me.

A few days later, with my court papers ready to file and arrangements in place with the kids, I was all set for my mid-week meeting with the parole officer. We met at a restaurant on the main highway running through Cranbrook, and I told him of my plans to go into Fernie. Dennis Larose balked, telling me I would be violating my parole condition if I went in without his permission, which he was not prepared to give.

"Dennis," I said, "I am going into Fernie to see my children and bring them back with me. If this system wants to throw me back into prison for being a good father, then that's what it's going to have to do!"

"If you go," Dennis replied, "the consequences could be severe. Give me some time and I'll see if I can get the condition dropped," he pleaded.

"I have already made the arrangements with the kids," I said. "The children's mother has given them permission to come back with me and I'm going into Fernie, with or without your permission."

Although Dennis was not pleased with me for challenging the board's authority, he relented and gave me verbal permission, suggesting he could not stop me from filing court papers in the community. On Friday, March 25, I drove to Fernie, and Aimee and Steven returned to Cranbrook with me. On Saturday we drove to Fairmont Hot Springs and enjoyed a great day in the hot pools. At the end of what was a terrific weekend, the kids took the bus back to Fernie, leaving with an expectation that we would spend more time together during the upcoming Easter weekend.

151

However, by mid-week I realized I could not afford the $75 it would cost me for bus tickets for all three of my children. On Good Friday I phoned and asked Jeff to let his mother know that I would like to come into town on Easter Monday, April 4, and take them to Sparwood. Gas for the whole trip would only cost about $20, and the community lay 20 miles east of Fernie, beyond the 10-mile restriction that the National Parole Board had put in place.

Jeff told me his mother wasn't home, but he would tell her about the plans we were making, and see if she would agree to them. When I called back Sunday evening, Jeff said he had talked with his mother, and that she had no problems with the arrangement. All she wanted to know was what time I was going to pick them up.

"How about 11 o'clock at the Park Place motel parking lot?" I said.

Later that same evening, Dennis Larose made an unusually late call, giving me short notice that he intended to come into town in the morning. At 9 am, I once again met him at a restaurant on the main highway, and he raised the subject of my challenging the 10-mile restriction.

I assumed he was still upset about the previous week, so without saying anything about my plans for this day, I took the opportunity to ask Dennis why he had not followed through with my request to have the restrictive condition dropped.

"I personally don't believe the condition is necessary," replied Dennis, "but the board has put it there, and they like to carry these things through to the end. Please don't force it right now, and I guarantee you I'll get it dropped." Dennis rose from the booth. "It's a done thing!" he said, then promptly headed for the exit.

I remained seated, finishing my coffee, my thoughts lingering on the day that lay ahead. I considered the fact that just 10 days earlier, I had made the trip into Fernie without any problems arising. Something I wanted to make abundantly clear to the National Parole Board, over and over again. I took into account Dennis's remark that he did not believe the fifth condition was necessary, and concluded that, at worst, the board might reprimand me for challenging its authority, if it did anything at all.

Regardless, the plans were set and I was not going to disappoint my children. I raised my cup and downed the last drop of coffee. An hour later I passed a sign indicating I was entering the city limits of Fernie, and shortly after that I pulled into the motel parking lot where my two sons were waiting. I stepped out of the car. "Hi, guys," I said as we hugged. "Where's your sister?"

"Don't know," said Jeff and Steven, flashing sly, mischievous grins at my disappointment. Just then I felt two arms wrap round my neck as Aimee jumped on my back with a heart-warming laugh. I gave my daughter a short piggyback ride and then the four of us jubilantly piled into the car and headed out of town.

When we arrived at the pool in Sparwood we discovered that public swimming would not begin until later in the afternoon. Since it was closing in on lunchtime, we decided to sit down to a hearty meal of burgers and fries at an uptown restaurant. When we were finished, instead of waiting around for the pool to open, we decided an afternoon of family bowling would be equally as much fun.

There was a response to each ball rolled: loud cheers for a strike or spare; moans followed every head-pin; and roars of laughter and even some woeful howls could be heard whenever a shakily thrown gutter ball dived off the lane. Jeff beamed with pride, as did I, when he scored over 200 for the first time, tying my score in doing so. We talked about his graduation, and he was obviously pleased that I would be home to witness that milestone in his life. Jeff had always been an honor student, and I was quick to let him know how proud I was of his academic achievements.

Aimee also scored her highest game ever and beat her older brother in the process. She spent the afternoon grinning from ear to ear, pumping her fist in the air, and joyously screaming, "Alright! alright!"

Steven remained close to my side through it all, fearful I might disappear if he could not reach out and grab hold of my arm at all times. Because he was so much younger, his scores were lower than those of his siblings. I could see the disappointment in his face at some of his gutter balls in the early games, but with constant encouragement from his family, he bowled over 100 in the final game. His face radiated with pride as his brother and sister lifted him into the air and we cheered the new kingpin.

There was no doubt that Steven had missed having these close times with his father, and I felt an unbearable pain whenever that thought crossed my mind. Steven had gone through his ninth and tenth birthdays without his father around to comfort him in the bad times, or cheer him on in the good. On this day he proudly announced that he was going to spend his 11th birthday with his dad. It was clear that he wanted a lot more days like this special Easter Monday.

The sun had sunk behind the mountain peaks by the time we arrived back in Fernie. We stopped for pops and discussed plans for Steven's birthday on April 11, just one day before the scheduled family court hearing. The kids then piled into the car and I dropped them off at home before heading back to Cranbrook.

I spent an upbeat evening, enjoying some television and reflecting on a terrific day with the kids. After the late news I crawled into bed and slipped into a night of pleasant dreams.

Early the next morning, on April 5, the phone woke me early. I crawled out of bed and made my way into the living room and lifted the receiver. "Hello, hello?" I said. A light click rudely told me the caller had hung up. I put the receiver back in its cradle and wandered into the bathroom. After taking care of business, I turned on the tap, splashed some water on my face and reached for a towel.

A knock on the apartment door startled me. Such an early morning visitor seemed unusual, and I hesitantly unlocked the deadbolt before opening the door a few inches.

"What...?"

"Are you David Howard Mitchell?" asked one of the three police officers standing in the hall.

"Yes," I said, regaining some composure. "Can I help you?"

"We have a warrant for your arrest, issued by the National Parole Board," said the officer as he rattled a piece of paper and pushed the door wide open. "It states that you violated a condition of your parole by entering within 10 miles of the city of Fernie, BC, yesterday!"

A blast of fear propelled me back a couple of steps. "This is garbage and nothing more then harassment by these people!" I hollered. "I spent the day with my kids! With their mother's permission!"

"Well, you'll have to explain that to them."

One of the officers stepped through the door and raised his handcuffs. My legs buckled ever so slightly and I suddenly felt the pit of my stomach churning. "Can I get dressed?" I asked shakily.

"Make it quick!" Came his harsh reply.

"You better make sure everything is turned off and locked up," the third officer barked. "You may be gone for some time!"

As upset and scared as I was, I told myself this was just another tactic meant to intimidate me. The thought helped me relax, and I convinced myself that Dennis would show up at the police station with a reprimand, and then have me released. "I won't turn any lights out. I'll just lock the door," I said confidently.

I was handcuffed and taken to the city cells. As I was being paraded into a waiting cell, I asked, "Will my parole officer be coming in to see me right away?" The sheriff prodded me forward, and the cell door closed without any response to my inquiry.

My anxiety grew as the day wore on and my repeated requests for information continued to be ignored. I asked for a phone and called Jeff, telling him to have his mother call Dennis and let him know that she had agreed to the family get-together. Jeff, who expressed his frustration at the turn of events, said he would talk with his mother immediately.

Two days passed, and still there was no sign of Dennis.

On the third day I was sent back to the Kamloops Regional Correctional Center, where I was to be questioned by the area manager of the Kootenay Parole Office.

When I arrived back at KRCC, Reverend Ray expressed his concern at my plight, and we spent some quiet time discussing my battle with the justice system. On April 11 (Steven's birthday) the area manager from the parole office came onto the tier and we met in a room located behind the unit officer's counter.

"Hello, Mr. Mitchell." The man extended his hand in a warm gesture. I quickly shook it, glad to have someone tell me what was going on. "Have a seat. My name is Jim Bartlett and I am the area manager of the Okanagan and Kootenay parole offices."

"Thank you," I said wearily as I seated myself.

"Well, we seem to have a slight problem here," said Jim Bartlett. "No one expected to see you back in prison!"

"I don't know why I'm here. Why didn't Dennis come and see me in Cranbrook? All I did was spend the day with my kids...It's my youngest son's birthday today, for God's sake!" I blurted out.

"Well, that's why I'm here -- to get this straightened out. We know it was just a minor violation. That's why I brought this wavier form for you to sign." Jim Bartlett pulled a piece of paper from his briefcase and handed it to me. "What it does, is allow us to make a quick decision so you don't have to wait to get before the board, which can take up to 45 days. That is the amount of time they can hold you before they have to give you a hearing."

Jim Bartlett looked directly at me and flashed me a reassuring smile. "If you sign it, we can have you back home within a week." I quickly signed the form and he stuffed it back into his briefcase. "Because you are a federal inmate, you will have to be sent back to your last federal institution until you are released. You will be transferred back to Ferndale tomorrow."

My lungs deflated, and I desperately fought to breathe. The thought of being sent back to that abusive institution horrified me. No doubt Bartlett knew that only four months after leaving Ferndale I had openly condemned the prison and its case managers during a family court hearing. For me, the minimum-security institution was a place of evil deception, hiding behind a carefully crafted façade of rehabilitation, highlighted by a golf course, tennis courts, and picnic tables.

"Ferndale? Ferndale?" I said as a combination of emotions rushed through me. "I would rather stay at KRCC for a few days and go home from here," I pleaded.

"Don't worry," Jim Bartlett replied. "We'll get you back home and you'll see your kids in a few days."

It was late in the afternoon the following day when the sheriff's van slowed and turned into the Ferndale Institution. A distant image of me running to my freedom filtered through as we moved up the narrow roadway. I quickly consoled myself with the thought that I would not be around long enough for case management to put its hooks into me once again.

"Mr. Mitchell, you liked the place so much you couldn't stay away, eh?" said the duty officer, sprouting a wide grin. "There's no need to go over the rules with you. Here's the key to your room. It's in the first trailer. You know where it is."

Early the next morning the camp speakers boomed to life. "Mitchell, report to the case management building!" I retraced the familiar path to the back door, well aware of what lay ahead. When I arrived at the inmates' entrance, Carter Alexander was waiting for me.

"Mr. Mitchell," he grinned, "I see you've come back to visit us!"

"Just for a couple of days, Carter," I said somewhat defiantly.

"Well, we'll see," said Carter. "We were told that you were just on suspension and therefore you cannot be put on any official caseload. But you should look at this report I just received from the Kamloops parole office."

I looked at the document with astonishment. It suggested I was a high risk to society and recommended that a transfer to higher security should be considered.

Carter smiled. "I'll see what I can learn about this and call you back when I find out." His wide grin eerily broke into muffled laughter, and he walked back up the stairs.

"God, what's happening!" I cried out as I headed back to my room, panic-stricken. As much as I hated the thought of calling my mother, who had done everything she could to help me out, I knew I had to let her know what was going on. She had just finished helping me furnish the apartment in Cranbrook, and would most certainly be calling any day to see how I was doing, if she hadn't done so already. I sensed Mom shudder as I told her that I was calling from prison. Although she had only her pension to live on, she quickly took $2,000 out of her retirement fund and sent it down to a lawyer in Cranbrook, along with a request that he look into matters, and get me back home.

And I started a new diary.

WED. APRIL 13/94 10 A.M.

I have been thinking about Carter, and I will be called to see him and what will happen if I don't succumb to his abuse.

I already see a report stating that I should be sent somewhere else for the risk of higher security. This will be a typical abuse tactic that they use.

Later in the day I called Ron Buddenhagen, the lawyer my mother had contacted in Cranbrook, and told him what had happened. I gave him the kids' phone number and asked him to get their version of the day we had spent together. He said he would call and then told me he would try to find out what was going on with the National Parole Board. He also asked me to keep him up-to-date on any new developments.

I frantically waited out the rest of the day and then called the kids early in the evening.

WED. APRIL 13/94 7:30 P.M.

I just got off the phone with the kids and found out from Aimee that her mother did not complain about me picking the kids up and taking them to Sparwood. I told Aimee that it looked like I was going to pay a price for my honesty and wish to clear my name of this allegation of abusing her mother throughout our marriage.

I asked her to be open and honest with my lawyer when she talked to him. I told her I loved her. She

158

said, "and I love you too." At these words, I broke down and started to cry and thanked her.

I asked her to tell Jeff and Steven that I would call later. Again tell her I love her and said good-bye.

My brother Donald called the next day and told me he had talked with case management. According to Donald, Carter had suggested to him that I would most likely be released in a day or two if I calmed down, quit condemning the justice system, and started listening to the people who were trying to help. Donald then asked me to ease off on my condemnation of these people and kiss some ass for a day or two.

Over the next couple of days Carter Alexander and Julian Methot made a point of stopping me on the grounds. They both insisted that they had nothing to do with my parole suspension. In fact, Julian repeatedly built up my hopes by telling me he had heard I would be released in a day or two.

Carter never said anything more about the statement from the Kamloops parole office, and I started to suspect it had been nothing more than another ploy to intimidate me.

However, I was unaware of two other reports that had been faxed to the National Parole Board, and put into the hands of the Ferndale staff on April 18. The first one was from Dennis Larose, dated the same day I was taken back into custody.

SPECIAL REPORT

Reason leading to Suspension: David Mitchell has become increasingly challenging with respect to any obstruction to his access to his children. He views the additional condition of #5 [Not to enter within a 10-mile radius of my ex-wife's residence in the Fernie area] as an unjust obstruction to his access to his children.

Overall Assessment: He had consistently resented the criminal justice system for what he views as character assassination and obstructing access to his children. His resentment grew to near obsession during the past two months.

My supervision experience with David has been a combination of either quite civil and co-operative, or threatening and confrontative. We have ventured into some significant debates concerning David's perceived injustices at the hands of the criminal justice system. David may conceivably have some valid complaints. He is, however, unwilling to appreciate the views and concerns of those that he perceives as his oppressors, leaving little room for reasonable compromise.

He had no appreciation for the National Parole Board's decision to alter the condition to permit travel into Fernie to attend his son's graduation.

David was attending counseling sessions with Kevin Kennedy. He informed me that Mr. Kennedy had advised him that should he feel the need for further counseling he should contact Mr. Kennedy.

I contacted Mr. Kennedy to "confirm his dismissal of David for further sessions". Mr. Kennedy states that David used the sessions to vent his frustration with the criminal justice system. He portrayed himself as a victim of several atrocities of abuse of authority. Mr. Kennedy was unable to make any progress with moving David beyond "venting" and "plotting revenge". He does not view David as ready to deal with any of his issues. Mr. Kennedy's observations were very similar to my own.

Dennis Larose
April 5, 1994

The second report was from Jim Bartlett and read in part:

SPECIAL REPORT
KAMLOOPS AREA PAROLE OFFICE
Post Suspension Final Report
Introduction

I refer the board to the Special Report dated April 5, 1994 by Mitchell's supervisor, Dennis Larose. Mitchell was suspended following the violation of an additional condition of his release requiring that he "not enter within a 10 mile radius of (his) ex-wife's residence in the Fernie area".

Interview With Offender: Mitchell was interviewed at Kamloops Regional Correctional Center on April 11, 1994. Post-suspension procedures were fully explained, and Mitchell elected not to have a post-suspension hearing.

Mitchell, throughout our conversation, focused on how mistreated he feels by the actions of the justice system in general and by his ex-wife in particular. Rather than expressing any empathy or understanding of how victimized his wife must feel, he repeatedly expresses how, in his view, she is treating him with unwarranted vindictiveness.

When I later read the report it not difficult to see the ploy Jim Bartlett used. He had taken my condemnation of the justice system and transposed it over an image of Geri, thereby portraying her as the one who was the target of my anger.

While to his credit, Mitchell has not verbalized direct threats to those involved, one has to question his ability to look at the situation in a realistic and sensible manner. It is of significant concern that Mitchell seems incapable of any understanding of his ex-wife's anxieties and fears: he seems only to see her as a person who is seeking revenge against him through making access to his children as difficult as possible.

Bartlett then gave the report its finishing touch, a clear message to me that when the time came, my release would depend on my willingness to play the parole game one more time!

...His view that many outside forces are conspiring to get him, in my view, could well border on paranoia. If this is in fact the case, the issue of risk needs to be thoroughly addressed, psychiatrically and psychologically.

In light of the above, revocation is seen to be an appropriate course of action. The N.P.B. might wish to leave the door open for a release in the future should Mitchell be able to present evidence that he has changed his attitudes and that he has a clean bill of mental health.

RECOMMENDATION: Parole revoked.
Completed by: Bartlett, James
Area Manager--Kamloops

The next day, April 19, unaware of the reports, I was ordered to attend a meeting in the administration building. Assistant Warden Glen Cross and about a dozen other staff members greeted me at the large conference table once again.

Carter Alexander was the first to speak. "What's happening with your parole suspension?" he mocked.

"I just spent a day with my kids," I said. "I was told it was a minor violation and that I will be released any day now. Probably tomorrow!"

Chapter 15

Dehumanization, Degradation, and Revocation

A few days after my meeting with the Ferndale hierarchy, I received an envelope from the Provincial court registry in Fernie. There was an array of documents inside, including a letter that stated there had been an ex parte order (a court order made in the absence of one of the parties, in this case, myself) made on March 31, which forbade me from contacting my ex-wife and my children. There were also two affidavits in the package, one signed by Geri and the other by her lawyer. They were loaded with inflammatory innuendo and suggested I had been annoying, harassing, and molesting Geri and the children while I was in the community on parole.

However, my ex-wife's affidavit also held one statement that seemed to be meant to appease me, probably inserted in hopes that I would abandon my search for answers in family court. It read, "I know why what happened, happened and it is something I will have to live with for the rest of my life and will never leave me."

I phoned Jeff, and asked him to get an explanation from his mother on the court order, as well as the affidavits. Jeff told me that his mother refused to discuss anything with him, and that she had threatened to have him taken away by the police after he angrily denounced her for betraying him. This threat came after he broke some furniture, expressing his anger at her support of my reimprisonment, after giving what he and we all saw, as her agreement to a family outing on Easter Monday in Sparwood.

I told Jeff to let it go and that I would take his mother back to family court when I got home. We said our good-byes with hopes that I could still get back for his graduation. Then I called Buddenhagen and informed him of the affidavits. He told me not to worry, and that he was looking into matters. He then instructed me to mail him back the documents.

Meanwhile, out on the grounds of the institution I continued to bump into Carter and Julian on a regular basis. "Are you still here?" Julian snickered one day. "I guess you better be nice to Carter!"

On Friday, April 22, I was called over to the case management building and one of the office staff asked me to sign a document that had arrived from the Kamloops parole office. Next to the heading DECISION, I read "Parole Revoked." I looked for a signature, but there was none.

"No! I'm not going to sign that!" I yelled, pushing the document back across the counter. Gasping for air and fighting back tears, I made a hasty retreat out the back door. When the numbness in my legs finally dissipated I slowly made my way back to the trailer and called my brother, Donald, to give him the news, letting him know I wanted to talk with the media. After saying good-bye, I walked down the hall to my room, and opened my diary.

> Friday, April 22/94 10:45 (A.M.)
> Today the deception and dishonesty of the System has taken another step.
> Today after leading my family and myself on, that I would be released, about 1/2 hr ago I was called to the Case Management building where the girls brought out the report that states the absurd, and revoked my parole.
> Today my faith in this country and the Justice System has hit an absolute low.
> I have let my family know that I need their support in taking this matter before the media and the public.--I took my kids bowling!
> They have taken Jeff's Graduation away from me and Jeff. I think that is one of the saddest things of all. My heart aches for him. I wonder if they will take Aimee's from me as well.

I felt the weight and pressure of the system crushing me as I stretched out on my bed and searched for answers. How angry were these people with me? Were they upset because I had challenged their authority? Was the Ferndale Institution incensed because I had condemned it in open court? Did they now want to see me on my knees and groveling at their feet for my release?

Later that day, Julian, once again confronted me. "I see you're still here," he said, showing me a wide pleasing grin. "Eighteen months is a long time!" (This was a reference to the amount of time left on my sentence.) He then repeated his earlier remark, "I guess you better be nice to Carter!"

On Saturday I was numb, thinking about the prospect of spending another year or more in prison, when one of the inmates asked why I looked so distressed. When I told him that the Kamloops parole office had revoked my parole, he informed me that only the National Parole Board had that power.

"Of course," I thought to myself. "How soon we forget!" I had been shown the document on Friday, and then left to stew in anguish for the weekend!

On Monday I failed to see Carter around the institution. As the day wore on I began to suspect he was not about to make an appearance. That meant I would have to wait another day for an explanation about my parole revocation.

On Tuesday morning I noticed Carter's car in the parking, and hastily made my way over to the case management building. When the receptionist said Carter was too busy to see me, I decided to hang around for a while, knowing he would eventually come outside for a smoke.

About mid-morning my surveillance paid off. Before Carter could test the wind, I was on top of him, asking about the document I had been shown on Friday.

"I'll go and get it," he said. Five minutes later he reappeared, quick to point out that the document only "recommended" that my parole be revoked. I also noticed this particular copy had James Bartlett's signature on it.

"Maybe you should consider applying for a hearing before the National Parole Board," said Carter, in a tone that suggested my parole would most assuredly be revoked if I did not.

"Why?" I angrily replied, convinced they now wanted to take me before the board at their leisure, and strip me of my dignity by having me play the parole game once again. "So you people can take your false reports into the hearing? I was promised a quick decision on my suspension and then told I would be home in a few days."

"Well, going before the board may be your only chance now."

"And if I apply for a hearing after having waived my rights to one, what date would my hearing be set for? A month from now? Two, three, or six months from now?" I replied bitterly.

I stepped around Carter and headed back to my room thinking about Jim Bartlett's report. He had also mentioned a report by Dennis Larose. This knowledge of two reports being sent to the National Parole Board set of alarm bells. I had no idea what Dennis's report said, but Bartlett's was damaging, so I decided I had better send a letter of my own to Board. In it I included the last words Dennis had said to me about having the 10-mile restriction removed, emphasizing his phrase, "It's a done thing!" I disputed the accusation that Kevin Kennedy had dismissed me from further counseling sessions, and I mentioned our agreement to continue sessions after the family court matters had been settled. I also described the circumstances surrounding my day with the kids, including the fact that Geri had given her consent to the family outing. I closed with, "I ask for your understanding and good judgment as it relates to your decision in regards to my full parole being reinstated under the circumstances of this violation."

On Thursday, April 28, Carter approached me once again. "Are you going to ask for a hearing?" he demanded.

"No," I answered. "I sent my response in to the board yesterday, and there is nothing more I can add."

"When's your warrant expiry date?"

"November 1995," I shot back, aware that he already knew the date.

"In that case, you better ask for a hearing."

"Why should I ask for a hearing? The board has my response. They had me waive my hearing so I could receive a quick paper decision and get back home."

Again, I stepped past Carter and continued on my way, growing more concerned about the possibility that I may not be released in time for Jeff's graduation. Distraught and depressed, I began to grow more nauseous each day while my stomach ached with sickening regularity.

A few days later I was walking past the duty office when Julian shouted out, his now less than impromptu line, as he stood on the landing, "You're still here! Eighteen more months is a long time. You better be nice to Carter!"

"I'm not doing anything wrong! And Dennis told me he was going to have the condition dropped anyway!" I shouted back in frustration. The correctional service's detestable and relentless toying was having its designed affect. As Jeff's graduation date drew closer, my nerves deteriorated a little more each day.

Early in the first week of May, Carter stopped me between the lunch trailer and the duty office. "I'm asking to be taken off your case because of your bad attitude," he said bitterly.

I had understood that I wasn't on anyone's caseload because I was only on suspension, but this request was one I could accept. "Put it in writing," I said, "and state your reason why. Because all I'm doing is standing up for my rights as a citizen."

"You have a warped sense of what your rights are!" Carter yelled as I turned and walked away.

When I returned to my room later that afternoon, I quickly realized someone had manipulated the lock on my door. A thumbtack had been inserted into the doorframe and wedged up against the plate in a way that rendered the locking bolt useless. I removed the small obstruction, wondering if the inmate who had moved into the room next to mine had anything to do with it.

Early the following morning I was awakened by the noise of prison staff milling about next door. During breakfast I learned there had been an escape from the institution -- a "walk away," as they call it when it happens at a minimum-security camp. Two inmates had left sometime during the night, and the man who had moved into the room next to mine, was one of them. His partner in the escape was assumed to be the more dangerous man, a convicted cop killer who had apparently worked his way into easier prison time by becoming a rat and informer for the system.

After the disappearance of the two inmates, a few days later, my room was searched and my notes and documents were thrown about.

I started to fear for my earlier diary notes and other documents that were free for the taking back in my apartment. I called Jeff and asked him to make a trip into Cranbrook to get my briefcase so he could take it back to Fernie and keep an eye on it.

Then one evening while I was watching television, a news flash scrolled across the screen. "Two escaped inmates from a minimum-security institution in British Columbia are suspected of killing a man in the United States." The next day all hell broke loose at the Ferndale Institution as the administration staff prepared for damage control. The shredding machine went into high gear, and bags of shredded paper were hauled away. Inmate passes were canceled and everyone was confined to work within the prison. Glen Cross called all the inmates into a meeting and told us to stay away from the front area of the prison and out of sight of the media who were swarming like bees outside the front fence.

While the prison crawled into its shell, Julian replaced Carter as my new case manager. He immediately summoned me to a meeting and spoke apologetically about the way things had gone during my suspension. I listened intently as he attempted to move my case from the judicial and correctional process into the political arena. "Things don't look good for you!" he said. "The Board will be using the report from Kamloops to decide your fate. And Dennis won't be there to confirm what he said to you, and since you're only on suspension, corrections is not involved, so I won't be submitting anything."

I confronted Julian with what I believed was really going on. "You people aren't interested in justice, or the truth, Julian. You people are interested in one thing, incarceration! If you are not going to submit anything to the Board, then why have I been put on a caseload? And even if Dennis can't be at the hearing, all they have to do is call him up!"

Julian shrugged his shoulders. "It's out of our hands," he replied. "Because of the heat on the institution right now, it will be a political decision, and that doesn't look good for you."

"It's only a fair and just decision, based on the facts, with good judgment that I'm hoping for," I said.

"Well sometimes, in political decisions, good judgment is not necessarily used," said Julian as he paused and reestablished eye contact with me. "What are you going to do if they revoke your parole?" he asked.

"I will continue to fight for my rights in the courts," I answered. "My mother has paid for a lawyer."

"Don't do that!" Julian said, displaying a sudden burst of emotion. "A lawyer will just take your mother's money." He pushed himself from his chair. "That's all. You can go and I'll try to find out what's going on."

After another restless night, Julian called me back to the case management building. "Come down to the office," he exclaimed. "I've got some good news!"

"They're ready to let you go!" Julian said, his voice bubbling with enthusiasm.

My heart skipped a beat and my emotions tumbled out as I realized that I was going to make it home for Jeff's graduation. "Thank you, thank you," I whispered hoarsely.

"We aren't your enemy, David," said Julian, continuing as he settled himself deeper into his chair. "We don't hide behind any crystal ball as you once told me. Corrections isn't evil. It just follows the will of the people. Our job is to protect society and rehabilitate," he said softly. "Some people might not agree with how we do our job, but we deal with what we're given, and that's all we can do."

Still feeling the effects from the good news, I wiped the tears from my eyes and continued to listen. "We aren't allowed to use physical punishment in corrections because society won't allow it to be used the way it is administered in some countries. Take the Philippines," Julian said as he leaned forward. "They use caning as a form of punishment, and that society has very little crime! And the people are behaved and advanced in what is a civilized society today."

I took a breath and got a hold on my emotions, realizing I had read everything correctly. The suspension had been nothing more than an act of intimidation. The end of the maximum 45-day suspension period was near, and they were now being forced to let me go.

169

"The emotional abuse administered by our system is not the answer," I said. "It must find a way, as difficult as it may seem, to deal with individuals as individuals and quit group labeling everyone in these institutions. It must stop forcing people to play this deceitful and dishonest parole game. If it doesn't change, this system will continue to be haunted by the same kind of incident that just happened with those two inmates who walked out of this institution a few weeks ago. Someone is dead because someone played the game, and the correctional service had no idea who, or what, they were dealing with!" I took a breath and looked more intently at Julian. "This system is a paper maze of cover-your-butt strategies and it has to stop!" I sensed my emotions rising again, and I had no desire to let my anger and frustration at the system destroy the moment. Instead I asked, "When am I to be released?"

"I understand tomorrow or the next day," answered Julian. "I'll let you know as soon as the decision is brought over to the institution. And remember, don't take this thing so personal!"

"It's hard not to!" I replied, and we shook hands like two parting friends.

The next day passed with no word on my release, and I nervously anticipated the big event would take place the following day...or the next... But to my dismay another week passed, and Julian dismissed all my inquiries. "I haven't heard anything yet," he would say, brushing me aside like an annoying gnat.

The correctional service's abusive tactic of raising my hopes one-minute, and dashing them the next had finally taken its toll. After days of waiting and hoping for my release, only to be disappointed, I started having bouts of uncontrollable shaking, similar to those I had experienced while on day parole in Victoria.

On May 18, National Parole Board members were engaged in parole hearings at Ferndale. I purposely positioned myself on the walkway leading to and from the hearing room. After a lengthy wait I confronted Julian as he left one of the hearings. "What about the Board's decision?" I pleaded. "You told me they were going to let me go home!"

"Haven't you heard anything yet?" Julian taunted.

"You must know what the decision is," I hollered. "It's 45 days tomorrow! You have to know by now!"

"No," Julian said, with an amused look, "I just have a flimsy on you."

Not knowing or caring what a flimsy was, I responded, "I don't care about that! I just want to know the decision. They have 45 days from the time my parole was suspended to give me a decision!"

"I don't know about that," answered Julian. "You probably won't get an answer this week, either, because the board has hearings at other institutions as well."

"I waived my right to a hearing so I could receive a quick paper decision," I begged, "as I was promised."

"Well," replied Julian, "they shouldn't have said you would get a quick decision."

"That's the point of waiving a hearing. So a quick paper decision can take place," I shouted after Julian as he walked away.

Another week passed with no word, and I made another entry in my diary.

> Tues May 24/94 11:45 A.M.
> I still have had no word on the parole decision. The stress level is extremely high as I try to hang in.
> This game of emotional abuse is the very thing I have written about and talked about in court. The frustration and abuse laid upon people in this system, before releasing them back into society is not only detrimental to the inmates, but to the people at large.
> It reiterates my suggestion that it is 'punishment of the individual' and 'not punishment of the crime and rehabilitation' that is at the forefront of the Judicial and Correctional System of this Country.
> I pray for Mom today. I know she is going through the same kind of stress today, waiting to hear from me on what the decision is.

I pray also for my children as they too are hoping their dad will be on his way home today.

I also pray for this System and the Sanity of a correct decision and not one based on Vengeance and Anger.

The following day I tried to bury my frustration and growing depression in my work. It was late in the morning, and I was spreading mulch around some shrubs next to my trailer, when Julian stepped out of the duty office and called to me. I jabbed my pitchfork into the mulch and started walking towards the man I now despised. As I drew nearer, Julian held out an envelope. "I've got your decision," he said, showing me a serious look.

My heart leapt into my throat and I reached for the envelope.

"Are you sure you want it?" asked Julian, withdrawing his arm, just as my fingers were about to grasp the envelope.

I lowered my hand and stood silently as Julian started toying with me like a child. "No, I don't think he wants to see it," he said, turning to another staff member standing behind him. They exchanged menacing grins and then Julian looked back at me. "You sure you want to see it?" he said and held the envelope up one more time.

This time I raised my arm more cautiously before extending my hand towards the envelope.

"No," said Julian, and he withdrew it once again, "you don't want to see it!"

I stood motionless as Julian became enthralled with his game of take-away. "Maybe you want to see it?...No, you don't want to see it!...Do you want to see it?...You don't really want to see it!" When he finally realized he was playing the game alone, he extended his arm and held the envelope steady. "Yeah, I guess you want to see it!" he laughed.

My heart and mind raced with jubilation at the thought that I now had a hand on my release papers. I turned without saying a word and rushed back to my room, ready to prepare for my trip home. As I was lifting the flap on the envelope, I nervously glanced through the slatted blinds dangling over my window. The duty office was the closest building to mine. Several correctional staff had gathered outside and joined Julian. My trailer appeared to be the focus of their attention.

I looked at the envelope, hesitated, and then, with trembling fingers, slowly pulled out the document that was neatly folded inside. I unfolded the paper and read the heading NATIONAL PAROLE BOARD DECISION. My eyes locked onto the words "DECISION(S): Full Parole Revoked."

A tear blurred my vision. *"Why! Who! What!"* I blinked away the increasing moisture, and went on to the next line, DECISION DATE: 1994 May 17. The correctional service had sat on the notice and allowed me to beg, twist, and squirm for an additional eight agonizing days before letting me know my parole had been revoked.

I continued to scour the document, searching for an answer, a reason. *"Why? Why??"* I focused on a part of the document with the heading ASSESSMENT OF RISK

> 1. Assessment of behavior during current release: --Your file indicates that you are obsessed with the idea your wife, C.S.C.[Correctional Service of Canada], N.P.B.[National Parole Board] and the justice system are conspiring to make your life difficult. You have been unable to find employment. You attended counseling, however, you were dismissed from further sessions as you were using these sessions to vent your frustration with the criminal justice system, and plot revenge. He is of the view that you are not ready to deal with any issues.

> 2. Comparison with previous pattern of criminal behavior: --Your criminal record is limited, however, there are indications that you have been involved in spousal abuse.

> 3. Professional opinions regarding current release: --Your Case Management Team are of the view that your behavior is such that your Full Parole should be revoked.

> 4. Other information regarding current release:-- Your ex-wife is very concerned about your behavior.

Horrified, I turned to the next page and read REASONS FOR DECISION(S):--

> You were released with a very clear explanation of your additional conditions and your need to abide by them. You are serving a sentence for a very violent crime that severely impacted on your family. You continue to obsess about the system and be a victim rather than abiding by the conditions of your release.
>
> ...The Board is extremely concerned about your lack of regard for the law and your inability to resolve issues through therapy. The safety of the public is paramount and the Board is of the view that at this time you present a risk to re-offend, therefore, Full Parole is revoked.

I looked up and focused on the crowd of correctional staff outside the duty office.

"No! no! You bastards," I screamed as an overpowering desire to confront the crowd engulfed me. I lunged into action. Pulling my cap down over my forehead, I headed back outside. With a firm grasp on the pitchfork, I jabbed it into the mulch and went to work, spreading it over the ground at a furious pace. The curious crowd of onlookers stood silently in front of the duty office, uncertain how to react to my display of vigorous activity.

I used it all, the anger, the pain, the frustration, and even the fear that threatened to collapse me on the spot. I fed off its energy, throwing mulch and spreading it about at breakneck speed. Finally the crowd dispersed and Julian was the only one left. With my tears flowing freely, I stopped and stared at my former cognitive living skill instructor, until he, too, turned and walked away.

Now alone, frightened and shaking, I walked back into the trailer and called Ron Buddenhagen, my lawyer in Cranbrook. Much to my dismay, he showed little concern, saying only that he was continuing to look into matters. My faith in him had been waning because of his apparent lack of initiative, and his latest response did nothing to make me feel better.

174

A feeling of absolute hopelessness set in and my physical pace slowed dramatically over the next couple of days. I shuffled about the institution like a zombie, looking for peace and quiet in a world that had none.

The next piece of confusion arrived in the mail. It was an unexpected package from George Majic. I opened the bulging envelope and pulled out copies of what appeared to be the same affidavits that I had already received from the court registry -- documents that I had already mailed back to Buddenhagen. As I was going through them, I picked up on what appeared to be changes in the sentence structure and content of my ex-wife's affidavit.

In the earlier one, sent to me by the court registry, I had recalled reading, "I know why what happened, happened and it is something I will have to live with for the rest of my life and will never leave me." This statement, which I thought was meant to appease me, had now been replaced with, "I saw the wounds that he suffered, I knew why he suffered these wounds, and the trauma that I suffered as a result of that attack will never leave me."

There also appeared to be a statement that was not included in the earlier collection of affidavits. In reference to my assault on Rob, I read, "In the attack, Mr. Mitchell was wearing a balaclava…"

A copy of an application for a restraining order was also mixed in with the affidavits, and I read: "Below is a summary of the important facts: The respondent is presently on Parole. The applicant fears for her safety and the safety of the children."

I immediately called Ron Buddenhagen to tell him about my suspicions that there were changes in the documents. I then asked him what a "balaclava" was. He said it was similar to a ski mask. I told him I was not wearing any mask on the night of the assault, and complained bitterly about the wording in the affidavits and restraining order that insinuated I had been molesting, annoying, and harassing my ex-wife and the kids while on parole.

I knew something else wasn't right as well, but I couldn't put my finger on it. Frustrated and angry about this latest turn of events, I told Buddenhagen I would call him back and hung up the phone. I went back to my room and looked over the new documents as carefully as I could.

The first page was a note from Geri's lawyer. It read "Re: Ex Parte Order; Enclosed herewith please find a filed copy of an Order which we obtained on March 31, 1994."

I turned the page and looked at the ex parte order. It showed that Majic had gone before Judge Carlgren on that date. This was the same judge who had presided over the family court hearing on November 2, 1993.

I asked myself why George Majic would have gone into court on March 31 and filed false documentation that indicated I had worn a mask during the assault, and more recently had been harassing my ex-wife and children while on parole. Why? He knew he was scheduled to be back in court with his client in less than two weeks, on April 12. He certainly knew I wanted to ask Geri questions about the victim impact statement that had been discussed in court on March 9. But he would have had to realize I would want to ask her to explain the new filings from March 31. And both Majic and Geri would have known that our children would certainly dispute any suggestion that I had been harassing them or their mother. Also the criminal court transcripts clearly showed that I had not been wearing any mask on the night of the assault! On top of that, this application for a restraining order had been stamped and dated as court documentation on March 23, 1994, when I was still in Cranbrook. And I had received no notice of this application, which had been brought before Judge Carlgren, supposedly on March 31, again while I was still in Cranbrook.

I quickly suspected that everything had been written and backdated after my suspension in an effort to support the revocation of my parole.

I concluded that the justice system, aided by Geri's lawyer, had fabricated a case to support the revocation of my parole. And all of it had been done while I was safely tucked away in prison, unaware of the manipulation.

The correctional service and the National Parole Board now had a record to support my suspension, something that suspiciously prevented me from proceeding to court on April 12, and a record to support the revocation of my parole as well. It portrayed Geri as a terrified ex-wife, a mother who was out to protect her-self and her children from a violent, abusive husband and father who had supposedly come back to the community, plotting revenge!

I woefully realized that my counselor, Kevin Kennedy, had been right. The justice system would stop at nothing to protect itself. I suspected everything could be traced back to the system's desire to keep the unethical manipulation of the plea-bargaining process from being exposed.

There was also something else I was certain of. The correctional service was determined to put a stop to my condemnation of its abusive rehabilitation process, better known to the public as parole!

Confident that I had it figured out, I called my lawyer back, and explained what I thought was going on. I asked him to look at the first affidavit so we could compare it with the one I had just received from Majic.

"Just send me the new affidavit!" he said and ended the call by telling me to stay in touch.

I hung up the phone, sensing more danger and betrayal at the hands of the legal system. I cautiously decided to hang onto the new affidavit, then sat down and made my first attempt to write a book.

A few days later Assistant Warden Glen Cross walked up beside me as I solemnly strode along the road next to the duty office. "If you're quiet and behave yourself, you will be able to do your time in comfort here," he said quietly. He slowed his pace, almost coming to a stop, and looked directly at me. "I'll tell you again. I've seen people who have fought this system do their entire sentence in a more secure and harsher environment than this."

"I'm not doing anything but writing about my experience with this system," I replied.

"That's another mistake!" snapped Cross.

On June 8, I was asked to walk over to the Mission medium-security prison, located right behind Ferndale. When I arrived at the institution, staff informed me that Corrections Canada had gotten rid of

177

my prints and I now had to have them re-done, along with a new mug shot.

After I was printed and photographed, I returned to Ferndale, where I was given a gas-powered weed cutter and told to clean up the edge of the road that ran from the Mission prison to the highway, a distance of about half a mile. I methodically went to work. When I reached the highway, I realized I was out of sight of Ferndale. The security towers at the Mission prison were unoccupied, as security was maintained with pickups that roamed the perimeter. I saw no vehicles in the immediate area.

I considered the possibility that I might have purposely been put in a position where I would be tempted to simply walk away in frustration. Such an attempt would certainly give Ferndale staff the justification they needed to support their suggestion that I should be transferred to higher security. I quickly worked my way back to the institution, making my presence known as soon as possible.

About 10 one evening, a week later, I was called over to the duty office. One of the correctional officers, Jackie, informed me that the head of security, Jack Nelson, had requested that she and another guard, Jerry, do a search of my room. I was ordered to stand outside the duty office and wait while the two of them went over to my trailer and conducted the search.

"What are you going to do?" I asked. "Plant something in my room?"

Jackie, who appeared nervous and upset right from the beginning, quietly replied, "We wouldn't do that."

After they had left for my trailer, a member of the inmate committee, the group that worked directly with administration on behalf of all the inmates, walked up and told me he had overheard the request that I remain behind while the search was conducted. He then told me I had a right to be present during a specified search like the one they were conducting.

I hustled back over to the trailer in time to catch the two correctional officers reading my most recent diary notes and my mail.

"What do you think you're doing?" I asked.

"Get out of here!" yelled Jerry. "We told you to stay at the duty office!"

"I was just told I have the right to be present when you do this kind of thing," I replied angrily. "Those are my diary notes...and that is legal mail!" I pointed at the document in Jerry's hand.

"Leave!" he shot back. "If you don't, I will cite you for disobeying direct orders!"

Right or wrong, I knew if I did not comply, I would be sanctioned in some manner. Upset and frustrated, I turned away and headed back to the office. Minutes later the two officers reappeared.

"If they are that concerned about my personal notes and want to read them," I said, "all they have to do is ask me!"

I headed back to my room and straightened up before returning to the duty office a half-hour later. I sensed Jackie might be willing to talk about the orders she had been given.

"You know, Jackie," I said, "if Jack Nelson wants to read my personal notes, all he has to do is ask me. There's no need to send you in to do it."

"I know," she replied. "And I don't know what they're trying to do."

The next day I packaged together some of my diary notes and other documentation and gave them to Richard Engle, who took them out of the institution, including the array of affidavits and court documents mailed to me by George Majic. A few days later I confronted Nelson. "What was the reason for the search of my room and the reading of my personal notes and legal mail?" I asked the man who headed Ferndale's security.

"I'm sorry, I had no choice. Your case management team ordered it," he replied.

"It figures," I responded dryly, walking away in disgust.

Despite the justice system's constant pressure, I continued to keep in contact with the kids, defying any orders that might exist which would have made even phone calls a violation. Jeff told me that his graduation ceremonies had gone well and that he had some pictures for me. I congratulated him and told him how sorry I was to have missed it.

On Thursday, June 30, 1994, I was summoned to a meeting with an institutional psychologist who, I had heard, had a reputation for being extremely abusive and more than willing to support whatever position case management wanted to take.

"Mr. Mitchell, my name is Mike Stoian and I've been asked to talk with you. It's strictly voluntary, and you don't have to talk if you don't want to. But I understand you're under a lot of stress and maybe I can help."

My immediate response was suspicion. When I had first come into this institution almost two years earlier and asked to speak with one of the institutional psychologists, my request had been denied. I had made no such request this time.

"What did you want to talk about?" I said cautiously.

"Tell me about the assault on your victim."

I gave a brief summary of the case and waited for the next question.

"What about your feelings towards the justice system and corrections?" he asked. That question initiated a 10-minute discussion of my thoughts surrounding what I saw as a lack of integrity throughout the justice system and its legal and correctional process.

Stoian suddenly became more confrontational. "Your counseling sessions while on parole were terminated by your counselor because you refused to address the issues surrounding your violent nature," he said forcefully. "Your counselor said you were even plotting revenge against your ex-wife!"

"That's not true," I replied. "In fact, Mr. Kennedy believed I posed no threat to her at all. And we had both agreed to postpone our sessions until after the family court matters were settled."

"What about the physical abuse of your wife?"

"In the 17 years of marriage there was one slap by each of us, and I pushed her once."

"What are your feelings towards your ex-wife today?"

"What happened back in 1991 is in the past," I replied. "It's over. I don't hate her. I probably still care about her somewhat. After all, she is still the mother of my children." I searched for the words that I hoped he would understand. "I do not wish to interfere in her life, and I respect her right to pursue it in any way she chooses to do so. But I also love my kids, and I want to be a big part of their lives and have them remain a big part of mine."

"What are you going to do when you get the chance to rejoin society?"

"Move back to Cranbrook," I answered, "get a job, and spend time with my children."

"How are you going to get a job?" Stoian replied in a tone that suggested he felt the possibility didn't exist.

"Like everybody else," I answered. "Like anyone who is out looking for work."

"It has come to my attention that you were involved in sexual misconduct while on day parole," he snapped, throwing me a curve from left field.

I looked at the psychologist, unsure if I had heard correctly. "What are you talking about?" I sputtered in disbelief. "Who said that?"

"There is a report that shows you were masturbating in the living room area," he replied coldly, "and especially doing so on more than one occasion during bed checks while at the halfway house in Victoria."

"That's a lie!" I yelled as I bolted out of my chair. "You know something? You people are sick as hell. This is nothing more than another sad attempt to degrade and dehumanize me! I have the reports from the Manchester House that clearly state my behavior was exemplary!"

My comment bounced off Mike Stoian and he remained stone cold. "What about your wife and kids?" he said icily. "Did you ever sexually assault or molest them?"

My anger swelled and I stepped towards the institutional psychologist, coming to a stop directly in front of him. "What the hell kind of game are you playing?" I shouted. "What gives you the right to ask such disgusting questions and make these unwarranted accusations? I would never do anything like that to my family!"

"Well," he replied, retreating slightly, "when we have information about other sexual misconduct we are obligated to ask these kinds of questions."

"This meeting is over," I said, letting out my disgust as I turned and stepped towards the door, then paused, "And I want to know who said I was involved in sexual misconduct at the Manchester House."

"I don't have that information with me," Stoian answered, "but I'll get Julian to get it for you."

I angrily stormed out of the duty office and called Ron Buddenhagen again, this time asking him to summon me into court. "I want it all exposed! The dishonest reimprisonment, and the false affidavits. Everything! All of the abuse that's been going on," I blurted out.

My lawyer told me there was no way to do that due to the fact that my parole had already been revoked. Exhausted and ready to collapse, I hung up the phone, convinced that the only thing left on the system's agenda was my transfer to higher security.

Even though I made sure I didn't break any rules, I was called into the duty office and falsely accused of missing several meal counts. Virginia Deardon also called me in and accused me of missing what she called a special count.

The hopelessness of my situation was becoming unbearable. I fought nausea 24 hours a day. When there was nothing left to vomit, dry heaves kept my stomach boiling. Exhausted and rapidly losing the will to live, I curled up on my bed around nine o'clock on the evening of July 3, 1994, and wished the world away.

After drifting into a restless sleep I stirred, conscious of a dim illumination in my otherwise dark room. I sat up, my body silhouetted by a sliver of light coming from the duty office's outside night-light filtering through the blinds. Without bothering to turn my own light on, I ran my hand along the dresser, locating my tobacco pouch which held a couple of rolled cigarettes and a pack of penny matches. My thoughts carried me 500 miles away, back to my children. I lit a smoke, put on my coat, and stepped outside.

After walking past the duty office I made my way over to the duck pond, slowly ambling around the watery sanctuary. I walked across the golf course, eased myself onto a bench, and stared off into the night, feeling completely lost and alone in a world that had recklessly discarded me. I shuddered and wrapped my coat a little more tightly around me. My eyes closed and a light breeze rocked me back and forth. Above me, a tree branch rustled its leaves, as if trying to comfort the lonely figure that huddled on the bench below it.

It was too late. Everything around me was dead, even the comforting night air failed to bring me back from my personal painful world. "Home, home..." I whispered as I shuffled back towards the distant lights of the institution.

"David?" The inquiring voice held a familiarity that I recognized. Marjorie, the duty officer who had briefly been assigned to my case during my first stay at Ferndale, emerged from the darkness. I slowly turned, hearing my own quiet response, *"Yessss."*

"We have you listed as missing," said Marjorie. "The police are out looking for you right now!"

"I --was--o--ver --attt --tthe -- ponddd."

"You know, the guards are probably going to take you out of here tonight and over to Matsqui?"

"Thaaat'ss ok'kkkay."

"Follow me. You can sit and wait for them in the duty office."

"Thattt's ffffine," I answered politely.

Marjorie picked up the phone, my eyes closed, and her voice trailed off. "Mitchell...found...send Matsqui...Okay!"

Lost in a world of hopelessness, I looked up at the bars of the cell. My arms pulled the bed-sheet tighter around my neck. My thoughts turned to my children.

"JEFF...AIMEE...STEVEN?" I screamed.

"David! Fight these people, fight back! Don't let them hurt you, Don't let them hurt your kids!...Stand up and fight back!"

"What's happening? What's happening? I can't breathe!"

I relaxed my grip and a blast of cold night air rushed down my throat. I felt a tear come to rest on my upper cheek. Exhausted, I unwrapped the sheet and dragged it over me, then slowly curled up on the floor, in the Hole at the Matsqui Penitentiary.

Chapter 16

The Profiling of an Inmate

A cool breeze stirred the damp morning air, ruffling the bed sheet that half covered me. Roused by the scent of dew, I rolled over, opened my eyes, and looked up at the gaping holes that separated the large triangular bars above my head. Slowly, pictures of the passing night rolled through my mind, coming to an end on an image of a twisted bed-sheet wrapped around my neck.

I pushed myself upright, removing the sheet. "Yes, I know this place. I have been here before," I said, recalling my experience a few years earlier. I gently rubbed at the soreness around my neck. "No more," I whispered. "No more!"

I had arrived at a crossroad, a place in my life where I had only two choices left. I could either give-in, and accept the abuse of power I was being subjected too -- a choice that would almost certainly lead to my release. Or, I could stand my ground, knowing full well that that route led to an uncertain future.

About mid-morning, a psychologist by the name of Pierre Ouellet came up to the Hole to evaluate my state of mind. I quickly gave the justice system my answer. "You people can do whatever you want because I'm not playing the game any longer," I said, fighting to hang on to what little strength I had left.

My take-it-or-leave-it attitude appeared to unsettle the psychologist. "Why were you out on the grounds so late?" he asked.

"I couldn't sleep and I was feeling pretty low with everything that's been going on," I said quietly.

"I've talked with some people in the system, and your brother, Donald, as well," he said. "I think there may be a way to work things out that could get you back home."

Pierre said Corrections Canada wanted me to accept a transfer to a maximum-security institution, known as the Regional Psychiatric Center (RPC) for an assessment. "If the National Parole Board could be given a favorable assessment from the best doctors in the system, they would almost assuredly have to release you," he said enthusiastically. "I talked with your brother, Donald, this morning, and he agrees that it may be the way to get you out of here."

Prepared to let the justice system do as it pleased, I accepted the correctional service's offer, and the transfer occurred on July 6, 1994. My new commitment to refrain from challenging the justice system at every turn quickly materialized into a strength that surprised correctional staff. Doug Hampson had been right when he told me not to give these people more power over me than they already had! Even though I was now incarcerated in a maximum-security institution, my dignity and sense of self-worth returned, and my sessions with one of the institution's psychiatrists, Dr. Caldis, gave me a place to quietly vent my frustrations.

Shortly after my arrival at RPC, Mr. Soon, a social worker at the institution, asked me to sign a form. After carefully reading it over, I realized my signature could lock me into the psychiatric center for an indefinite period of time. The document had me agreeing to a release, only after I had completed counseling that was deemed necessary by the correctional service.

Leaving it up to the justice system to determine what was necessary and what constituted completion was an unsettling proposition under the circumstances. I crossed the wording out and wrote along the edge of the form, "I agree only to an assessment by institutional doctors for the purpose of determining if any treatment or counseling is necessary." I handed it back to Mr. Soon and he stormed off, muttering under his breath.

The following day he returned with more documents and pointed out one particular form. "If you sign it, you will be given the opportunity to oppose the involuntary transfer to higher security," he offered.

"I have made the decision not to challenge anything the system does. Whatever you people do is your choice," I said, handing him the document back, while keeping the others.

Mr. Soon again left in an angry huff, and I returned to my cell, where I started reading the remaining paperwork.

The first document was titled, Notice of Involuntary Transfer Decision.

> You were recently assessed by the psychologist [Mike Stoian] in order to evaluate your suitability for a correctional treatment program. The findings from the psychologist were twofold:
> --First, in conjunction with previous psychological/psychiatric assessments, you remain largely untreated/unchanged due to your continued denial and rationalization.
> --Secondly, your risk to re-offend in a violent manner remains moderate to high unless you are involved in an intense treatment program, i.e. the R.P.C. Personality Disorder Program.
> The latest psychological finding coupled with your recent behavior at the Ferndale Institution has resulted in an upgrading of your security classification to medium security. As result, my recommendation is for involuntary transfer to medium security (Matsqui Institution).

The transfer notice had been signed by Warden Weibe, who had recently been appointed to Ferndale, replacing Warden Dillon. The transfer notice was dated July 5, 1994.

I then read a progress summary report, written by case management from Ferndale.

> You continue to be obsessed about the system and be a victim---the Board is extremely concerned about your lack of regard for the law and your inability to resolve issues through therapy. The safety of the public is paramount and the Board is of the view that parole is revoked. Until Mr. Mitchell successfully completes intense treatment, he should be seen as a high risk to be violent. Mr. Mitchell is presently unsuitable for the Criminal Thinking Errors Program, offered at Ferndale Institution, due to serious untreated personality disorder.
> In Mr. Stoian's opinion, Mr. Mitchell should be seriously reviewed for possible detention.

[Detention, also referred to as "gating," is a process that allows the correctional service to hold inmates beyond their statutory release date (two-thirds of their sentence), effectively keeping them incarcerated until the end of their sentence, taking away any possibility for early release through parole. This form of continued imprisonment is allegedly used by the government, in only the severest and most warranted cases.]

He also demonstrated an unwillingness to abide by the rules and regulations of Ferndale by failing to be present for count.

ESCAPE RISK: MODERATE

Mr. Mitchell has no history of escape. However, his latest unexplained behavior (wandering the grounds of Ferndale Institution at night) is an indicator of escape potential.

PUBLIC SAFETY CONCERN: MODERATE

Mr. Mitchell has a history of family violence and substance abuse. His current offence involves use of violence and is viewed as very serious. The latest psychological assessment sees Mr. Mitchell as a high risk to return to the use of violence towards those he believes have conspired to prevent his full access to his children.

APPRAISAL AND RECOMMENDATION
Appraisal:

[While on full parole] he once again used his "free time" to harass his ex-wife and find reasons to be with the children...Mr. Mitchell focused on how mistreated he was by the actions of the Justice System in general and by his wife in particular.

(Once again the justice system had taken the anger and frustration I had directed towards it, and shifted it onto my ex-wife.)

His behavior on Full Parole is extremely alarming. It is consistent with his pre-offense behavior and has to be addressed. In his psychological assessment of June 30, 1994, Mr. Stoian clearly indicates that Mr. Mitchell represents a high risk to re-offend in a violent fashion (especially towards his ex-wife) and if he doesn't successfully complete intense treatment, he should seriously be reviewed for possible detention.

As a result of Mr. Mitchell's erratic behavior in the last few days, coupled with the concerns expressed in Mr. Stoian's psychological assessment, his security classification has been upgraded to medium security.

> Recommendation
> Medium Security--APPROVED

This document was signed by Julian Methot and Marilyn MacNeil and was also dated July 5.

I reached for the next document, titled "PSYCHOLOGICAL SERVICES REFERRAL REPORT" and read "Reason for Referral:--SUITABILITY FOR CRIMINAL THINKING ERRORS PROGRAM." I had absolutely no idea what it meant. I found this report to be one of the most abusive and degrading of all the reports submitted. I suspect it may have been written to portray me as a depraved being beyond hope of redemption, to be used if I dared to challenge the system any further.

The first part of the report used the Crown's spin on the evidence from the preliminary hearing on May 1, 1992, suggesting my suspicions about Geri's affair bordered on delusion and paranoia, and then it went on to say:

> MORE RECENT EVENTS: Mr. Mitchell received Day Parole to Vancouver Island. During the present interview, Mr. Mitchell stated he behaved appropriately while on Day Parole. However, in personal communication with Mr. Dennis Larose, Parole officer, I was advised of verbal reports that Mr. Mitchell engaged in inappropriate sexual behavior while on Day Parole. Specifically I was advised that Mr. Mitchell masturbated on more than one occasion in the common TV room of the half way house, and also masturbated in his room, especially during security checks. During the present interview Mr. Mitchell denied any inappropriate sexual behavior and stated that once he received such allegations in writing he would pursue legal recourse.
> On 94/01/11 Mr. Mitchell received Full Parole to Cranbrook, BC. Although he attended counseling,

sessions were terminated by the counselor due to Mr. Mitchell's refusal to address issues and persistence in believing that his wife, National Parole Board and the Justice System have conspired against him. During the present interview, Mr. Mitchell categorically stated that the counselor's stated reasons for terminating treatment were lies. [In fact, I never said Kevin Kennedy had lied. Rather, I had told Mike Stoian that the reason attributed to Kevin in the report, was false.]

Mr. Mitchell further stated that in fact the counselor terminated sessions because the counselor believed Mr. Mitchell was "...Absolutely no risk to anyone..." Mr. Mitchell's reality testing would therefore seem somewhat questionable.

INTERVIEW IMPRESSIONS
Mr. Mitchell was interviewed on 94/06/30 for approximately one hour. (A gross exaggeration of the 15 to 20 minutes I had spent with Mike Stoian before walking out on him.) He presented himself as somewhat emotionally flat and definitely evasive, avoidant and vague. Comprehension and vocabulary indicated he is likely of at least average intelligence.

Two and a half years earlier, the forensic report had stated that I had a superior level of intelligence. Now, according to Mike Stoian, I had gone through Corrections Canada's institutions, taken some courses, and was about to be released back into society with a reduced level of intelligence! Certainly not a resounding testimonial for the justice system!

Mike Stoian's report continued on with some of the correctional service's most often used labels and impressions.

The predominant interview impressions were:
1.Denial
2.Projection of blame
3.Rationalization and Minimization
4.Rigidness
5.Persistence of maladaptive values and attitudes.

He then went on to misrepresent our discussion in a clumsy effort to support his labels. A couple of paragraphs were made up of

190

innuendo and suspicions meant to leave the impression that I was out to harm Geri. He even added a few false quotes attributed to me in an effort to inflame prejudice and fear in all who would listen. He ended his report with: "Mr. Mitchell is in my opinion presently unsuitable for the Criminal Thinking Errors Program due to serious untreated personality disorders...In my opinion, Mr. Mitchell should be seriously reviewed for possible detention."

The report was signed: M. Stoian, M.A., Registered Psychologist, Ferndale Institution

The documents were a clear indication that Corrections Canada had no plans to wait for Dr. Caldis to submit an assessment report!

However, a few days after receiving this condemning paperwork, the social worker returned, this time showing me a document that suggested staff at Ferndale had concluded that my actions on the night of July 3 were not serious after all.

I viewed this new document with great suspicion. I believed it was meant to tempt me to dispute the involuntary transfer. If I took this route, one of two things could happen. Since the justice system had just finished manufacturing several damming documents that would support a transfer to higher security, they might be trying to entice me into challenging the involuntary transfer so they could use the manufactured documentation to slam the door in my face. Or they might be offering to drop the pretense that I was a flight risk, something my ill-timed wandering on July 3 had supposedly initiated.

I carefully considered my options and concluded that if I went back to Ferndale and stood up to case management, my tenure at the minimum-security camp would be short, ending with a transfer back to Matsqui. I decided to stick to my earlier decision and leave it up to Corrections Canada to do as it pleased. As I saw it, they didn't need my permission to send me back to Ferndale.

Once again I informed Mr. Soon that I was not going to challenge the involuntary transfer. Instead I continued on with my sessions with Dr. Caldis, hoping his report would eventually force corrections to release me.

Caldis tried desperately to convince me that I should back away from my challenge to the justice system, and let everything go. He wrote a case summary report that carefully straddled the line between supporting my release and echoing the justice system's character assassination.

His report lacked the demeaning and accusatory innuendo that infected the reports from Ferndale. He challenged Mike Stoian's major argument for my continued imprisonment -- the assertion that I was suffering from a delusional disorder -- and concluded there was no evidence to support such a diagnosis, stating, "Projective and other psychological test have shown a superior intelligence, but no paranoid traits."

However, Dr. Caldis also inserted catchwords and phases that could be used to support Corrections and its rationalization of my parole suspension.

"What do you mean by 'adjustment disorder with depressed mood'?" I asked.

"It just reflects your resentfulness and depression in relation to your present incarceration," he answered. "It's understandable."

We also discussed his reference to my moderate level of stress.

"I assume it would be pretty normal in this situation," I said.

"Absolutely! Under the same circumstances, anybody's stress level would be up. And in fact, that is the point I make in stating that your level is only moderate," Dr. Caldis explained. "I believe you are handling it better than many others, and about the same as most people would under the same kind of stress. That in fact is what I show in my next statement." he continued. "The general ability to function, shown at 65 percent, is in the range and area where the majority of society functions. The fact you are doing it under these circumstances is a plus for you."

A few days after going over this report with Dr. Caldis, I was summoned to a conference room. When I entered, I noticed a tall woman sitting stoically at one end of a lengthy boardroom table. To her left sat Mr. Soon, while on her right was the institution's recreational director, *Christy Long.

At the opposite end, well separated from the trio, sat Dr. Caldis and one of the ward supervisors, *Earl Clark. Although I liked and got

192

along well with the recreational director, I quickly seated myself across from Dr. Caldis, at what I knew, would be the friendlier end of the table.

The tall woman, whom I had seen around the institution on a couple of occasions, introduced herself as my case manager, *Barb Fenton.

"Mr. Mitchell, this is a meeting by your case management team, and doctor, to review your assessment here at RPC," she said. "We have Dr. Caldis's report and he will now give us some insight into it and the results of the discussion I understand he had with you about it."

She quickly turned to the psychiatrist, who acknowledged her with a nod. "Mr. Mitchell and I have discussed the report and it is really just a preliminary report," he replied. "Mr. Mitchell asked many questions about parts of it he did not understand, and I cleared some of that up with him and we are going to discuss it some more." Dr. Caldis then focused all of his attention directly on my case manager. "Mr. Mitchell has been very cooperative and we have a good working relationship."

*Barb Fenton winced, then turned to *Christy Long and asked her about my participation in activities at the institution.

"Mr. Mitchell has been a pleasure to work with. He has participated in both indoor and outdoor recreational activities and has demonstrated a willingness to be helpful to the other inmates, and shown good sportsmanship."

"Thank you," said *Fenton as she turned back to me. "Mr. Mitchell, my concern is with your actions during parole. Your counselor said you used that time to harass your ex-wife and plot revenge!"

"Both those allegations are false," I answered politely, "and I think you know it."

"Let me tell you something, mister!" *Fenten screamed. "Your practice of denial has been well documented! There is a well-documented history of several physical assaults against your ex-wife! And do you continue to deny that as well?"

"There was one slap and a pushing incident in the 17 years of marriage," I answered, leaning forward and calmly resting my arms on the table. "If you're going to sit there and accuse me of something, then be specific. I will be more than happy to respond."

"I don't have to be specific!" she yelled. "It's written down in every report I've seen!"

"Well," I replied quietly, "tell me what you've seen written down and I'll respond."

"Mr. Mitchell, the reports repeatedly confirm the ongoing physical abuse of your wife, and I don't need any more than that! If I were your wife, I'd be terrified of you!"

Dr. Caldis appeared alarmed at the direction the discussion had taken, and he quietly interjected, "I don't think the rhetoric is going to help us get anywhere. There appears to be a misunderstanding about the abuse in the marriage. Mr. Mitchell has admitted he was insecure to a degree in the relationship. He realizes and accepts responsibility for that and understands how it contributed to the breakup of his marriage." Caldis then added some firmness to his soft words. "I did talk with Geri. Mitchell and she confirmed to me what Mr. Mitchell has said. She mentioned only two incidents that happened early in the marriage, a push and a slap."

The case manager reluctantly dropped her attack, turned to *Earl Clark, the ward supervisor, and asked for his input.

"Mr. Mitchell's behavior on the ward has been exemplary," he answered. "He has never been confrontational or threatening, and has demonstrated a willingness to be helpful to others on the ward."

After the ward supervisor's comment, the real power in the room had heard enough. "Let me be blunt and come to the point, Mr. Mitchell!" said Mr. Soon, who had remained quiet up to this point. "We don't like the way you continue to attack the system and the people who are just trying to do their jobs. If you were to step back and stop your denials about everything that is written, stop the attacks and confrontational attitude that you continually display, I can guarantee you that the reports would be much more positive, and you could find yourself out of these institutions and back home." He raised his voice up another notch. "In short, Mr. Mitchell, we don't want to listen to, or hear any more about your feelings towards the justice system while you are incarcerated. You can deal with that any way you like when you get out."

I was certain Mr. Soon's outburst was tied directly to the correctional service's realization that I was steadfast, in my refusal to beg and plead for my release.

"My understanding from what you just said is that you people do not wish to discuss my feeling in regards to the abuse and dishonesty that has gone on in this case," I responded. "And you want me to deal with it when I get out. Have I got that clear?" I asked, wanting to make sure I had heard correctly.

"That's right!" snapped the social worker.

I thought to myself, "Boy, that *was* blunt!"

I noticed a shocked look on Dr. Caldis's face, and heard it in his response. "Well, I think what Mr. Soon is saying, uh, is what you and I talked about. If you accept in good faith what people write, and accept in good faith what your ex-wife says about her fears, then the confrontations that arise out of your objections to the written reports will disappear. And that is what the reports will ultimately reflect."

"It's all been said then," responded Mr. Soon. "There is nothing else to add. That's all, Mr. Mitchell. You can leave, and I suggest you think about what I said, and let us know your decision."

I left the conference room, still convinced that Dr. Caldis's final report would support a recommendation that I be released. I stayed my course, and my refusal to give in moved Corrections Canada to put yet more pressure on me.

On July 21, Ferndale Case Management sent over another recommendation for a transfer to higher security. They also confiscated four-fifths of my institutional pay, telling the psychiatric center that they had overpaid me while I was at their institution.

I was certain this latest action was an attempt to attack my self-respect by leaving me without any means to buy cigarettes. In order to feed my nicotine habit, I started lifting butts out of ashtrays and off the breezeways throughout the institution, a demeaning action that left me loathing my addiction.

Another three weeks passed, and on August 11 I received a document that clearly indicated the correctional service was not going to wait for Dr. Caldis's final report:

> Ferndale Institution is requesting an Involuntary Transfer to Matsqui Institution due to information in a Psychological Assessment [Mike Stoian's report] which indicates that he remains largely untreated/unchanged due to his continued denials and rationalizations in regards to his current offense. In the Psychological Assessment, Mr. Mitchell's risk of re-offending in a violent manner is described as being moderate to high unless he involves himself in intensive treatment at the Regional Psychiatric Center. This information, coupled with his behavior during his Full Parole release and Mr. Mitchell being missing from his room during a routine count at 0045 hours caused concern for the management of Ferndale Institution. His Security Classification was re-assessed resulting in determinations of Moderate in all 3 factors."

My immediate reaction was disbelief. How could they do this without Dr. Caldis's final recommendation? Heartbroken by the decision, I waited out the afternoon and caught Dr. Caldis as he was leaving the institution. I quickly pointed out the reference in the report that stated I was largely untreated/unchanged and in need of intense psychiatric counseling.

The psychiatrist shook his head. "You and I both know that you do not need the counseling they are suggesting. And there are no courses here at RPC that you need."

The same helplessness I felt could be seen in Dr. Caldis's expression as he spoke. "I'm sorry they've decided on the transfer to higher security, but I'll be submitting my final report very soon and I'm sure it'll help."

On August 16, a few days after my chat with Dr. Caldis, I was escorted over to Matsqui and assigned to a cell on the lower level. The following day was spent going through the rules of the prison, after which I was assigned work with the prison labor crew. Again, almost all of my institutional pay was confiscated by the Ferndale Institution. With no money to buy cigarettes, which I needed for prison currency, my bargaining power within the penitentiary was practically non-existent. The going price for a small black and white television set was three pouches of tobacco, and it would take me a month to pay for that simple luxury.

Each day I made my rounds throughout the prison, attending to my assigned duties, which included emptying ashtrays. At the end of each day, with my pockets full, I went back to my cell, removed the tobacco from the cigarette butts, and rolled myself a couple of smokes, using the cigarette papers that I could afford to buy from the canteen.

On September 15, a month after my placement at Matsqui, Dr. Caldis brought over another report and called me into a private meeting in the administration building. He had carefully inserted wording that suggested my return to prison had been warranted at the time, but his personal recommendation clearly stated that I should now be released. What was also clear was the obvious conflict between his conclusion, and his struggle with the correctional service's authority. He wrote:

> It is not the writer's opinion that at present Mr. Mitchell should be detained. As to whether parole suspension should be continued or not, although the writer does not feel Mr. Mitchell constitutes a high risk of reoffending in a violent way, this was not a unanimous feeling amongst our treatment team [case manager, Fenton, and social worker, Soon]. All agree that suspension at the time was necessary and therapeutic.

Dr. Caldis then assured me that he felt I should be released from prison.

However, I also noticed that the report still contained the word "paranoid." I had picked up on his use of the word in the first report, and when I had questioned the psychiatrist about it, he had indicated it could easily be replaced with the word "sensitivity." I had a strong suspicion that the word had been inserted to refute my allegations of abuse in the system by suggesting my claims were coming from someone with a paranoid personality.

One could argue that this simple belief I held was paranoid in itself, but I knew the truth and understood the deception that could follow. The question was, would I ever be able to convince anyone else that this kind of manipulation was going on in Canada's correctional and parole services?

Dr. Caldis told me he would re-evaluate the use of the word, along with the rest of the report, and then left, leaving me the unsigned copy. Little did I know that I would never hear from him again during my incarceration.

As time passed at Matsqui, it became clearer to me that an imprisoned person, who does not ask for something from his captors, cannot be denied anything that has not already been taken -- namely, freedom! With that in mind, it was easy to see how a prisoner's natural tendency to long for freedom can easily be abused by the justice system with tantalizing promises of reduced security or early release through parole. This is why Corrections tries to keep inmates requesting things -- a transfer, a new work assignment -- anything that Corrections can control and use as leverage.

My choice to refrain from engaging the system on any of its recent decisions had taken that power away, and Corrections Canada wanted it back! With my refusal to play the game, the only way it could regain that power was to threaten to take away more of my freedom -- to hold me beyond my statutory release date.

To better understand this, one must understand the workings of parole. Let me take a minute to explain. After a revocation, parole dates are recalculated based on the time remaining in the sentence. For example, inmates may once again apply for day or full parole after one-third of their remaining sentence has passed, or they may be forced to wait for their release until their new statutory parole date is achieved after two-thirds of their remaining sentence is served.

With eighteen months left to go on my sentence, from the date of my revocation, that meant my new statutory release date was approximately a year into my reimprisonment. In this case, that date was May 6, 1995. If the system wished to detain me, (Gating) it could hold me until the conclusion of my sentence, expressed as a warrant expiry date. That date was November 1, 1995.

A few days after I saw Dr. Caldis, for the last time, I was given notice to appear before the prison program's board. I was unsure of the nature of this particular panel, and when I asked what it entailed, I was told it was to discuss my work assignments while I was at Matsqui.

When I arrived, a dozen staff members confronted me, including my new case manager, Thelma Graham. The meeting had nothing to do with work. Instead, it turned out to be a hearing on the subject of detaining me beyond my statutory release date. I sat and listened as I was ridiculed for attacking the justice system, chastised for challenging its integrity, and, finally, threatened.

"There doesn't appear to be enough substantial evidence for the board to gate you...at this time!" said one man who had taken charge.

I had already started counting down the months to my statutory release date, so this meeting had its desired effect. I panicked, and once again the Correctional Service had me asking for something. On September 22, I sent in a frantic request to the National Parole Board for a re-examination of its earlier decision to revoke my parole. In the request I informed them that I had Dr. Caldis's favorable assessment, which included his stated belief that my incarceration need not continue.

I also contacted Prison Legal Services, where Beth Parkinson dismissed my request to meet personally and discuss the manipulation that had gone on with my revocation, opting instead to mail me a letter explaining my options. Sometime in mid-October I received her correspondence, it indicated I had let too much time pass for a re-examination of the revocation decision. She suggested I apply for parole instead.

Thelma Graham also took advantage of my new activity. "Why don't you apply for a transfer back to a minimum-security as well?" she asked, in a tone that suggested she would give her support for such a move. "If the Board won't review its revocation decision, you'll still have that application to fall back on."

"If that's the case, I'd rather stay here than go back to the abuse at Ferndale," I said sullenly.

"It doesn't have to be Ferndale," Thelma replied. "Elbow Lake is another camp you could apply for."

A couple of weeks went by without any response to a review of my revocation, and I started mulling over the thought of spending my remaining prison time at another minimum-security camp, as Thelma had proposed. I decided it was a proposition I could live with and filled out the transfer application on October 26. The very next day I received a letter from the National Parole Board, dated two days earlier, rejecting my request for a revocation review. It also indicated I had the right to apply for a brand new hearing.

I took up this option as well, something that both Prison Legal Services and the National Parole Board had now suggested. On October 31 I filled out an application for a new parole hearing. Sometime in the third week of November, the National Parole Board sent a letter back, dated November 16, indicating it would give me a hearing sometime in April 1995, less than a month before my new statutory release date.

Frustrated, I now understood why I had grown stronger over the last months. The simple fact was, if I wasn't asking for anything or demanding something, the system could no longer play with my emotions. Offering me a hearing just days before it had to release me by law (unless they went ahead and "gated" me) only highlighted the abusive nature of the correctional and parole system of justice.

I wrote the board to say I would not put my family or myself through the abuse of the system any longer. Although fearful, I suspected the threat of gating was a hollow one. With my statutory release date set for early May, I declined the offer.

I called my lawyer, Ron Buddenhagen, whom I had almost given up on. I asked him to arrange for a new date for the family court hearing that I had been denied due to my parole revocation. "Get a date set for sometime in June or July so I can discuss the case with you as soon as I get back home. My statutory release date is on May 6," I said, keeping my bitterness hidden.

On December 12, Jim Wilson, the man who had introduced me to Richard Engle and Doug Hampson, mailed some more of my legal correspondence and correctional documents, along with some of my diary notes, to Ron Buddenhagen. In the attached letter he wrote, "He seems to be receiving unfair treatment following his parole revocation."

I received no response back from Buddenhagen, and it appeared that the only thing left to wait on was my application for a transfer to Elbow Lake. When Thelma Graham sat on that request, I angrily admonished myself for falling into a trap that had me chasing another one of the Correctional Service's cherished carrots, a transfer to minimum-security!

I quickly took back as much control of my life as I could, and gradually adapted to the harsher and more secure environment of the Matsqui Penitentiary. As I had done throughout my incarceration, I continued to attend church services and struck up a friendship with the prison chaplain. Visits by Richard and Ruby Engel became weekly highlights and also gave me some much needed and appreciated support.

The institution went through a couple of lengthy lockdowns in December and January. The guards took advantage of it. All day and all night, they would set off the deafening fire alarms, letting them clang for up to five minutes at a time. Inmates swore and cursed, banged their cell doors, and vented their frustration while the guards used the excuse they were testing the alarm system.

My telephone access was restricted to one call a week and I hunkered down in my cell where I continued to work on my book and write in my diary.

> Wed Jan 4/95 10 pm
> Today went slow and it seemed like kind of a 'blah' day. I sure miss that second call to the kids. With four months to go to my release date I am also beginning to wonder what this system will do to emotionally abuse me before that date. I am trying hard to prepare myself for it, but even knowing it is part of the incarceration and would be consistent with how case management works, it is still difficult to accept, and it hurts. I hope it is not something that will also hurt mom and the kids some more.

In early January there was a prison escape. Two or three inmates hid in the back of a truck that left the institution, unsearched. Their bid for freedom was short-lived as they were captured a couple of hours later. Due to this incident and a confrontation between a guard and another inmate, we were locked down for an additional two weeks in January before the institution returned to a degree of normalcy in February.

While I waited patiently for my statutory release date, now only three months away, Corrections Canada decided to move on my transfer to Elbow Lake. Matsqui staff put together a progress summary report that portrayed a successful rehabilitation, supporting my transfer to lower security. Like all the other reports, it was carefully crafted to give just enough support for an about face if the correctional service felt a need to haul me back. Their sudden approval of a transfer to minimum-security did not surprise me. Presenting a successful rehabilitation to the public, while promoting the parole process is critical to the prison industry's success and continued growth.

Case management covered themselves by claiming my association with the chaplain filled Corrections' mandate of providing ongoing counseling, though they did not stipulate what the counseling was for. (Reverend Gehrs and I did discuss the topic of abuse in the correctional service, and he allowed me to vent some of my frustration, which probably was helpful, though not in a way Corrections was willing to admit too.)

Under the heading DISCIPLINE/SECURITY CONCERNS, the report read: "Mr. Mitchell has not received any institutional offense convictions. For the most part, he is not considered a behavioral management concern. The only concerns surround those times when he is clinically depressed. This is usually anticipated when he feels his access to his children is being curtailed or limited."

Under TREATMENT AND /OR PROGRAM PARTICIPATION it stated: "Mr. Mitchell is presently receiving counseling on an ongoing basis with Fred Gehrs, Chaplain. Reverend Gehrs is supportive of a transfer to Minimum Security and does not view Mr. Mitchell to be at risk to escape or cause harm. He indeed believes that he is stronger for being able to survive in the environment at Matsqui Institution given that he is non-criminally oriented and does not hold the values of the pro-criminal."

PROPOSED PLANS: The time at Elbow Lake Institution would be used as a defusing period prior to his release.

SECURITY RE-CLASSIFICATION
Institutional Adjustment-Low
He has not presented any security concerns
other than his depressive state after his return from
R.P.C. --He receives good work reports. During the last
three months there has been marked improvement in his
mood state. The brief therapy he received at R.P.C. and
ongoing support from Rev. F. Gehrs, Chaplain, has
stabilized him.

What I saw under the next heading was particularly interesting.

Escape Risk: Low
Mr. Mitchell has never been convicted of any
offenses that would indicate he was a risk in this category.
The incident at Ferndale Institution did not result in a
Disciplinary Charge.

This might have made some readers of the document wonder
what the involuntary transfer to higher security was all about.

PUBLIC SAFETY CONCERN-Low
The risk Mr. Mitchell presents is viewed as low.
He is resigned to the breakup of his marriage and harbors
no resentment towards his ex-wife. His primary concern
is his access to his children and this has been mitigated by
their advancing ages, his two oldest children are in their
late teens and his youngest son is now thirteen years of
age. The courts have granted him access to the children.
His ex-wife is not interfering with his access to them.

OVERALL SECURITY RATING- Minimum
Security

RECOMMENDATION: Transfer to Elbow
Lake Institution approved.

I signed the document and put the day's date, February 15, next
to my name.

The following day I talked with the chaplain about the report. "I
told them that you showed a great deal of strength in surviving the

environment of Matsqui," Fred said. "I did not say you achieved that strength because you were put here...you survived despite it! I don't think there would be many people out in society who could come into the Matsqui institution under your circumstances, and survive the way you have." Fred Gehrs leaned back in his chair and calmly reflected on my relationship with the justice system. "You maintained your self-respect and gained the respect of the prison population, as well as a lot of the staff. You haven't become a snitch or rat. Haven't gotten involved in any destructive activities, yet get along with just about everyone in the institution. You hung in there and stuck to your guns, and despite what these people write, I know they respect and admire your courage and conviction, as you know I do. Remember, David, surviving persecution is something God applauds, and even demands."

I maintained my regular routine over the next several days as I waited patiently for word on the transfer to Elbow Lake. On Monday, February 27, 1995, I went to my workstation and received the work pass I needed to move about the institution.

My first task for the day was to clean the security trailer inside the work compound. The job took about an hour and was one I had come to enjoy. The women in the office were friendly and went out of their way to show me some respect. The atmosphere helped take my mind off the environment outside, even if it was only for a brief period of time.

After I had finished cleaning the trailer, I showed my pass to the guard at the P-9 Security Gate and carried on with my remaining duties back in the main area of the prison.

About a half-hour later I was emptying the ashtrays when I heard a blast over the prison speakers. "Mitchell, report to P-9!" I used my pass to move through another security check and started down the breezeway.

I was still a considerable distance from P-9 when I was met by two security guards. "They're waiting for you over at P-9," said one of the guards, "and you're in big trouble, mister!"

"What's the problem?" I asked nervously. "I've just been doing my job."

"You're not supposed to be over here."

"This is my regular job," I replied defensively. "I have a pass."

"Your boss said you're not supposed to be over here, and they're mad as hell at your breach of security!" the guard yelled. "You're on your way to the 'Shew, in Prince Albert mister!"

My heart sank and I followed them down to the security station, where the manager of the works department greeted us. He asked for my pass and I turned it over to him, pointing out that it made no mention that I was restricted from my regular work duties.

"I'm keeping the pass and you're laid off from the works department," he said. "You were supposed to stay in the work compound today."

"That's garbage!" I yelled.

"Follow us back up to the units," said one of the guards. "You're in lockdown until your transfer to Prince Albert!"

With a guard on each side, I was marched back to my cell. The heavy metal door slammed shut, and I slowly edged myself onto the bed, and considered this turn of events, -- a transfer to Prince Albert, a maximum-security prison in Saskatchewan, known for its harsh environment. "David, you understand this system and its use of threats and intimidation," I said to myself. "Yes, they brought you back to prison, and they have transferred you to RPC and here to Matsqui, but there is no way they could ever justify a transfer to Prince Albert. Never! Never! They're just playing the game. You know it, you know it, hang in there!"

A half-hour later the intercom box in my cell came to life. "Mitchell, you're wanted at A&D immediately! Stop at the bubble [the enclosed area for the guards] and get your pass!"

The cell door popped open and my heart raced as I rose and headed down the tier. The guard flashed me a large smile. "So, looks like you're about to leave us, eh?" he said as he slid my pass through the slot.

I walked up to the Admission and Discharge building and stopped outside its door. I took a deep breath, emptied my lungs before filling them to capacity once again, then nervously opened the door and walked up to the counter to await my fate.

"You Mitchell?" asked the man standing behind the counter.

"Yes," I answered, trying desperately to keep myself together.

"Here, take this form and get it filled out. I need it before I can get your stuff ready for your transfer…" After a deliberate pause, he added, "To Elbow Lake tomorrow." The man then flashed me a sly grin. "You look kind of pale," he said. "Thought you were going somewhere else, did you?"

Chapter 17

Reflections on a Mountain Top

It was February 28, 1995, when I left Matsqui behind and moved on to Elbow Lake. The sheriffs drove me to the minimum-security camp along a narrow gravel road that wound high into the Coast Range Mountains. Entering the camp, we drove over a plank bridge that led into a serene area just below the tree line.

Under the bridge's heavy timbers, a turbulent creek cascaded down a narrow mountain chute, en route to the Fraser River. Above us, the mountains displayed their snow-covered peaks, while a spectacular view of the valley to the east highlighted the institution's elevated remoteness.

I quickly settled in at Elbow Lake, spending my first few days enjoying the natural beauty that dotted the landscape. I was then assigned a job clearing away some of the undergrowth on the forest floor. It appeared to be work for the sake of something to do, but it served its purpose, keeping everyone busy.

Richard and Ruby Engel kept my spirits up as well, making the long and generous trip out to Elbow Lake twice a month. It was a friendship I knew I would cherish for the rest of my life.

The peaceful atmosphere of Elbow Lake gave me the chance to reflect back on my life, which included my lengthy relationship with Geri. After so many years together, having her support the justice system's dishonest attempt to label me as a wife abuser was something I found hard to forgive, and painfully impossible to forget!

However, I also understood it had been the justice system, and not Geri, that had pursued this character assassination with reckless zeal, using Corrections Canada and the parole service to further support the dehumanizing label.

While I was going through this time of reflection, I received notice that the family court hearing I had requested had now been set for July 25, a couple of months after my pending release in May. I quickly went to work on my court statement, condemning the legal profession's unethical manipulation of justice, and the correctional service's hidden abuses, including its vindictive revocation of my parole. As I wrote, I wondered, "Has it all been worth it? Has my refusal to play the parole game cost my children, and me, too much?"

After several drafts I finished the statement a couple of weeks before my release date, leaving just enough time for case management to pull me into one last emotional mind game.

I was called to the institution's administration building and informed the pre-release report expected from Matsqui had not been completed, and that my release date was now in doubt. I made another harried phone call to Prison Legal Services, asking for help, but the woman on the other end of the line only managed to raise my fears.

"It looks like the system is trying to detain you," she said.

"I don't see how they have the right to do that," I responded anxiously, "especially at this late date!"

"They could use what is called a commissioner's directive," she replied, "although I believe it's unlikely."

I hung up the phone and slowly calmed myself. "It's just part of the game, David. It's just part of the intimidation. You've been through it before."

On May 1, less than a week before my release date, another inmate approached me. I had seen him around Matsqui during my stint at that institution, and on a few occasions we had engaged in insignificant small talk. He was a young man in his late 20s, who I thought carried too much weight on his short frame.

This day he initiated a conversation, telling me he had just broken up with his girlfriend, who was now seeing someone else. "When I get out," he said, "I'm going to beat the hell out of both of them!" He smiled enthusiastically and then said, "I guess you feel the same way, eh?"

"No," I answered, "my ex-wife has the right to live her life as she wishes, and I respect her right to do so."

"I guess when you get out you're going to get drunk or do some drugs and unwind. I bet that'll be a relief, eh?"

"No," I calmly replied, "I don't drink or do drugs."

The inmate then told me he had waived his right to be released and had agreed to finish out his sentence at Elbow Lake. It was a curious comment, that sounded more like a suggestion than a revealing statement about himself. It made me suspect his earlier comments and questions had been carefully thought out. My sixth sense smelled the odor of a prison rat, looking for responses it could take back to case management. I turned down his request to join me in a walk around the perimeter of the institution, telling him I needed the time alone.

After my quiet half-hour stroll, I was summoned to the duty office and asked to check one of two boxes on a correctional service document. It appeared that my earlier intuition about the other inmate may have been correct.

The form was titled "STATUTORY RELEASE: Inmate Release Decision." Underneath were two statements, each preceded by a small check box.

[]-I advise that I do not wish to be released on my statutory release date.
[]-I advise that I wish to be released on my statutory release date.

I checked the latter, but I was thinking about the young inmate and wondering, "Why in the world would anyone check the first box?"

However, when I thought about the psychological harm that often accompanies incarceration, I began to see that many inmates might find life easier inside these work camps than out in society. The form was like a job offer, which many must have found hard to turn down, complete with the enticement of three square meals a day and a roof over their heads.

During my stay at Elbow Lake, about half-a-dozen inmates from the east, some from as far away as Ontario, found sanctuary at this minimum-security camp. Undoubtedly many were prison rats and informers, inmates whose lives were in danger, who had been transferred for their own protection, or who had been sent along like any employee on a regular job transfer, doing case management's bidding at their new institutions.

Cop killers, habitual drug addicts, rapists and other sex offenders, all looking for easy time, are a cost taxpayers are burdened with as the Correctional Service protects these individuals with their frequent us of this underground judicial railroad.

It was indeed a mixed-up system I was about to leave.

Because May 6, was a Saturday, I was told I would be released on Friday, due to the fact that inmates could not be released on the weekends. I arranged for Richard and Ruby to pick me up on May 5, but after doing so, Corrections Canada then refused to confirm my release. I felt I had to force its hand and get an answer, so I informed the staff at Elbow Lake that if I did not hear anything to the contrary, I would consider it confirmation that I would be released on Friday when Richard and Ruby came to pick me up.

On Wednesday, May 3, the National Parole Board held hearings at the camp. This, I suspected, was the date I would have been brought before the Board if I had gone along with its decision to give me a hearing sometime in April.

The next day passed without incident, and on Friday morning, May 5, 1995, I walked down the hill to the duty office and received my release papers. The previous condition that I not come within 10 miles of Fernie, BC, had now been set at 20 kilometres, but with only six months left until my warrant expiry date, I took the restriction in stride.

Richard and Ruby arrived at 8:30, bubbling with excitement over my release. Richard opened the trunk and I deposited my belongings inside.

"Richard," I said quietly, "I'm going to walk to my freedom one more time."

"I thought you might want to do that," Richard said, and he smiled warmly. "Go ahead, we'll meet you on the road."

I left my friends behind and walked until I reached the heavy wooden bridge. I paused for a second, letting my eyes rest on the planking that stretched across the fast-flowing mountain stream below. Then, cautiously, I stepped onto the timbers and moved forward.

I had not looked back when I left Ferndale in 1993, but this time I felt something tug at my heart and whisper in my ear. Was it a warning? Had I left something behind?

I stepped off the bridge, on the free side, then hesitantly turned around and looked back into the shadows of the institution. A bead of sweat rolled across my temple and a blast of windswept dust momentarily stung my eyes.

Through the blur, I squinted into the teary and bloodstained face of a quivering shadow. A ghostly image it was, filled with fear and riddled with pain and uncertainty. I closed my eyes and tried to shut out its woeful wails and lonely cries of despair. Suddenly, a tear dropped onto my cheek and I realized a part of me was missing. My childlike innocence, imprisoned in eternity...lost forever! Forever gone!

PART THREE

Chapter 18

A Father's Plea

I'd walked a fair distance from the Elbow Lake Institution before I heard the sound of vehicle tires rolling over loose gravel. I turned around, and Richard's car rounded the corner and slowed. A trailing plume of dust rapidly disappeared when he pulled alongside and stopped. I opened the back door and climbed in. Richard put the car in gear and we eased our way along the rocky surface, increasing our speed once we reached the paved highway that wound it's way through the narrow valley below.

A half-hour later we arrived at the bus station in Abbotsford. I embraced Richard and Ruby in a warm farewell and then started the journey home with a waiting friend, arriving in Cranbrook about midnight, some fifteen hours after my release from prison.

The next morning, after calling the kids, I went to the apartment block where I used to live, and asked about my car. Its disappearance had baffled my family and me. The apartment manager told me it had been towed away a few months after I was taken back to prison. I immediately checked with the tow services in town, but not one of them had any record of towing the car. I checked the vehicle impound and scrap yards, but again, no one had any records that indicated they had received it.

Frustrated by its disappearance, I carried on, renting an apartment in the complex next to my previous residence before heading back downtown to the commercial storage site where my family had stored my other possessions. I opened the locker and immediately realized the new television set I had purchased a year earlier had also gone missing. Any chance of a claim disappeared when the storage company informed me it wasn't on their list of stored items.

On Monday morning, unannounced, I dropped in on Ron Buddenhagen. I could not hide my anger at this man, for what I believed was his less than honest effort to get me out of prison. Now that I was out, I was determined to carry on where things had ended with Judge

Diebolt on March 9, 1994, and was looking forward to the new hearing, rescheduled for July 25.

As I sat across from Buddenhagen and asked about the hearing though, my worst fears were quickly realized.

"I'll let you know right now that I have no intentions of going into a courtroom and chastising the justice system," Buddenhagan said emphatically, before telling me he had used up most of my mother's $2,000.

I rose from my seat. "I don't think there's any point in you representing me. I don't see that you've done a hell of a lot to help me so far. You left me back in prison to rot. ...I would like my file," I said, terminating my association with the lawyer.

Once back home, I flipped through the documents and notes, looking for Geri's first affidavit, which had been sent to me by the Fernie Court Registry while I was still at Ferndale. I recalled the middle page of the affidavit held a statement of appeasement, ..."I know why what happened, happened and it is something I will have to live with for the rest of my life and will never leave me."

In a later copy, mailed to me by Geri's lawyer, George Majic, the statement had been altered, to read, ..."I saw the wounds that he suffered, I knew why he suffered these wounds, and the trauma that I suffered as a result of that attack will never leave me."

My notes to Buddenhagen also showed there had been no mention of a balaclava in the first affidavit, something that was present in the second copy. Putting them side by side, I would have proof of tampering with court documentation.

Halfway through the file I found what I was looking for, but was setback when I realized the middle page in the first affidavit was missing. I now had nothing to compare with the second one. ...But why was a statement, saying I had worn a balaclava during the assault been inserted into the second affidavit? That was untrue, and surely everyone knew the criminal court transcripts could prove the statement was clearly false!

I applied for legal-aid at the downtown office in Cranbrook. Due to new guidelines, however, I was told I would have to sign a form consenting to hand over any notes and evidence I had. Reason being, a case management team could determine if my application qualified for financial assistance from the government. Convinced that any more damaging evidence I relinquished would go missing, I refused to sign the form and immediately left the office.

At the end of the week, I called my children again. Jeff, who had just come home from the University of Victoria for the summer, assured me that my diary notes and the other documents that he had taken from my apartment a year earlier, were safe and secure in Fernie. Considering everything that had happened over the last three and a half years, I was thankful for this bit of good news. I now suspected that just about everyone involved in my case would do whatever they could to protect themselves.

But there was one man I believed would speak openly and honestly with me about his involvement. And his involvement was crucial! This was Kevin Kennedy, the counselor I had been seeing before my parole suspension.

My parole conditions had remained virtually unchanged, and my new parole officer, John, told me that I was still obligated to attend counseling with Kevin. When I arrived to renew our sessions, I showed Kevin the comments that had been used to support my re-imprisonment a year earlier. He shook his head and informed me that he had never told the parole service that I was out seeking or plotting revenge against anyone.

Confident of Kevin's support, I called the court registry in Fernie and asked for a copy of my family court file. I hoped this would expose any courtroom activities that had gone on in my absence. It would also give me an opportunity to check out all the affidavits on file, especially Geri's.

I was surprised and shocked when the registry informed me that legal-aid had asked them to forward my file to Buffy Blakley, and they had done so. The lawyer's office, located in Invermere, BC, a small town about an hour's drive north of Cranbrook, was well past the boundary imposed on me by my new parole officer.

It was deja vu! After rejecting one of my applications for legal counsel (supposedly because I did not wish to follow new guidelines), the

215

government had gone ahead and given me a lawyer, but one I would have difficulty meeting with to discuss my case, due to government restrictions on my movement!

Angry, confused, and uncertain, I called the lawyer and asked her if she had my file.

"Oh yes," Buffey Blakley replied. "The court registry in Fernie forwarded a binder filled with family court documentation dating back to 1991. I'll be in town in a couple of days on another case. Maybe we could meet in the courthouse library?"

"That'll be fine." I responded, still confused about how she had become involved.

A few days later, as arranged, Buffy Blakley met me in the Cranbrook courthouse library. I showed her the National Parole Board's revocation decision, pointing out their false statement that said my counselor had indicated I was plotting and seeking revenge a year earlier. I then told her that Kevin Kennedy had denied making any such comment.

Blakley's enthusiasm for challenging the justice system's deceptive and dishonest statement fell well short of mine. She ended our brief meeting with a promise to see me again in the near future.

A week later, I quickly realized I was once again talking with someone who was not willing, or prepared to question the integrity of the justice system, and after a rousing debate, Buffy Blakley and I remained at odds.

Despite my new focus on exposing the deception surrounding the revocation of my parole, and the manipulation of court documents, my concerns about living with the degrading label "wife beater" and having it associated with a dishonest criminal prosecution, remained on top of my list. I plodded on, ordering other court transcripts and searching through court registry documents, all the while, refusing to let any of it interfere with my children's trips into town, who came into Cranbrook almost every weekend. With funds scarce, we usually spent a couple of hours at the public swimming pool, before going back to the apartment to play board games.

I had also been given permission to attend Aimee's high-school graduation ceremony. I dressed up in my best clothes and beamed with pride as I watched my daughter end one phase of her life and move on to another. A wave of sadness swept through me as I recalled the pain of missing this joyful day with my oldest son, only a year earlier. So when Jeff got a summer job at a mill near Cranbrook, and called to say he wanted to come live with me for the summer, I was doubly delighted.

Jeff also brought my diary notes and other court documents back to Cranbrook. I went through them, and the complete November 2, 1993, family court transcripts I had applied for. As I read through George Majic's cross-examination of me at that hearing, I noticed some suspicious and disjointed dialogue. A few lines above Majic's, "No, no," where he had interrupted what was going to be my testimony about the manipulation that had occurred in the plea bargaining, I read, "Are you saying that someone else put the balaclava over your head and broke into that -- it's somebody else's fault that you broke into that place with a knife?"

I was shocked! Not only had I never heard Majic mention anything about a balaclava during this hearing, the double dash separating the disjointed statement looked all to fishy. What I had recalled Majic saying was, "Are you saying that it's somebody else's fault that you broke into that place with a knife." My response to his statement, had been to refer back to what Dr. Dilli had said. The psychiatrist believed that the cumulative impact of the events leading up to the assault, coupled with the alcohol consumed on the night in question, had pushed me beyond a point of self-control. But now, with a mention of a balaclave in the sentence, an impression could be left that I was fully aware of my actions that night, and had even conducted the assault while trying to protect my identity.

I realized I had to get Geri back on the stand and get her to admit that she never saw me wearing a mask that night. I would then have all the proof needed to expose the manipulation that continued to come to life under every rock I turned over.

Needless to say, I was extremely thankful for my present counseling sessions, which helped me vent my anger and frustration at the justice system. I had a good relationship with Kevin Kennedy, and asked him for a signed letter that disputed what the correctional and parole service had put into the record, using him as their source. He obliged and gave me a letter to that effect on June 6, 1995.

A few days later, Buffy Blakley made another trip into Cranbrook and I showed her Kevin's rebuttal of the statement attributed to him in the National Parole Board's document. To my dismay, she dismissed it and once again asked me to drop the matter. Undeterred, I stood my ground and told her I wanted to read my own prepared statement in court, and have her question Geri on the stand. "I want some answers and I want the record set straight!" I said, showing my frustration.

Leaving my statement hanging, Blakley once again put me off. "We'll talk some more in a few days," she said, "Right now I have to head into the courtroom."

Blakley's departure was not without purpose. Realizing I would settle for nothing less than a fair chance to clear my name of the degrading innuendo that graced government files, I had forced her to show her hand. And a week before the hearing she did just that. Blakley informed me that she had been declared ineligible to practice law in British Columbia, supposedly due to some mix-up with her licence. The justice system had made my choice clear. I could either adjourn the family court case, or proceed without legal counsel.

Not about to be turned back, I walked into the courthouse in Fernie on July 25. I was immediately asked to attend a meeting in the judge's chamber, along with Geri's lawyer and a few others that I failed to recognize. Judge Fabbro asked me to drop my request to be heard and forego any questioning of Geri on the stand. When I steadfastly refused, the judge angrily ended the conference, sending us all back into the courtroom.

As I approached the counsel table, I noticed Ron Buddenhagan sitting in an area set aside for lawyers. I gave him a disdainful look and then turned my attention forward as the clerk called our case before the bench.

I remained standing, showing my respect to the judge as he took his seat. Then without hesitation, a fuming Judge Fabbro, still upset over my refusal to drop matters, startled me by stating that he had looked at my application and was ruling that too much time had passed from the date of my original application. He then declared my case abandoned!

In shock, I stood glaring at the judge, searching for words to express my anger. Buddenhagan stared at me with an unreadable look on his face. It was possible he was in Fernie on some other case, but I suspected otherwise. One thing was certain, he certainly appeared poised to listen carefully to what I was going to say.

He didn't have to wait long. Looking for a place to direct my anger and frustration at the justice system, I hotly accused him of stealing my mother's money. Judge Fabbro quickly admonished me for my outburst.

Wasting no time, I stormed out of the courtroom and filed another application in family court, still hoping to have Geri put on the stand. After having a new date set for August 25, I received notice that the law firm of Majic Purdy had also filed for a no-contact order on behalf of Geri. The two applications were joined together by the courts, and the hearing in August was rescheduled for late September.

The summer passed, and Jeff returned to Victoria for his second year of university, joined this time by Aimee. Steven remained with his mother in Fernie, and in early September, just before the scheduled family court hearing, I received permission from the Kelowna Parole Office to travel into Fernie to watch Steven play in a soccer tournament. I contacted a lady friend who agreed to drive me into the community.

*Colleen and I met Steven at the concession stand about a half-hour before the match, and we bought some refreshments before Steven excitedly led us over to the soccer field.

Due to the allegation that I had been plotting revenge during my first parole stint, I knew the last thing I needed was someone suggesting I was back in town harassing my ex-wife. Although I felt somewhat protected by the fact that I was with another woman, when Steven told me that his mother might show up later on I decided we should make ourselves visible beforehand. That way, if Geri showed up during the match, she would be able to find a location well away from us. I suggested to Colleen that we take up seats at an isolated picnic table to the right of the spectator stands.

The game started and I immediately became engrossed in the action, focusing on Steven's movement out on the field. Near the end of the game he scored a goal on a magnificent shot to the upper left corner of the net. I leapt off the picnic table and cheered loudly, waving my arms wildly to let him know I hadn't missed his moment of glory.

After the game ended I started walking towards my son, who was already headed in our direction. As I drew nearer I heard a familiar voice calling out Steven's name. I stopped in my tracks and looked to my left, and noticed two women wearing large sun hats, sitting in lawn chairs, about 75 feet away. One of them rose from her chair and tilted back the large brim. I immediately recognized Geri.

I quickly backed away and rejoined Colleen at the picnic table. "Is that your ex?" she asked.

"Yeah," I replied. "Did you notice them arrive?"

"No, they weren't there when the game started."

I looked back out at Steven, who had stopped, and was now talking to his mother. A few minutes later, he joined Colleen and me and we headed over to the concession stand for hot dogs and pops. Geri and her lady friend tagged along about 50 feet behind, and continued to remain in our vicinity until we left.

A few days later my parole officer dropped in to see me at my apartment. I described how Geri had deliberately put herself close to me, and showed no fear at all. "This nonsense about a no-contact order is nothing more than another attempt to portray me as someone who is out to harm her," I said, "and you can count on me telling the judge about it during the upcoming hearing. It's all garbage what these people are doing!"

Despite the fact that my warrant expiry date of November 1, 1995, was fast approaching, it was the family court hearing scheduled for September 26, that filled my thoughts with anticipation.

Finally, the day I had been waiting for, arrived. I stood before my justice system and informed Judge Waurynchuk that I wished to have Geri put on the stand, but only after I had read my prepared statement.

Judge Waurynchuk, the same man who had presided over my preliminary hearing in 1992, motioned for me to proceed. I sat down, spread my papers out on the counsel table, took a deep breath, and started to read.

...“We must ensure that accused citizens who are tried before our courts have their rights of ‘due process’ protected. Setting aside this right can have a devastating impact on people’s freedom and rob them of their dignity.
...Our justice system is and must always remain the foundation of our nation. It must use all of its wisdom and courage to ensure that the legal rights of its citizens are protected, no matter their wealth or status in society.
...I have never denied the assault that took place on that tragic night in October of 1991. I in fact, turned myself over to the legitimate authorities within our community that night, and did so while in a state of shock and despair. Now, almost four years later, I find myself struggling to keep my head above the stench, rising from false and misleading statements and reports that have been manufactured by certain individuals, and condoned by others.
...I fought hard to hang on to my dignity and self-respect while imprisoned. I did so, in an environment where the resurrection of human spirit and hope is lost. In many cases, destroyed by a systematic policy of intimidation, degradation, and dehumanization.”

I felt my voice quiver and took a moment to relax before drawing in more air.

...“The unhealthy and unsafe practice of parole justice in our country must come to an end,” I said with renewed confidence. “To support this system with the experimentation of behavioral psychology within our correctional institutions is a dangerous game. Behavior therapy, using extrinsic motivation, a theory based on rewards and punishment, is neither healthy, nor safe. It leaves many of our incarcerated citizens languishing in a dysfunctional state, and sends back to society, human beings, who lack the positive and personal motivation they need to survive in the community.

...Like any other Canadian citizen, I have the right to question my justice system’s integrity and its values. According to the Auditor General, the suspension and revocation of my parole cost the taxpayers of my country approximately $100,000. Add to that the human cost in pain and suffering inflicted on a decent Canadian family, and I say the abuse of this power and control is too high a price to pay.

221

...I have to ask, where was the protection for my children when the institutional staff from the Ferndale Institution manufactured false and misleading documents, and then vindictively re-imprisoned their father for another year.

...Today, I am asking this court to allow whatever latitude is necessary to put to rest any false or misleading statements that could be used as a basis for any future incarceration or punishment of their father. By doing so, it could give back to my children a peace of mind, a peace of mind this system has so sadly taken from them.

...I only ask that lingering suspicions and innuendoes be discussed in order that they may be replaced with understanding and forgiveness. Only then, can this family begin its healing process."

I set the last page of my statement on top of the others and sat back in my chair, uncertain how things were going to proceed. I didn't have long to wait. Geri's lawyer broke the deafening silence. In an effort to regain control, he stood and told the court that I had been in town recently, and suggested I had purposely positioned myself close to the children's mother during a recent soccer match. Then without missing a beat, George Majic asked the court to grant a no-contact order.

Stunned and hurt by yet another false accusation, I immediately told the court what had truly taken place during the soccer match. I then produced Kevin Kennedy's signed statement that disputed the justice system's inference that I had been out in the community plotting and seeking revenge during my parole in 1994.

Judge Waurynchuk casually pushed aside the friction between Majic and me, and asked if I would accept the no-contact order. His quiet manner left the impression that it would be a positive act on my part, something that would indicate to everyone that I had no desire to interfere in my ex-wife's life. Judge Waurynchuk continued along his comfortable line, indicating the court would grant the order based only on Geri's personal feelings, and not for any other reason.

I considered the request. If the record reflected my conciliatory act, it would set aside any misleading suggestion that I was out in the community plotting revenge. And if the order wasn't being demanded by her, or otherwise based on the courts false documentation, it would be another admission that such allegations of abuse were false.

I had no desire to interfere in Geri's life, and wanted only to write about my experience in the justice system, so I took the judge at his word, satisfied that I had made my point with my court statement. Besides, the no-contact order did not bar me from coming into Fernie to spend time with Steven.

A little over a month later I left the movie theater in Cranbrook and sauntered back to my apartment. It was October 31, 1995, some 1,450 days since that fateful night in October 1991. The light on my answering machine was flashing and I pushed the play button.

"Hello, David, this is John. I just wanted to congratulate you on making it through to the end. Good luck!" The short message from my parole officer ended with a hesitant pause.

I pushed the erase button and headed for the bedroom, wondering, "Is it really over?"

Chapter 19

Revelations

When I woke on November 1, 1995, my legal ties to the criminal justice system were severed, but the previous four years had left memories that I feared would haunt me forever. The abandonment of due process in the legal arena, and the lack of integrity in the prison system had opened my eyes to a world of deception that had been unsettling to me as a citizen. My anger and my frustrations were overshadowed only by the shame I felt for a judicial process that I now understood was neither, honorable or just.

Exposing the corruptive power of the justice system, and writing about it in the book meant researching more court documents, going back over correctional files, and, most importantly, interviewing people involved in my case. People who might willingly, or unwillingly, expose evidence that had been suppressed in the criminal court, or who might reveal something that would highlight the manipulation used in the plea-bargain. There was also the challenge of finding support for my accusations of abuse in the correctional and parole service.

I now questioned my wisdom in agreeing to the no-contact order that had taken away my chance to get some of those answers from Geri, under oath!

I decided to try once again. I was making trips into Fernie to see Steven, and I also knew I would have to do some research in the community. I applied to have the no-contact order amended to apply to Geri as well. I realized that if she opposed the application, she would have to take the stand. And if she did not, at least I would have equal protection against any unplanned contact that might arise. Her lawyer, George Majic, no doubt understanding the danger associated with any opposition, did nothing to oppose the application. On December 5, 1995, my order was granted.

I accepted my small victory for what it was worth and went back to the court registry in Cranbrook, looking for any usable material that might be tucked away in my criminal file. While I was browsing, a memo from the Crown's appellant court lawyer, Carol Baird, caught my attention. It referred to the original forensic report that had been missing from the evidence bag during the first appellant court hearing on December 3, 1992. The memo asked the registry to clarify what document Justice Provanzano had examined at my sentencing hearing, while making a subtle suggestion that it might have been a photocopy of the report. Baird then wrote, "I do not wish to be sent the original of the report, as counsel for the Appellant will likely be making similar inquiries and ultimately, that document should be before the Court of Appeal."

There was no mention of Madam Justice Southin's concern that the report might have been highlighted instead of edited. And Baird's request, asking not be sent the original, while suggesting my lawyer would do so, did not fall in line with the Court's demand that she produce the evidence that was missing from the evidence bag. I requested a photocopy and left the courthouse. It was time to start doing interviews, and I decided to begin with Kevin Kennedy, the counselor whose alleged comments were used by the correctional service to support the revocation of my parole.

I showed my nervousness as our appointment began, but got right to the point. "I want to be up-front with you. I have a tape recorder with me, and I want to tape the interview."

"That's fine. I appreciate you asking me first," Kevin said affirmingly.

I set my tape on the desk and pushed the record button. "Can you explain how I became one of your clients?" I asked.

"You were referred to me by the National Parole Board."

"What treatment was I to be involved in during these sessions?"

"My understanding from Dennis [Larose, my parole officer during the first parole period in Cranbrook] was that you had been convicted of a violent offence, and part of my job was to meet with you and determine if in fact there was some need for behavioral adjustment?"

"What was your impression?" I asked as I followed the list of questions written on my notepad.

"My initial impression was that the files were somewhat confusing, in that there were a variety of opinions."

"What was the content of our discussion?" I asked.

"Mainly, you and I had discussions around the adequacy, inadequacy, justice, and injustice of the justice system."

"During these discussions or sessions did I ever relate to you or give you reason to believe that I was out for revenge, or out to do physical harm to anybody?"

"No!" said Kevin emphatically. "And I have given you a written letter to that effect."

"Did I terminate my sessions with you during this period of my parole?"

"No," answered Kevin. "I think your parole was revoked and as a result of that I didn't see you again."

"At one point during our discussions do you recall telling me that you believed the court system would make it very difficult for me to clear my name of false allegations, suspicions, and innuendoes that have followed me throughout the system?"

"I think I recall making a comment like that."

"After my parole was suspended and revoked, did you ever talk to anyone in the justice system, other than Dennis Larose?"

"No!" Kevin responded without hesitation.

"What was the content of your talks with Dennis?"

"Well, the only conversation I can remember having is after..." Kevin hesitated and rephrased his response, "when I phoned him to verify what you had told me about what others had said that I had said. I asked him about the statement that was attributed to me, that relayed that you were out plotting revenge, and he assured me that I hadn't made such a statement, and I was satisfied with that."

"And the only other time you talked to him was prior to me becoming one of your clients?" I asked.

"Yeah. There may have been an occasion when he may have phoned to ask if I was seeing you or not and I would have said 'Yes.'"

"No one ever approached you after I was taken back to prison, as to why?"

"To the best of my knowledge, no," Kevin replied. "I mean, you went back to prison and Larose let me know that that had happened, and I never saw hide nor hair of you until...or heard about you until you turned up in my office again when you got back out."

"He never asked you for any information as to whether or not you thought I was a danger to society, or the children's mother, or anyone?" I asked, amazed at the system's blatant disregard for my counselor's input into the suspension and revocation of my parole.

"No, no," Kevin said as he quickly confirmed my suspicions. "He just called and asked if I had any more appointments scheduled with David Mitchell and I said 'We have something set up in the future,' and he said, 'Well it's not going to happen because I've had to remove David back to prison.' So...end of discussion!" Kevin's shoulder shrug and turned up palms highlighted the point he was making.

His comments were strong evidence that the correctional and parole services had deliberately manufactured a record to support the revocation of my parole. By challenging their authority, I had incited their anger to the point where they turned a day of family fun into something dangerous and threatening. I felt certain that I could now show the revocation of my parole was nothing more than a vindictive act carried out by people in the justice system, simply because they had the power to do so.

They had not only, not asked the counselor for his input or thoughts on the matter, but they had deliberately misused his name and position to falsify their reports, and justify the revocation.

I shuddered when I thought about the words I had read in a pamphlet put out by the National Parole Board. "Based on our recognition of the dignity of the individual, the humane, fair, equitable, individualized, and impartial assessment of offenders is critical to achieving our mission."

I left Kevin's office and headed home, determined to make my former parole officer the subject of my second interview.

Dennis Larose had told me he had left the parole service and was operating an orchard in the Creston Valley, 150 kilometres west of Cranbrook. I borrowed a friend's van and made the 90-minute trip with a sense of anticipation.

During the interview, Dennis tried to put the best light on what had happened. He acknowledged that it was possible Geri's victim impact statement had been solicited after I had condemned the justice system during the family court hearing on November 2, 1993. Dennis then said the suspension of my parole had been initiated as a "scare tactic," a ploy meant to scare me into accepting the ten-mile restriction. "I called the National Parole Board a few days after your suspension and asked that it be lifted. They told me they weren't prepared to do that yet," said Dennis.

I asked him about the suggestion that I was "plotting and seeking revenge." Dennis said that was directly related to my pursuit for answers in a court of law. "That was intimidating and threatening to everyone," he said with a frown. "The courts, corrections and parole is like a three-headed monster. I wanted to steer you away from pursuing matters that I knew would only instill further frustrations. Maybe even to a point where you would lose the ability to get on with the rest of your life!"

Dennis reflected for a moment before continuing. "The revocation was 'overkill,' and if I had to do it over again, I would back out of it so fast, it would make your head spin."

"You have stated that if you had it to do over again, you would do things differently. I appreciate that," I said as I stared intently at Dennis. "Do you believe the revocation of my parole, even if the suspension was, as you said, a hammer to let me know, that I had to adhere to the condition, a wake-up call as you put it -- but the actual revocation of my parole..."

Dennis saw no need to let me stumble through the question he knew I was trying to get out. He understood it all too well. "Unnecessary!" he emphatically interjected. "Unnecessary!"

I let out a sigh and choked back tears as I recalled the nightmare my family and I had gone through after my return to prison. "Would you say it was unfair, based on suggestive, improper suspicion and innuendos, arising out of manufactured statements from that date on in order to support the revocation?"

"Yes, uh, I think that's a good statement. Yes, yes I would have to agree with that," Dennis concluded quietly.

During my drive back home, images of prison case managers and other correctional staff danced through my thoughts. Frame by frame, I relived the nightmare of the revocation, including a painful image of my oldest son staring out into the audience during his graduation ceremony, longing for his father's presence.

I relived the heartache of hearing my mother's voice crack as she told me she was sending $2,000 to Ron Buddenhagen, who then sat back and did nothing to question those who had returned her son to prison.

I tightened my grip on the steering wheel and screamed out loud, "Why?...Why?" Then I remembered the promise made to my children as I lay shivering in the hole at the Matsqui Penitentiary. "Yes...I'll fight back!" I screamed. "I'm out of your grasp you bastards! You can't lock me up now!"

Now, more determined than ever, I continued to work on the book until Jeff and Aimee arrived home for the Christmas holidays. Along with Steven, they came to Cranbrook and spent some time enjoying the winter break with me. It was a holiday I had dreamed about for a long time, and I enjoyed every single day of it. After the kids went back to school in January, I went back over my taped interviews with Kevin Kennedy and Dennis Larose. I then considered the possibility that there may be others, who would be just as willing to talk.

I decided to broaden my search for answers, and early in the New Year I visited Jeff and Aimee in Victoria. During the day, while they were in school, I dropped in unannounced at the Manchester House to tape an interview with my former federal case coordinator, Judy Chouinard.

"On a scale of one to ten, with ten being the mark for most worthy of parole, where would you say I sat on that scale?" I asked.

"In terms of being worthy of parole...abiding by curfew, having a job, um, respecting the rules within the house? A ten," she said forcefully.

"Do you believe there was any intimidation going on while I was at this house in the last two months before my parole?"

"You may have seen it in that way," said Judy, pausing to take a drag on her cigarette. "For me, it didn't appear to be what I would call intimidation. When someone says, 'I'm not going to support you,' no matter who you are, they want that person to say, 'Well! Okay, what do I have to do in order to get your support?' And then that person says, 'Well, you have to do such and such.' So the person who wants the support says, 'Okay!'"

"In other words, play the game or move on," I said.

"Yeah, yeah!" Judy replied.

"Did you ever receive any information that I had been involved in any sexual misconduct here at the halfway house?" I asked.

Judy looked confused and surprised. "Sexual misconduct?...No."

"As far as you know, my file was complete when it went before the National Parole Board?"

"That's the parole officer's jurisdiction," Judy answered. "It certainly should have been."

"In this house, my file was complete," I inquired more precisely.

"Oh, yeah," she answered. "Oh yeah."

"The statement you gave to the National Parole Board,...that was complete?" I asked.

"Yeah!"

"You had no concerns about my activities at the house?"

"No."

"When I went to [family] court while I was still on day parole, you asked me not to be hard on the system when I spoke. Do you remember that?"

"Yep, yep!" answered Judy.

"Can you explain that?"

"You were so angry that I felt it could be detrimental," replied Judy.

"What was I angry or upset about?"

The case coordinator hesitated, and I pushed a little harder. "Wasn't I upset about all the labeling?"

"Yes," she responded, "you certainly disagreed with that...yes."

"The more I spoke up, the worse the intimidation got. Isn't that true?"

"Yes!" answered Judy once again, and then hesitantly added, "Well, I don't know if intimidation is the right word."

I challenged Judy straight up. "If I had not expressed my concerns about the system, isn't it true that my imprisonment and movement through day parole and full parole would have been much easier?"

"Yes," she answered, "probably it would have been."

With that admission I decided to bring the interview to an end. "You didn't believe for one minute that I was a danger to society, or anyone out in society," I said confidently.

"No," she replied, "I didn't think you were a danger, no."

"Do you believe I was strictly honest and up-front with you while I was at this halfway house?" I asked.

"Yes!" she answered emphatically. "I do believe that, yes."

I returned to the halfway house a few days later and talked with Kathy Roy, who had also been involved in my case, and was now the House Director. I quickly brought up the subject of the alleged sexual misconduct.

"There was nothing!" Kathy blurted.

"You never heard about such activity by myself at this halfway house?"

"There wasn't any!" Kathy replied just as definitely.

"I understand that. But nobody ever talked to you about it?" I asked.

"No! There wasn't any. It was never discussed because there wasn't any."

After I left Manchester House for the last time, I headed for the Victoria Parole Office, located on the third floor of a downtown office building. I believed the fact that I had felt compelled to tear up documents and plead for my release back in January 1994 revealed a lot about how the parole system worked. And Dave Dystra, the head administrator in the local office, was the one person who could acknowledge that event.

With my tape recorder hidden safely in my pocket and already running, I waited at the counter until Dystra invited me down to his office. After some initial small talk, I brought the conversation around to my emotional state during my parole period in Victoria. When I described the day I ripped up the documents and pled for the office's support, Dave Dystra responded, "Yeah, yeah, you did that!" With his acknowledgement on tape, I drew the conversation to a close.

Bruce Monkhouse, the psychologist I had been seeing during my day parole in Victoria, also agreed to do an openly taped interview. I met him in his office at six o'clock, later that same evening. I told Monkhouse that my parole had been suspended in 1994 and then revoked after the correctional service had manufactured reports filled with innuendo and suspicions, using the same group labeling technique found in progress summary reports.

Monkhouse relayed to me what he saw happening in the system. "I think what's happening here is exactly what you said. They're lumping a lot of different guys together. If there's violence or sexual misconduct associated with an offence, parole is denied or revoked at a disproportionate rate."

"Sexual misconduct was another one of the false allegations made against me, are you aware of that?"

"No, no I wasn't. But it wouldn't surprise me. It wouldn't surprise me!"

"You understand that these people would go that far in order to support themselves?" I asked, excited by his frankness.

"Yeah, yeah, sure!" he said more emphatically. "I'm not telling any secrets. There are some absolute injustices done!" He leaned back in his chair. "It's a cover-your-ass kind of system. It's a political culture out there in CSC [Correctional Service of Canada] right now."

"But even in this case, where these people were aware that I was no danger to anyone, they still manufactured it. Why?" I asked.

"I don't know, I don't know," he said with disgust. "It's seriously unethical, it really is." Monkhouse leaned forward and rested his arms on his desk. "And I know of colleagues who have done this, through pressure from the institutions, uh, to say those kind of things."

I sensed he would like to have an in-depth discussion on the system, so I sat back and let him go where he wanted. Among other unsolicited information he offered me was the comment, "In 1994/95 the budget for Corrections Canada was just a touch under one billion dollars. You think about that, that is just a huge...it's a huge industry!"

After some discussion on my book and the concept of a judicial system without parole, the psychologist said, "I think you should write the book. I think you should write that, and make that argument!" he said excitedly. "I think it would be very worth while, having that discussion. I think it's a good idea, I don't support it a hundred percent, but it's a good idea and worth discussing. Do it now, write your book now that they can't touch you."

Monkhouse then reflected on how fear had overtaken the system. "There is tremendous pressure within the system. Nobody's going to criticize someone if they say, 'Well, I'm going to err on the side of caution."

"Would you be surprised if that happened in this case?" I asked.

"Sadly, no, because you were a shit disturber and you fit the profile."

I asked the psychologist if by "shit disturber" he was referring to my willingness to confront the system and stand up for myself.

"Yeah," he confirmed. "And others perceive that as a threat to the system, and a system will protect itself. The CMOs [Case Management Officer], COs [Correctional Officer], and wardens and deputy wardens, sure they will. And the National Parole Board. Because that's what the public wants [for the parole board to err on the side of caution]."

"I don't believe the public wants our system to be deceitful, manipulative, and dishonest," I responded.

"The public doesn't understand how to translate the difference," he replied. "If [the public is] not sure, then the longer the sentence, the better," he said with a sigh of resignation.

The next day I said good-bye to Jeff and Aimee, and headed home.

When I arrived back in Cranbrook, I again visited the court registry and thumbed through my file. This time I was looking for a request from my appellant court lawyer, Adrian Brooks, asking for the original copy of the forensic report. The memo from Crown Counsel had indicated he would likely make such a request, but I couldn't recall seeing it when I had looked at the file earlier. As I suspected, it wasn't there.

I was now convinced more than ever that Madam Justice Southin had been right on the mark when she voiced concern that the original document may have been highlighted rather than edited. I concluded that when the court asked Baird to come up with the original, the justice system had no choice but to have the allegedly edited document disappear. As Bruce Monkhouse had said, a system will always protect itself.

It was now March 1996, and four months had passed since my ties to the criminal justice system had been severed. Although free from restrictions preventing me from living in Fernie, I concluded that with job opportunities bleak in the depressed coal mining town, it made more sense to look for work elsewhere. If I could get myself established, I could apply to the courts for custody of my youngest son. I knew he still dreamed of living with his father, so I let him know my plans and headed off to Calgary, Alberta, where I stayed at my sister's while I handed out resumes. Unfortunately, my years of incarceration left a hole in my neatly printed handout. I sadly recalled Ferndale case management's threatening words, "Eighteen more months will sure set you back!"

Now penniless, with hopes of a normal life dwindling, I sought refuge in my old hometown of Vanderhoof, a community in northern British Columbia, where I'd spent the first 25 years of my life. My father had been born in the community in 1919 and had remained till his death in 1984. My mother still lived in the same house where she and Dad had raised seven children.

Chapter 20

A Search for Truth

I quickly buried myself in my writing till late July, when I drove to Fernie and brought Steven back for a month of his summer holidays. I was surprised when Geri engaged in pleasant small talk with me before Steven and I headed back to Vanderhoof. As the end of August approached, a sense of sadness enveloped us as our time together ran out. I drove my son back to Fernie, realizing I wanted and should return to Fernie. Such a move would give Steven and myself the time together I felt he not only needed, but was something we both deserved.

Before I made the move, however, I hopped on a bus to Vancouver and dropped in on Dr. Dilli, the psychiatrist from the forensic institute.

I started the interview by reminding the doctor about the phone conversation that we had in 1992, while I was incarcerated at Ferndale. "When I talked to you on the phone," I said while showing him my copy of the forensic report, "you mentioned to me that the part of this report you did was the summary and conclusion."

"That's right, yes," he replied.

"And anything to do with any of the other stuff, I had to talk with the social worker. He was the one that prepared it?"

"Yes, exactly."

"So he was the one that prepared that," I quickly confirmed.

"Yes, he did."

"He just prepares it, and then you read everything over and then sign it?"

"Yes, yes."

"You based your summary and conclusion on seeing me and on some of the information he has given you?"

"Exactly. Yes, yes."

"And if there are any questions I have about anything other than your summary and conclusion, you would say that I would have to talk to the social worker, and that's what you told me on the phone in the fall of '92."

"Yes, yes. It's very important information that the social worker gathers."

When I pointed out many of the false and damaging statements inserted by Marc LeBlanc, Dr. Dilli became quiet and then expressed his regret that I had spent four years in prison.

I asked the psychiatrist if he had ever been contacted by the courts or by any of the lawyers, either my own or Crown counsel.

"No, no one called me," he answered.

I ended the meeting with the sense I was being drawn in deeper and deeper. The interviews raised more questions about the actions of my lawyers and the justice system's social worker at the forensic institute. I left Vancouver and headed for Kamloops. The time seemed right to confront the legal-aid attorney who had represented me at the sentencing hearing on May 1, 1992.

When I arrived at Mike Vannier's office next morning, his secretary asked if I had an appointment.

"No," I answered, "but I only need a few moments."

"Well, he does have an appointment set for this morning," she said hesitantly, "but they are not here yet." She glanced toward one of the office doors. "Who should I say is waiting?"

"David Howard," I answered.

The secretary rose from her chair, walked over to the office door, and knocked before opening it. "A Mr. David Howard is here to see you. He said he only needs a moment."

Mike Vannier emerged from his office and approached with a brisk stride. His pace slowed and he gradually came to a halt as recognition set in.

"David Howard Mitchell, just in case you don't remember me," I said, stepping forward to close the distance between us.

Vannier twitched. "Yes, ...yes, I remember," he said, avoiding eye contact. "What can I do for you?"

I stretched out my arm and placed a hand on his shoulder. "This will only take a minute," I replied, then firmly nudged him back to his office and closed the door behind us.

"I think you know why I'm here," I said, purposely stiffing my tone while we took seats at his desk. "Four years ago you handed me a bouquet of roses. You went into a back room with the prosecutor, made a deal, and sold me down the river. Now I'm here to get some answers."

I reached into my coat pocket and Vannier recoiled at the sight of the black object that appeared in my right hand. "I am writing a book about my case and recording all my interviews," I said, placing the recorder on his desk. "Now, you don't have to talk to me, and that's fine. I'll just write in the book that you refused to discuss the matter with me." I reached into my briefcase and pulled out a notepad. "I have some written questions I would like you to answer, and you can do so in whatever manner you wish." I reached forward and pushed the record button on the tape.

The lawyer eyed the slowly rotating wheel, gathered himself, and began a defensive monologue. "What I would like to say to you is that I worked very hard on your case. I did the best job that I could. You said earlier that I gave you a bouquet of roses and sent you up the river." He took his eyes off the recorder and looked at me. "I don't know if those are the exact words that you used?"

"Pretty close," I answered.

"But, uh, that's not my read on it...You figure that I went in the back room and made a deal with the prosecutor. That's not true. I mean that's the furthest thing from the truth and I'm insulted by you saying that."

"Well, you can be insulted, but I'm insulted by what happened in this system, to me, and to my family," I replied. "I'm insulted by what you said to me outside the courtroom here in Kamloops in order to get me to plead guilty to a charge of aggravated assault, only to leave me hanging in a courtroom."

Vannier shifted nervously in his chair, "Well, there was no doubt you were guilty, and the Crown read in the particulars about how the offense happened. What the evidence of the various people would be, that sort of thing. And what my job...was to provide an explanation as to why this happened. And what I told the judge was...that it was a situation where, uh, as I recall it, you were provoked by this guy. He...he goaded you and flaunted his relationship with your wife in your face, and that's basically what initiated this."

"That's not what's in the court transcripts," I shot back. "You know what I ended up being labeled as, as I went into prison? A wife beater!"

"Well I don't see how that could happen," Mike Vannier replied, "because you weren't charged with that."

"Well, it happened!" I replied angrily. "It doesn't matter whether I was charged with it or not. The allegations were left wide open."

"Well, you see, I don't have any control over that. I mean, I don't have control over what happens in the prison system."

Vannier then denied there had been any agreement with the Crown on the length of my sentence and my frustration quickly surfaced. "When you talked to me outside the prisoner's door at this courtroom here in Kamloops, you said and explained to me the deal the Crown was offering, and asked me to accept it." I leaned forward, my body covering a good portion of his desk. "You suggested that I take the deal and I said yes."

"No!" The lawyer protested as he moved back in his chair and stared at the tape recorder. "I...I disagree with that!"

"You came to me and said, 'That's the Crown's deal.' And I said, 'Okay, I'm tired.'" I searched for words that I felt best described what had taken place. "...I was purposely kept in remand without bail, solely for the purpose of wearing me down until this system could obtain a guilty plea to a lesser charge, so they wouldn't have to go to trial."

Fighting to get my anger out in a controlled fashion, I reminded Vannier how he had remained silent while the prosecutor asked for a sentence of four to five years. This, after I had been led to believe there was a sentencing agreement in place that would have seen me released within months.

"This discussion is over," Vannier spat, denying any wrongdoing.

I headed for the Kamloops Parole Office and my next interview.

I was certain Jim Bartlett would never talk to me if he knew he was being taped, so I pulled the recorder out of my coat, put in a new cassette, pushed the record button, and quickly stuffed it into my upper vest pocket before entering the parole office. "I'm here to see Jim," I said politely to the approaching secretary.

"What's your name?" she asked, showing me a cold crustiness.

"David Mitchell," I answered just as rigidly, confident my name would give Bartlett a stiff jolt. However, I also knew he would recover quickly, and a sense of invulnerability would draw him out to talk to me.

The secretary disappeared into one of the offices and closed the door behind her. She emerged a long minute later with Jim Bartlett following close behind.

The area parole officer walked up to the counter and enthusiastically greeted me. "How are you doing?"

"Not too bad," I answered. "How are you?"

"I'm fine," he replied confidently, "Come on in!"

Once inside the office, his enthusiastic front disappeared and he became more reserved and tense. "What can I do for you?"

I handed him the special report he had faxed to the National Parole Board on April 18, 1994. "Do you recognize that?"

Bartlett took longer than necessary to look over the report he had written, recommending the revocation of my parole. "This was a couple of years ago and I don't have much of a recollection about it...So, what can I do for you?" he repeated.

"As my regional parole officer, after looking at that, can you explain how and why my parole was suspended and revoked in the spring of 1994?"

Bartlett's innocent demeanor quickly turned into bitter hostility. "I'm not prepared to get into a discussion as to what decisions were made or how they were made, because it's two and a half years ago," he snapped.

"Fine," I said calmly, "if you don't have the answers, or do not wish to answer, I have no problem with that..."

"Tell me what you're doing," he said, cutting into my response. "It's like you're on some kind of a quest here or something."

"I'm just inquiring about the validity and the strength of what you people wrote," I replied sharply.

"Well, I can't, uh, I can't defend this or not defend this, because I can't remember."

I watched with some pleasure as Jim Bartlett squirmed for answers. "Well, if you don't remember," I replied, "that's fine with me."

My take it or leave it attitude appeared to unnerve the parole supervisor, and he reluctantly responded, "I've looked at it. I have some vague recollection of some of the circumstances, but that's all I have at this stage."

"Do you recall interviewing me up at KRCC [Kamloops Regional Correctional Center] when they brought me here?"

"I don't specifically recall it. Some of these facts are familiar to me, so I guess I must have."

"Okay, so you wouldn't have any recollection of telling me it was a minor violation, and if I waived my right to a hearing that I could get this over with and be back with my family in approximately a week?"

242

"I would doubt very much that I would have said such a thing," he replied.

"You don't recall saying that?" I snapped.

"I certainly don't," Bartlett said more defiantly.

"You don't deny saying it?"

There was lingering silence in the room and then Jim Bartlett said, "Listen, I'm sorry, I'm not going to sit here and go through what is your idea of some kind of a cross-examination."

"Okay," I said as I reached for my briefcase.

His uneasiness increased with my apparent willingness to just walk out. "If there's some...some, uh..."

"You people sent me back to prison for thirteen months," I said angrily, cutting him short. "It was based on false and misleading statements of innuendo and suspicions. I knew it! You people knew it at the time..."

"You're suggesting to me that I..."

"I'm suggesting to you that you manufactured this," I said as I held up the report.

Bartlett rose from his chair. "Get the f-- hell out of here!"

"Get out?" I said, showing my amusement at his outburst.

"Get out! I'm not going to sit here and listen to these kind of accusations."

"They're not accusations and I can prove it," I said as I also rose from my chair. "You refuse to answer the questions? Is that right?" I asked, pausing just long enough to let him know I was defying his request to leave.

"I refuse to listen to these accusations," he said as he pointed to the door. "Now get out of my office!"

A sense of satisfaction engulfed me as I watched Jim Bartlett struggle with the realization that he no longer held the power of imprisonment over my head. I smiled and headed back to the bus station and my final destination.

When I arrived in my old community of Fernie, I took a job cleaning and painting a motel owned by some friends. In exchange, they gave me a motel room and one meal a day at their restaurant. Steven came over almost every day after school, and on the weekends we made use of the local parks.

My return to Fernie also led to more interviews. With my tape recorder running and safely tucked inside my coat, I went to see Dan Sliva, the first legal-aid lawyer involved in the case.

After a few minutes of chitchat, I brought up the matter of the plea-bargain. "You told me you had been talking with the Crown, and the plea-bargain of two year's less a day," I said.

"I remember that," Sliva replied.

I then reminded him about the phone conversation we had while I was incarcerated at the remand center in Kamloops. During the call he had told me that Geri's lawyer, George Majic, had said that I should be elated at getting that offer from the Crown.

"You said that he had a lot of background in this. And that you were recommending to me that I accept it. Do you recall saying to me that you were talking to the Crown about this?"

"I was talking to the Crown, yes, that's right," Dan Sliva answered.

"And it stands to reason that you were talking about the sentencing?" I said, looking for a more specific answer.

"Yes, yes," he replied nervously.

Satisfied with the response, I asked if I would be right in understanding that the sentence was to be two years less a day.

"No, you could be right," said the lawyer.

"You were talking to the Crown about two years less a day?" I said more firmly.

"Yeah," replied Sliva reluctantly.

Satisfied that I had the confirmation I was looking for, I left the lawyer's office and made my way to the victim assistant coordinator's office which was located on the upper floor of the police station. The coordinator's reaction was one of surprise, along with disdain when she realized who I was.

I informed the coordinator that I had come to find out how Geri's victim impact statement had suspiciously appeared right after I had condemned the correctional service during the family court hearing on November 2, 1993. ...I asked Wendy Damstrom if she had approached Geri on behalf of the correctional service, and asked her to submit the victim impact statement. She acknowledged that she had been involved in my ex-wife's statement, and had discussed it with the Correctional Service, but she refused to elaborate on who had initiated the action.

When it became clear that I was not going to get any more out of the tight-lipped coordinator, I excused myself and headed back downstairs.

Earlier, while still in Vanderhoof, I had phoned the Fernie RCMP detachment and talked with the officer who had found me huddled by the back door of the police station on that frightful night in October 1991. She had agreed to speak with me about it,

245

so I stopped at the front counter and asked if I could speak with Constable Magnus. A few minutes later she came around the corner, wearing her ever-present smile.

"There she is," I said gleefully as she approached. "How are you?"

"Not bad," Magnus replied pleasantly. "How are you, Mr. Mitchell?"

"Not bad. You told me you wouldn't remember much..."

"Not the questions you would ask me anyways," she said, as her grin widened and she let out a short laugh.

Acknowledging her abrupt honesty and quirky response, I erupted with a hearty laugh of my own. "Okay...well." Her honesty tugged at my conscience. I reached into my pocket, pulled out the recorder, and quickly informed her that I was taping all my interviews, something I had failed to tell her during our phone conversation. I sensed her uneasiness as I continued, "The night I assaulted the victim in this case, I was found by one of these doors?"

"You were found by the back door," the constable answered quietly, "crouching down by the back door."

"You found me?"

"I found you."

"What happened then?"

"I brought you into the office and then to the hospital...I don't think I put you in a cell," she said and then paused to look over her left shoulder. "Let's go in the other room," she whispered.

I followed her into a small room off to our right and she closed the door. "Was I violent or anything like that?" I asked, picking up where we had left off.

"No!" she replied swiftly. "You were just sort of incoherent. That's why I took you to the hospital, you seemed very out of it."

"Okay," I replied, now ready to move the interview to the area where I wanted some clarification. "At one point when I was in the cells here, I remember you coming back to see me."

"It was probably the next night," she offered.

"I think you understood that I was out of it, and you had come to see how I was doing?"

"Okay, I know what you mean, yes."

"You asked me if I remembered what had happened, and I said I wasn't too sure, but I knew I had hurt this man."

"Probably, yeah," she nodded.

"And you explained to me kind of what happened, and told me he was going to be all right, 'he needs stitches.' You informed me he wasn't going to die or anything like that."

"Yes," replied the constable, with some uncertainty creeping into her voice.

"Now, I don't know if you remember that or not," I said, searching for more conviction in her response. "Do you?"

"No."

"Okay," I replied dejectedly.

There was a short pause, then the constable piped up, "Knowing me, I probably did say that."

"Okay!" I replied, my spirits rising again. "I think you were trying to reassure me that this man was going to be all right, and I appreciated that! And I remembered saying to you that I was grateful, and that was basically the end of the conversation, and you left...What I'm trying to get at, do you have any recollection of coming in to see me at all?"

"Not really," she replied.

"No? Is it possible..."

"Yeah!" the officer responded, cutting me short. "Yeah, probably, because knowing me, I would have come in and seen you. Yes. I think I would have gone back to see you, because I was working that night. Yeah, yeah, I could have done that."

I left the station, sensing there was more truth to Constable Magnus's opening quip than she would have cared to admit. I liked the strength I saw in the officer and I truly believed she wanted to help as much as she felt she could, without putting herself on the spot. Her mention of taking me to the hospital because I was, in her words, "incoherent and very much out of it," also suggested an idea for another interview.

I recalled that the forensic report in 1991 referred to Charles Bertholf, the counselor I was seeing before I assaulted the victim. The reference left the impression that, Bertholf, felt I hadn't dealt with the consequences of the assault in an insightful manner, and the judge, in his reasons for sentencing, had made use of this. But Bertholf's statement made no sense, because I had only spoken to him on two brief occasions, prior to the assault!

I made an appointment with "Chuck" Bertholf, and with my tape recorder hidden I read him the statement from the forensic report. "Mr. Mitchell may again exhibit violent behavior in the future as he has had extreme difficulties in coming to terms with the reality of his situation, and has not dealt with an insightful fashion in regard of the consequences of his recent actions."

"I said all that?" The counselor was surprised. "I don't usually..." He reached for the report. "Can I look at that? ...I don't usually say stuff like that."

"Do you recall keeping any kind of record of that?" I asked.

"Actually, my record keeping is a bit sloppy." Chuck replied. "My record keeping tends to be brief, very brief."

I tried to focus our discussion on the fear I had of hurting the victim prior to the actual assault.

"A big part of you didn't want to do that," Bertholf said.

"But I was scared it was going to happen."

"Well, it did happen."

"And I think I was relaying that to you...I wanted to be able to get through this somehow without hurting this guy, and I didn't think I was going to be able to make it."

"Uh-huh," said Chuck as he nodded. "I remember concerns about that. There was a struggle between wanting to beat the guy up and not wanting to beat the guy up."

I recalled that I had told Bertholf that I had shown up at Rob's apartment a couple of months before the assault, wearing a ski mask, and doing some damage to his vehicle.

Chuck now indicated he was not certain I had mentioned a ski mask, though he did recall me telling him I had shown up at the guy's apartment one night, unsure of my intent. I then asked Chuck if he had talked to any lawyers or Crown prosecutors about the substance of our sessions. He told me the only one he would have talked to without my consent would have been Dan Sliva -- and he said he might have done that.

I now considered the possibility that Sliva could have passed on information about the ski mask to Geri's lawyer, George Majic. That would explain how the mention of a balaclava had found its way into the family court record, two years after the assault.

It was disturbing to think that Majic had deceitfully taken that information, and introduced it into the family court case. Putting the "balaclava" over my head during the night of the assault was deceptive to say the least. I wondered if it had been done purposely, designed to leave behind a court document that would support the government's suggestion that the assault was a planned, premeditated act, carried out with considerable forethought? If the mention of a balaclava was indeed on the November 2, 1993 court tapes, as the transcript showed, it raised an intriguing question. Had I missed the comment altogether, or had it been inserted into the transcript afterwards?

The later mention of the balaclava in Geri's 1994 affidavit, after I had been sent back to prison, suggested yet more deception on the part of the justice system. I wondered whether Geri had knowingly signed that affidavit, supporting this deception, or if the detail had been altered on the second page without her knowledge. I was considering that possibility when, Bertholf, ended our discussion, telling me he would look for any records he had, and get back to me in a few days.

It didn't take that long. Late the following afternoon he called the motel. I sensed a growing urgency in his voice as he asked to see me as soon as possible, saying he wanted to show me a file he had just come across.

I suggested we make arrangements for the following morning, but that wasn't soon enough for Chuck. He insisted we meet at a restaurant next to my motel, right after work that day. I hung up the phone, inserted a new tape into the recorder, and made a short notation. "Obviously all this has got some people worked up. It'll be interesting to see what they come up with in this case to support themselves."

Just before six o'clock I greeted Bertholf outside the Chinese restaurant and followed him into the dimly lit establishment. He asked the waitress if we could be seated in a quiet area against the far wall. As we walked over to a secluded table, I reached into my coat and pushed the record button on the tape.

I was still settling into my chair when Charles Bertholf handed me a six-page computer printout. I was amazed at the length of the report, especially since Chuck had told me that he had kept poor records and took no notes during our two short sessions. I noticed a date of October 16, 1991, on the document, indicating it had been written two days before the assault.

The waitress brought us coffee and we quietly prepared our cups as I flipped through the document, titled "Mini Assessment and Termination." Chuck looked on with eager anticipation. After a few minutes had passed, he asked me what I thought of the three hypotheses, suggesting why I had committed the assault.

The first hypothesis indicated I was an angry man, intoxicated by various combinations of alcohol and drugs, who charged my victim's apartment with testosterone-fuelled intent to show who was the better male.

The second portrayed me as someone who planned his revenge in a manner consistent with the dynamics of paranoia, rather than an enraged and wounded male. It suggested I stalked the victim and planned the attack with significant forethought.

The third hypothesis was particularly degrading, and I sensed its purpose was to embarrass me into silence. It suggested that I had a fantasy of wanting to watch my wife make love to another man, and had assaulted her lover because I was angry about not being invited to join them in their activities.

I also noticed that the report held references to events that had happened well after my imprisonment. As I read through the report, I briefly discussed some of it with Chuck, but kept my suspicions to myself. One thing became clear as I read the report, it supported the justice system's suggestion that I was hell-bent on doing harm to this man and 'damm the consequences. What was suspiciously missing from the document was any mention of my severe depression, or my open discussion with the counselor concerning the intense fear I harbored about not being able to refrain from hurting the victim, a discussion and fear Bertholf had confirmed just the day before.

"When was this written?" I asked.

"That's a really good question," said the counselor, "because I looked for that." He reached for the document. "Um, I think it says..."

I placed the printout on the table and turned it at an angle we could both read. Chuck quickly pointed at a date. I quickly informed him he was pointing out my birth-date.

"This is probably the date," h said, now pointing at the date I had picked up on earlier.

"October 16, 1991?" I said inquisitively.

"That's probably the date," he exclaimed, more boldly this time.

"October 16, 1991?" I repeated in disbelief.

"Um, ah, what?" he waffled. "There's a date of the evaluation..."

I cut his rambling short. "This was written two days before I assaulted this guy?"

The counselor cringed as he realized that some of what we had just discussed had happened well after the date on the report.

"No, I wouldn't have written it two days before," he stammered. "Uh, it was actually, it was, no, it was written after...it was pretty much well after the fact. It was almost certainly all written at the same time," he added defensively, "and probably well after the time."

"How could you be writing this a year after?" I asked with a sense of heightening suspicion.

"Oh," he answered, "that's the way I...I...I run behind."

My suspicions about his three hypotheses continued to grow. I was convinced the report had come into existence since our discussion the previous day, and probably with outside help and influence.

"It looks like this was strictly written in order to support the justice system," I said snidely, still somewhat amused. Then I abruptly challenged him. "Corrections and Parole, wanted this, no?"

"Oh, really," Chuck replied nervously, sensing I might be seeing through the façade.

"In fact," I mused out loud, "this could have been written and put together yesterday."

"Well," Chuck said with some resignation, "that's probably true."

I let out a small laugh at his forced but truthful statement. Bertholf grasped the report, searching nervously for an explanation he could use. The waitress came up to the table with her coffee pot. I pointed at the cups without saying a word, keeping my eyes focused on the man across from me, who was trying desperately to determine how he was going to explain the glaring error between the date on the document and the content. Five minutes passed before he broke the silence.

"A part of it was almost certainly written a few days to a week after I saw you," Chuck said defensively, "and printed out on a computer much later."

"Do you have any written notes?" I asked calmly.

"Not any more."

"Did you do this based on notes that you took while I was talking to you?"

"No," he answered, "I probably didn't make any notes. I rarely take notes."

"You didn't take notes, and this is what you basically wrote up...a day or two later?" I said, trying to pin down his story.

I noticed his hand trembling as he pointed at a section of the report. "This part was probably written from memory," he replied sheepishly.

I wasn't too sure what part he was pointing at, but I assumed it was the hypotheses. I bit my bottom lip to keep from laughing. "A couple of days after?" I chided.

"A couple of days after or a week after...probably?" he insisted, with even less confidence.

I recalled his earlier comment that the entire report had most assuredly been written on, or near the same date. I picked up the document and pointed randomly at sections. "And then the rest of this was written a year, two years, three years, four years later?"

"Well, no," Chuck said, frantically choking back his words. "Not that long later."

I had picked up on a line in the report that proved the document had been written much more recently than the counselor was letting on, so I replied confidently, "Well, it was definitely over a year later!"

Bertholf finally crumbled, and I noticed a bead of sweat trickle down his left temple. I felt for this man, whom I truly liked. I saw him as basically, a sincere and honest man who was being used by others who were more powerful and less ethical.

"How did you tell?" he moaned.

I pointed to the incriminating statement and read it out loud. "As it turns out, Dave is in prison on the lower mainland, and there is evidence that the victim probably left for Calgary some time ago." I told Chuck that the victim had not moved away from the community until a year or maybe two after the assault. The comment "and there is evidence that the victim probably left for Calgary some time ago" indicated that the report had been written a considerable time after his move -- and much closer to the present date.

I ended my meeting with Bertholf, now certain the justice system had deliberately suppressed evidence surrounding my emotional state in 1991, and had, and were continuing to build a record that would degrade and dehumanize me as I continued my search for answers.

It all pointed back to a prosecution, bent on ignoring mitigating circumstances such as provocation, emotional stress, depression, and alcohol. All these factors are, and continue to be contentious matters in the criminal justice system. None of them lead to a defense of innocence as far as I am concerned, but if combined, they could support a reduced sentence. At the very least, if all the facts had been fairly accounted for and had not been replaced by the justice system feeling a need to degrade me, the turmoil of the last years could have been avoided.

A few days after this second meeting with Bertholf, I ran into Dan Sliva on a downtown sidewalk and asked him if he had talked to Charles Bertholf prior to my sentencing.

"I have nothing more to say to you," Dan Sliva replied, then high-stepped it through the cross-walk.

A week later I received a threatening phone call from a woman who indicated she was a friend of Geri. She warned me that if I stayed in town, my life would become a living hell. "I'm just letting you know, you're not welcome in this town," she said. "So go, you're not welcome here!"

"Who says I'm not welcome here?" I responded, quickly holding the tape recorder up to the phone.

"I'm telling you, you're not welcome here! You will not be comfortable here!" the caller threatened.

"What are you going to do?" I asked.

"Make your life not very much fun if you stay in this town. You won't be able to work anywhere. You won't be able to show your face anywhere!"

A few days after this conversation, the receptionist at the motel where I worked, received a similar disturbing call. A woman who identified herself as someone from the victim assistance program suggested that I had "just" returned to the community in violation of a parole condition. The suspicious caller hinted I was back in town to do my ex-wife harm, and that the motel should reconsider giving me future employment.

When the receptionist asked the caller to leave her full name and phone number, she refused and hung up. Fortunately the owners of the motel, who knew my children and me, dismissed the not-so-subtle suggestion.

Despite the barrage of intimidation, I was determined to stay close to my son. But I realized if I wanted to accumulate any funds, I would have to move into a cheap apartment and look for more work while I continued on as a part-time employee at the motel.

Without a car, and little funds, I got a place in a cheap apartment block, conveniently located in the main section of town. It's nickname, 'The Getto, said it all! One day I was having coffee in a nearby fast food outlet, going through the help wanted ads, when the owners of the restaurant told me they were looking for someone to do some cleaning, three nights a week.

I quickly accepted the position and added a second source of income. The timing could not have been better. The painting job at the motel was near completion and my hours were about to be substantially reduced. Then good fortune shone on me once again. I was offered the job of on-site manager at the apartment block in exchange for rent and a wage of $100 a month. I now had three sources of income, even if they were all meager.

I gave Steven a key to the apartment so he could come and go as he liked. Despite the threats and intimidation, my endurance was paying off and life was moving on.

Chapter 21

The Setup

It felt great to be living the life of an everyday father again. But being back in the small East Kootenay community also meant contact with Geri was going to be unavoidable. One day as we walked by one another on the main street, I nodded and said hello. She remained stone-faced and breezed by in silence. Shortly after that, I noticed a pattern of unnecessary contact. She would show up at the restaurant where I worked, and sit down to breakfast, something the owners told me she had never done prior to me becoming an employee. When I arrived to enjoy my free morning coffee, I felt compelled to turn away and head for the doughnut shop down the street.

Most afternoons I turned the quiet tables at the public library into my writing retreat. One day Geri walked in, looked toward me, then stayed, hanging around the front.

With the no-contact order still in effect, I began to suspect a possible set-up, where she would accuse me of breaching the order, resulting in more hassle from the justice system. I had no desire to pursue her obvious violation of the order, although I had a right to do so. I had already decided to solve any potential problem by applying in court to have the mutual no-contact order taken off the books.

My application for legal-aid was turned down, and I went ahead on my own, making two other requests of the court as well. One was an application to listen to the court tapes of the November 2, 1993, family court hearing. I wanted to hear if a reference to the balaclava was on the tape, something I suspected was not, and on top of that, I also felt there had been some other subtle manipulations in the transcript. The second additional application dealt with arrears of maintenance. A sum of about $4,000 had accumulated over the last couple of years while I had struggled through imprisonment and unemployment.

I was also aware, if Geri's counsel came into court and opposed my application to drop the no-contact order they would have to put her on the stand to face cross-examination, something I hoped would happen. It was my best chance to question her on the false affidavits and accusations of spousal abuse that materialized after my imprisonment in 1991.

I arrived at the courthouse on December 12, 1996, with my tape recorder tucked away in my upper vest pocket. My concern over alterations in earlier transcripts had spooked me to the point where I now felt I had to protect myself from any further manipulation of court documentation.

I entered the courthouse and approached the registry, where I was informed that Judge Waurynchuk was the scheduled judge this day. I was then told that a previous court order could only be changed by the judge who made the order. The court clerks no doubt knew, as I did, that it had been Judge Carlgren who had made the maintenance order when he presided over the November 2, 1993, hearing.

Sensing an attempt to discourage me from proceeding into court this day, I said that I still wanted to go into the courtroom and deal with the no-contact order. Judge Waurynchuk had made the initial order, and I was suspicious about the validity of the court staff's contention that only a judge who made an order, could change an order. Judge Carlgren's amendment of Waurynchuk's original no-contact order certainly suggested otherwise.

When we were called before the bench, Geri's lawyer, George Majic, informed the court that my ex-wife was at work and would not be attending. I immediately suspected some collaboration between court staff's attempts to discourage me, and Majic. I quickly accused him of showing up at the hearing without Geri so he could protect himself from being exposed for filing false affidavits.

"I'm going to object...I'm going to..." George Majic stammered.

259

"No!" I hollered, angrily cutting him off. "You can get up and start talking in a second. It is people like you, sir, that have taken what was once a proud and honorable profession, that dinned with kings and queens..."

"Whatever..." Majic muttered.

"...to the point where it is today," I continued, glaring angrily at the lawyer, "where you're only invited to the ball behind the loan sharks and carpetbaggers of this world!"

"Mr. Mitchell, you're out of place! You're totally out of place!" yelled Judge Waurynchuk.

I turned away from George Majic and looked up at the bench without missing a beat, "Well, I'm not going to apologize for standing up and defending myself when this justice system, and this country won't give me legal representation!"

"Okay!" the judge uttered threateningly.

"And I won't apologize for standing up and telling the truth in a courtroom in my country!"

Judge Waurynchuk had heard enough. Infuriated, he stopped the proceedings and set my case ahead a week so it could be heard by Judge Carlgren.

Seven days later, on December 19, with my tape recorder hidden in my vest pocket once again, I stood up to answer Judge Carlgren's question: "Why do you want to listen to the court tapes?"

"I suspect the transcript of the hearing has been altered," I replied.

George Majic hastily jumped into the discussion, letting loose with a barrage of rhetoric. He argued that I should not be allowed to listen to the tapes due to what he called "consideration for the security of the tapes." He ended his onslaught by suggesting to the provincial court judge that only the Supreme Court could grant such an order.

Judge Carlgren set my case down, stating he wanted to finish hearing a couple of other matters first. A few hours later we were called back before the bench and the judge said he was denying my application to listen to the tapes. Then he attempted to move the proceedings onto my other two applications, dealing with maintenance, and the removal of the no-contact order.

However, I felt I had not received a sufficient reason for his denial on the matter of the tapes, so I asked the judge if he would agree to give me a copy of the original tape. Again my request was denied, and I angrily accused Judge Carlgren of knowingly signing off on the false affidavits, that I believed had only been written after my parole suspension in 1994, and then mailed to me, pre-dated, while I was imprisoned at Ferndale.

The judge erupted from his bench and angrily threatened me with a contempt charge.

Without waiting around to hear more, I gathered up my papers and headed for the door. "There are people in contempt of the justice system, in this court, and in this country...sitting on the benches around here," I said angrily, shouting back at the judge as I stepped out of the courtroom.

"All applications are dismissed!" I heard the infuriated judge holler as I stormed off and disappeared down the hall.

*****

A few days after the December 19 hearing, Jeff and Aimee came home for Christmas. Over the holidays Jeff and I sat down and discussed a conversation he'd had with his mother a few months earlier. At that time, Jeff had told me he had expressed concern to his mother over some of the things he had read about me in government documents. (I freely shared documents and other material with my children, not wanting to hide anything from them.) Jeff had then told me that his mother had said, that she had also seen some things that looked like they were written for no other purpose than to make people feel better about what they were doing.

However, now Jeff informed me that his mother had gotten angry with him when he had tried to discuss the matter in more detail. Although I wanted to pursue a civil suit against the justice system, I did not want to strain the relationship between my son and his mother any more than it already was. I decided I would look into the matter on my own, and told Jeff not to worry about it.

Jeff and Aimee returned to Victoria after the holidays, and I resumed doing research for my book, which included a few more interviews. One was with my long-time family doctor in Fernie. Needless to say, I was shocked to find out he had a complete and unedited copy of the 1991 forensic report stuck away in my medical file, a document I had been told, had been edited. He said he had no idea how it had gotten there, and I asked him if he would look into the matter, inquiring of his clinic staff. Doctor Geddis promised me he would do so, and asked me to meet him outside the clinic the next day.

I headed home, recalling Madam Justice Southin's comment that maybe the report hadn't been edited at all, but highlighted instead! This document in my family doctor's file, had several underlined and highlighted sentences, but nowhere was there any sign of editing or deletions. Also, the fact that my ex-wife worked at the clinic where the report surfaced did not escape me.

Outside the clinic the following day, Doctor Geddis handed me the original report with a signed note attached, stating that no one at the clinic knew how the document had gotten into the file. It appeared it was going to remain a mystery.

Next I interviewed one of the nurses who had been working at the hospital during my admittance in 1991, beginning on the night I had rushed to the hospital after hearing voices, just a few months before the assault occurred. Her recollection was that I had been admitted for several days. This fact had also gone missing in the case.

When the head nurse heard that I was making inquiries, she came down to the nursing station and asked the younger nurse to join her in a private conversation. When they reappeared out of a back office five minutes later, the nurse who had been so eager to help, suddenly showed signs of severe amnesia.

Undaunted, I continued to make notes and store away the tapes. I mixed my writing with my three part-time jobs, while also doing everything I could to support Steven. During the first week of February his scout troop went on a five-day outing into the Rocky Mountains. I volunteered as a supervisor and Steven and I enjoyed the week immensely.

On February 12, about a week after we returned, I was walking back to my apartment, which was just a block away from the post office. As I approached the front doors, I noticed Geri was about to come out. I was only a few steps away from the entrance and made a split-second decision.

I stepped to my right, opened the door for my ex-wife, and took a chance. "Jeff told me what you said about some of the misleading reports, ..about people writing things just to make them feel better about what they were doing, and I need to know what statements you were referring to," I said politely.

Geri stepped by me and started crossing the street. "You're not supposed to talk to me," she said without looking back.

Her cold tone let me know there would be no further comment on the matter, and I continued down the sidewalk toward my apartment.

The next morning there was a knock on my door. "Police!" boomed a loud voice. Startled, I opened the door to find two officers standing in the hall.

"Mr. Mitchell, you're under arrest for violating a court order," said the shorter officer.

"You've got to be kidding!" I shouted back in disbelief, recalling the horror of a similar scene that had been played out a few years earlier.

"We have a complaint from your ex-wife that you talked to her at the post office yesterday."

"I asked her a question in regards to a statement she made to our son," I exclaimed, and my shock quickly turned to anger and disgust. "That no-contact order was made a year and a half ago. She has violated that order herself!"

The second officer reached toward me with a pair of handcuffs and I was hastily led past the tenants who had stepped into the hall to see what was happening. For the next couple of hours I was left to stew in the city cells...and stew I did! "Arrest, jail, court...all for making a simple inquiry. There has to be more to it!" I screamed to myself. "Has the system been sitting in the weeds, looking for something they could use against me, waiting for something...anything?"

After I had worked myself into a state of utter contempt for the justice system, the local RCMP escorted me to the neighboring community of Sparwood, twenty minutes east of Fernie. The same town the kids and I had gone bowling in, just before my re-imprisonment in 1994.

Once inside the courthouse I was shown a document signed by Geri. It accused me of accosting her at the post office. The typewritten format suggested that the victim assistant coordinator had given the document a helping hand. Seething with anger, I tossed it across the room. The sheriff grinned, grabbed me by the arm, and paraded me into a packed courtroom where I was told to stand in the prisoners' box.

264

On the bench sat Judge Waurynchuk, one of two judges who had recently admonished me from the bench. Standing on the far side of the courtroom was Geri's lawyer, George Majic. He glanced at me and flashed a satisfied grin.

I looked at the nearest counsel table. My former legal-aid lawyer, Dan Sliva, turned and showed me a pleasing smile. On his right, only a few feet away from where I stood, sat a man I sensed I had seen before. Ron Webb looked up, stirring memories of a distasteful prosecution six years earlier. Co-incidence or not, my mid-day interruption of the court's scheduled proceedings, held an altogether, too familiar audience.

Judge Waurynchuk hastily informed me I had been brought to court for violating the no-contact order.

With a blast of anger I denounced the proceedings as nothing more than a kangaroo court. My outburst heightened the bemused look on Webb and Sliva's face. I straightened my arms on the railing that separated me from the two men, and angrily accused them of conspiring with one another on my criminal case in 1991. A stoic look replaced their amused grins, and I turned back to the bench, demanding that Geri be put on the stand so I could question her about the complaint. But Judge Waurynchuk inferred that was not necessary, saying it was the court, and not my ex-wife that was charging me with contempt of a court order.

"Not guilty," I yelled. "I plead not guilty!" I echoed, blasting out my contempt for a packed courtroom to hear.

Perplexed, Judge Waurynchuk ended the proceeding, stating it would be improper for him to sit in judgment due to his previous involvement in the case. The sheriffs escorted me to Cranbrook, and I spent the night in lockup. In the morning I was brought to the courthouse where, to my surprise, I faced Judge Waurynchuk once again.

I remained defiant, again demanding that Geri be put on the stand. Realizing I was prepared to stay in jail, Waurynchuk softened his stance. He indicated that he did not believe Geri was prepared to pursue matters, and he relaxed his interpretation of the no-contact order. Verbally dismissing the distance requirement, he indicated that if I simply agreed not to speak to her again, he would release me and set a new date to deal with the breach of the no-contact order.

I agreed, but asked for his assurance that my previous applications, concerning maintenance and the removal of the no-contact order would be discussed at the same hearing. Judge Waurynchuk indicated it could all be discussed before a different judge, and a new date was set for April 7.

Sensing I was only being harassed, and that the breach of the order would eventually be dismissed, and that everything else would be settled, I got on a bus and went back to Fernie.

Sensing that I now had to stay more alert, with my tape recorder in my coat pocket, I walked over to Ron Bentley's law office. My previous dealing with this man had left me skeptical, but he headed the legal-aid program in town, and I definitely needed a lawyer.

"Dave," Bentley said in his booming baritone. "Come on in! What can I do for you?"

"I guess I need a lawyer," I said, displaying a half-hearted laugh.

"What did you do now?" Bentley said, laughing back.

"They said I violated a court order."

"Did they charge you with anything?"

"I don't know," I replied, still not sure what was happening. "I have no idea!" I added, emphasizing my confusion.

I then inquired of Bentley, asking about the validity of an eighteen-month-old no-contact order that had been violated by both parties, without any previous action being taken.

"I'll look into it," he said, and the meeting ended.

When I returned the next day, Bentley again greeted me with a large smile. "It's a very frivolous, frivolous thing," he reported. "I don't know what they're doing, because it doesn't seem like they're following any procedure here."

"What do you mean?" I asked, sensing he knew more than he was telling me.

"What they're trying to do is lay a charge against you for a breach of this order. But I don't know if they've done it properly."

"Who's trying to bring a charge against me?"

"Well, we don't...I don't know," he said. "I can't find out from the registry whether the procedures been followed properly or not. I don't know what's going on. I'm trying to find out. We're trying to get approval from Vancouver to get this covered for a lawyer."

"Why would they not give me a lawyer?" I asked, fearful that I was once again going to be railroaded into a courtroom without legal counsel.

"There's been no charge laid against you," replied Bentley.

I considered how ridiculous it all sounded. "There just has to be more to it," I thought to myself. "I've been put in jail, brought before a judge, put back in jail, and then let go with a court date pending. All without a charge laid against me?"

"It looks like there's procedural problems with this," the lawyer continued. "The thing that it looks like to me is...this is being blown out of proportion."

Irritated by Bentley's alleged lack of knowledge, and loud bouts of laughter, I cut in, "If they're going to charge me, I want them to charge her!"

I stomped out of Bentley's office, confused and bewildered by the conversation I had just engaged in. I decided if I wanted answers, I would have to go get them. I turned north on the main street and headed for the police station. I was greeted at the counter by two officers, one of them Constable Magnus. I hastily asked if either my ex-wife or the police were charging me for talking to her.

Neither officer had an answer, but their indecisive humming and hawing warned me there was a threat hanging over my head, that would be acted on if I did not back off the justice system.

I walked back to my apartment, sensing there was some unseen force out there, haunting me, stalking me, following me wherever I went. Was I being paranoid? What was it that continued to move about in the shadows of my world?

Over the next weeks, a steady stream of strange phone calls kept me on edge. A few, I supposed, could be dismissed, but the regularity and the number made them suspicious. I would pick up the receiver and sometimes there would be an eerie silence on the other end. Other calls involved strange clicking noises, and on some occasions a phone on the other end would start ringing back at me.

I called Jeff and Aimee, who expressed their concern. "Dad, I think the justice system and Mom will do anything to make your life hell if you stay in Fernie," Jeff said. "I talked with Mom about what happened at the post office and asked if you had done anything to harass her. She just screamed, 'That's not the point, he's not supposed to talk to me!'...Dad, Mom's not thinking rationally.

She just screams whenever we try to talk to her. Aimee and I think you should move to Victoria, look for work, write on your book, and spend some time with us."

Jeff also mailed a statement back to Fernie, relaying to the court what his mother's response had been when he had asked her about the incident. I wrote out my own statement and filed them both at the court registry. But when I informed Ron Bentley that the statements were on record, he hastily and nervously suggested that this response might not have been necessary.

"It may not even get to the point of a hearing, because it may not be a valid charge," he said.

I had heard enough -- or maybe I was tired of not hearing enough. Between the harassing phone calls and being kept in a state of deliberate limbo, I decided the kids were right. It was time to move.

Once again I had to tell my youngest son that I was leaving. Steven and I spent the last couple of days together, reassuring one another that things would work out. As far as I was concerned, I was being run out of town, pressured to leave my youngest son behind, as well as a community I loved. It was a hard choice to accept. What made it even more difficult, was the probability that it was being orchestrated by my country's justice system, something that only added to my heartache.

With a heavy heart I told Bentley that I had decided to make the move to Victoria. This information produced a jubilant response, and he suddenly let me know that my request for counsel had been approved by legal-aid. He then gave me the name of a lawyer in Cranbrook, who had just agreed to take the case.

The next day at the bus stop, Steven and I hugged and said our good-byes. A little over an hour later I walked into Murielle Matthews' office in Cranbrook, leaving her copies of the statements I had filed in Fernie, along with a clear message that there would be, absolutely no plea-bargain with the court on the matter of the breach. "There is nothing this justice system would like better than to have documentation that indicated I had been forced to leave Fernie based on a complaint made by my ex-wife," I said, ending my brief contact with the attorney before heading on to Victoria.

Chapter 22

Hijacked

A week later my new lawyer accepted a collect call. "Yes! You made it to Victoria," Murielle Matthews said pleasantly. "Have you got an address for me?"

"No, not yet." I said, seeing no need to inform her I was temporarily bunking in at a friend's place. "Was that complaint dropped?"

"I haven't had a chance to deal with it yet," replied the lawyer.

"Well, it's a frivolous and unwarranted complaint as far as I'm concerned, and if they don't drop it, I want you to ask for a new date so I can be present during any hearing. Okay?" I said, knowing I would need time to make some travelling money for the trip back.

I then asked Ms. Matthews what she was going to do about the false affidavit Geri had signed, claiming I was wearing a balaclava during the assault.

"The first thing and the only thing I'm going to do at this point is see if I can convince them to drop the whole thing. Okay? If we get them to drop this, there's nothing else to do. Right? If they don't, then we will talk about what we do about the affidavit. Okay? Give me a call in a week."

A week later I placed the call as instructed. "What's happening out there?" I asked.

"Nothing yet," Ms. Matthews replied. "I'm waiting to hear from you about an address."

Not sure what an address had to do with my immediate legal problem, I hastily gave her my son, Jeff's, mailing address, then got back to the matter at hand. "If this is not dropped by the end of the week, I want you to file a charge against her for filing that false affidavit," I said sternly.

There was a hush on the line before Matthews replied quietly, "You're talking about perjury charges and I can't deal with that. Let's see what we can do about this other problem first. Besides, how would you question your ex-wife on the affidavit and prove she was lying?"

I swiftly rehashed the facts of the case, starting with the hand-to-hand confrontation with the victim. I told her about the witness who identified me as I came out of the apartment and stumbled up the stairs. Geri had also seen me on the street after the assault. I told Ms. Matthews that all three witnesses had identified me, and not one of them had testified that I was wearing anything over my head.

"I have a copy of the criminal court transcript and it makes no mention of a balaclava," I added. "And the reason for that is a simple one. I wasn't wearing anything over my head during the assault!"

The legal-aid attorney excused herself for a moment and put me on hold. My tape recorder picked up seven long minutes of silence before she came back on the line. "Yeah, David, I got talking a bit longer than I thought I would on the other line. Okay? Well, listen, uh," she sounded hurried, "you let me know if you change your address, make sure you keep in contact, and I will find out what's going to go on with all this."

The sudden brush-off irritated me and I considered asking her, who she'd been talking with for seven minutes while she put me on hold. However, I didn't want to strain what already showed signs of becoming a difficult lawyer/client relationship, so I said I would call again the following week, making it clear that if the charge of breaching the no-contact order was not dropped, I would file a civil suit.

272

At this news, Ms. Matthews, who had been so anxious to end the call, took another twenty minutes to tell me the complaint would be dropped due to the fact that I was now living in Victoria.

I knew that did nothing to clear my name. It also left the correctional service with an opening to suggest that the revocation of my parole had been justified. It could point to a court record that indicated I had come back to Fernie a few years after my second release, and harassed my ex-wife.

I stood my ground with Ms. Matthews and insisted that the record must show that the complaint was dropped because it was frivolous and unwarranted. Matthews argued that it did not matter why the complaint was dropped, as long as it was dropped. "No one will know why it was dropped," she said. "We don't have to give a reason, and it'll just be dropped. Won't even go into court."

I knew the manipulative nature of the justice system, and had felt its deadly sting before. Knowing I could not accept a dismissal of the complaint under any conditions other than what I had indicated, I told Matthews that I would show up at the hearing, even if I had to borrow money from my family.

"No!" Matthews screamed and ended the call abruptly.

As the scheduled hearing date approached, I contacted the lawyer again, only to be told that the hearing had been postponed and rescheduled for sometime in mid-June. The sudden postponement confirmed my belief that members of the justice system were searching for a way to leave behind a record that would support their earlier actions.

However, the delay would also give me time to save some money. I had just landed a job at a building materials store, and with my mother's help, I had bought another used car. I searched the papers and found a place to live, then called Ms. Matthews with the address. The conversation turned sour when she suggested there would be no need to question my ex-wife on the false affidavit if the breach charges were dropped. "Going after her and attacking her is not the issue!" Ms. Matthews blurted out angrily.

"I'm not attacking her! I'm just trying to get at the truth and clear my name from this garbage violent wife-beating crap!" I insisted, not wanting to leave open any implication that the charge had been dropped, simply because I had moved to Victoria.

"That's not going to happen in June," the attorney snapped back. There was dead silence for a moment, then, "That will never happen!"

"So my only option is to go into a lawsuit against her?!"

"Well, for what purpose? You're getting yourself re-established, aren't you? Trying to get back in court is not going to help that. You need to go on!"

"Yeah!" I shouted frantically. "So this system's allowed to use me, and abuse me, and use her to support it? And get away with it after four or five years?"

"The problem is, you're looking at a really big picture. And it's way too intimidating for everybody," Matthews groaned. She reminded me that the courts had not allowed me to question the integrity of the system before, and would not allow it in the future. She then added that I needed more than one false affidavit to sue someone in civil court.

I quickly reminded her that there were other false statements: most notably those that suggested Geri had been an abused spouse throughout the marriage.

"So, you're going to have your day in court in June, and you will not try to resolve it out of court ahead of time." Matthews paused, and then once again suggested the case would not proceed. "They will drop it!" she said emphatically.

274

Still concerned that the justice system, particularly the correctional service, would point to my move to Victoria, as being the only reason the charge was dropped, I pushed for clarification. "All they have to do is drop the frivolous complaint and agree that I do not owe the past family maintenance that accumulated while I was incarcerated, and this thing would be over, just like that!"

"Well," said Ms. Matthews at a level slightly above a whisper, "you did technically breach the court order."

The lawyer's response confirmed my suspicions that this breach was something the justice system wanted on file, with a notation that it had not been pursued due to my leaving the area. "They will drop it!" was deceptive. They would drop it, ...but only as long as I remained out of the Elk Valley.

My suspicions were confirmed a week later when I received a letter from Murielle Matthews. "If proof of your employment and continued residency in Victoria is provided to me, this hearing will not likely go ahead at all. George Majic has agreed not to proceed with the application if proof of your continued residency in Victoria is supplied.

"Thus, if you provide me with the information I have requested herein, we may be able to immediately resolve both issues outstanding in this matter, without a court hearing."

The letter suggested I would likely be found guilty if I insisted on proceeding.

> ...if there is a hearing, it is very likely that the judge will make a finding that you did breach the no-contact order, and that you were therefore in civil contempt of a court order. The judge will then penalize you accordingly. Incarceration is a possibility. Thus it is my advice to you that you should avoid a court hearing of this matter by negotiating a settlement if at all possible...I will not represent you at a court hearing where your sole purpose is to cross-examine your ex-wife on the evidence she gave at the last family court hearing.

275

I considered the possibility that Ms. Matthews could be looking for a way around her legal and ethical responsibilities to defend me in court. Hoping to protect myself with a written record, and not have her walk away from the case, I contacted another lawyer in Victoria. I asked him to immediately inform the Cranbrook lawyer that I was sending the requested information. The letter also made it clear that Ms. Matthews was not to commit me to any agreement without my approval. I inserted statements of support from Jeff and Aimee and sent the sealed envelope off to Murielle Matthews.

After receiving it, Matthews sent me a copy of a draft letter she had now given to Geri's lawyer, George Majic, which indicated she was prepared to proceed into court if matters could not be worked out. However, I was not convinced she would carry on as the letter suggested. I suspected she was leaving a paper trail that could suggest she was prepared to do something, that in fact, she had no intention of doing. I grew even more suspicious when she told me she did not think it was appropriate to insert Jeff and Aimee's statements into the record.

It was mid-May when I dialed Ms. Matthews office again. When the automatic operator asked, "Do you accept the charges?" I could hear Matthews replying "Yes" somewhat reluctantly, and when the connection was made she said, "You have to stop calling me collect!"

"Oh, okay...Why is that?" I replied.

"Because I would rather you didn't."

"Legal-Aid's not paying for that?"

"Uh," Ms. Matthews hesitated, "they do, but it's too difficult for me to keep track of the cost."

"Oh, okay," I said. "The other day you indicated you didn't want to include the kids' statement in anything?"

"No, I didn't think it was necessary."

Without knowledge of the deception involved in my case, most people would have considered my lawyer's response, baffling. One would think that the statements and feelings of children, especially older children, would be of importance in court proceedings involving their family. But when you knew the facts behind the case, it was easy to understand why the justice system did not want a visible record that highlighted the children's support for their father.

"What was the reason for that?" I asked Ms Matthews.

"I just didn't think it was necessary," she answered, without giving any specific explanation.

In frustration I replied, "What I would like you to do is forward to George Majic, the statements Jeff and I gave to the courts."

"NO!" Matthews screamed. "I'm not here to do what you want me to do! I've told you that already."

I held back my anger, determined not to let her off the hook by firing her. "Okay," I said calmly, "so you refuse to represent me in the way I ask?"

"I think that's what we're going to have to do. You're not following my advice."

"Okay, well, I'll show up in court, and if you're not there I'll just explain what's going on and look after myself then."

"I don't think it's necessary to do this," Matthews said as she craftily tried to lay the decision back on me, "but if that's the way you want it, then fine..."

I refused to take the bait. "No, it's not the way I want it!" I shouted, now venting my frustration at the entire legal community. "I wish you's' would do your jobs!"

"I am doing my job," Matthews replied angrily.

"No, you're not doing your job," I sighed.

"Yes I am. I'm not here to be a lackey for you."

"Well, you're not there to be a lackey for the system either."

"I am not doing that," Matthews said defensively. "I'm acting in your best interest."

"No," I replied, "you're not acting in my best interest if you leave it up to them to determine that I was harassing her, or leave it open to an insinuation that I have been harassing her."

"That's not what we're doing," the legal-aid attorney retorted. There was deafening silence, then a thunderous, "I won't be acting for you anymore!"

A prolonged silence told me that yet another legal-aid lawyer had left me hanging onto a dead line.

Overwhelmed with frustration and a sense of helplessness, I called up Jeff and Aimee and informed them that it looked like I was being forced back into court without a lawyer.

I could not dismiss the children's fear, or my own, as the kids and I walked along the ocean beach later that day. They had felt the heavy hand of the justice system before, when forced to watch on helplessly as I was sent back to prison less than a day after a family outing a few years earlier.

Distraught, Aimee phoned Ms. Matthews, and the attorney assured my daughter that she would stay on the case. But despite the lawyer's apparent change of heart, nothing seemed different.

Ms. Matthews phoned to tell me that my hearing had been postponed once again, and was now scheduled for July 22. She still insisted that she could get everything dropped because Judge Waurynchuk (who was still involved in the case) was demanding that the other side settle the matter without coming to court. Everything I heard suggested that it was no longer the court pursuing the matter, but my ex-wife.

A week before the hearing, I found myself short of travel money and told Murielle Matthews that if she could not get an agreement, I might need her to go into court and ask for a delay until I could afford to make the trip.

Matthews now suggested the hearing could still go ahead, and she came back to her old argument. "If they drop it there doesn't have to be a reason why," she said quietly.

"Then they can use any insinuation they want?" I replied dryly.

"That's right," said Murielle Matthews. "But it doesn't mean anything!" She then informed me that Geri might be at the hearing, but it would be highly unlikely for her to take the stand.

I spent the next few days stewing over the probability that I could be harpooned at the hearing if I did not make an appearance. My uneasiness moved me to ask my family for some financial help, and my older brother quickly sent me five hundred dollars. With the money in hand, I called Matthews back and informed her I would be at the hearing on July 22 if the matter was not dropped.

The next day she phoned to tell me she had not reached an agreement with Majic. She then added that she would not proceed if I insisted on going into court, and suggested I seek out other counsel.

I hastily called the registry in Fernie. The clerk told me it was too late to cancel the hearing, and added that if I did not show up, the judge would decide what to do when the case was called before him. I was then told that he could make an order in my absence, or issue a warrant for my arrest.

I called legal-aid in Victoria, but learned they could not help because my case was registered outside their jurisdiction.

I hung up and frantically called Ron Bentley in Fernie. He told me he was unavailable for court, then indicated that it was too late to find anyone who could appear on my behalf.

The system had me trapped! Legal-aid had set me adrift with a threat of incarceration hanging over my head. With nowhere left to turn, I nervously made the long drive across the province to address the court, needing to ask for a delay in proceedings until I could find legal counsel.

Chapter 23

Banished

I arrived in Fernie on July 21, took a room at the motel I had worked at earlier and called Steven. My son came over and we spent some time playing cards and watching television before he headed back to his mother's place for the night. The following morning I made my way to the courthouse, all set to ask the judge for a delay until I could find legal counsel.

Even though Judge Waurynchuk had admitted it would be inappropriate for him to sit in judgment in this case, he was presiding in the lone courtroom that highlighted the colorful history associated with one of the province's oldest courthouses. He started proceedings with a request that Geri's lawyer and I spend a few moments discussing matters in private. George Majic agreed to meet, and I could see no reason to refuse to hear what he had to say. We went off to a side room and he quickly offered me a reduction in the accumulated family maintenance sum I owed, if I would agree before the court that I had breached the no-contact order.

Most of the $4,000 owing had accumulated during my incarceration, and I believed had increased unfairly due to those circumstances, legal or not. Besides, I wasn't about to plead guilty to the frivolous breach and allow Geri to escape answering questions under oath.

I promptly dismissed his offer.

We went back into court and a disappointed Judge Waurynchuk asked to speak with me. Once again I stepped into private chambers for a meeting. Judge Waurynchuk insisted I settle the matter without taking it before the court, reminding me that the amount owing for outstanding maintenance was a considerable amount for someone in my position.

I knew if I accepted this offer, my challenge to Geri's complaint would go unheard, and the justice system, particularly Corrections Canada, would have ammunition to support the dishonest revocation of my parole back in 1994. They would do so, simply by pointing to a record that indicated I had indeed came back to Fernie and harassed Geri after my sentence had expired. With that in mind, I informed the judge that I had a right to question her on the honesty and truthfulness of any accusations she had ever made, including those in the past that had never been questioned. I specifically mentioned the false affidavit, telling Judge Waurynchuk that I believed, in this case, it was entirely possible that she was not aware of the false statement in that document, asserting that I was wearing a balaclava during the assault. I then said I was going to request a postponement until I could find competent and honest legal counsel.

I had made it clear that I would not plead guilty to a breach of a court order in exchange for a reduction in accumulated family maintenance. And upon hearing the news that I had arrived in town seeking a postponement so I could proceed with legal counsel, Judge Waurynchuk angrily announced that come hell or high water, he was going to proceed with the hearing on this day. He rose from his chair and stomped down the hall to another room where Geri and her lawyer were waiting.

"Just tell them all they have to do is drop the frivolous complaint!" I yelled, following him into the hall. The infuriated judge stepped through the open doorway and into the other room, paused to look back at me and then slammed the door shut. I shook my head in dismay and stepped across the hall into the courtroom, seating myself behind one of the counsel tables. A few minutes later Geri and her lawyer walked in, seating themselves at the adjacent table.

The clerk called, "All rise!" Everyone stood as a seething Judge Waurynchuk strode across the wooden flooring of the old courthouse and lowered himself into the huge chair.

The case was called to order and I addressed the bench. "Today I have no lawyer here to represent me, and if the complaint is not withdrawn, it is my desire to ask for a postponement of the hearing on this matter, until such time as I can obtain competent counsel who will represent me in a manner consistent with my rights as a citizen of Canada."

Then, taking advantage of my opportunity to address the justice system, I angrily admonished it for its abuse. "But there is another matter that is even more important in this family court. I am talking about three children who have gotten lost and been forgotten in this process while the justice system pursues its own misguided agenda of vilifying the children's father!"

Judge Waurynchuk winced and pushed himself back in his chair. "Mr. Mitchell, you're here because you're making an application to cancel a restraining order. That's number one."

"Well, the first thing, your Honor..."

"Just a minute! Listen to me. You also have an application to cancel maintenance and arrears. That's number two, and number three, you're charged with a breach of your restraining order...Now I take it that Ms. Matthews is not here today because you've dismissed her as counsel?"

"Yes, there could be no agreement reached between the lawyers," I said, with no desire to go any deeper into my entanglements with Ms. Matthews. Judge Waurynchuk then suggested it was my own applications that had brought me into court on this day.

"The original reason I am here, your Honor, and I think you're well aware of it, is this complaint. I did not have to be here with these other matters. And I did not need to pursue them. I'm here under the threat of a bench warrant for my arrest!"

"Well," the judge barked, "if that didn't go ahead and it was dismissed and not prosecuted, what are you doing with regards to your other applications?"

"I'm waiting to deal with this matter first," I replied.

"No!" said the judge irritably. "What are you going to do if there's no prosecution on the breach? If that's withdrawn, what are you going to do about your application to cancel the restraining order?

"I want to be able to get legal counsel to go ahead with it. I have never been able to question any of the reports, affidavits, and especially the false affidavits filed in this courtroom."

Realizing I was not going to drop my other two applications that could force Geri onto the stand at a later date, even if the civil contempt matter was withdrawn, Judge Waurynchuk pushed aside my request for a postponement, stating the case would continue as scheduled.

I then protested the contempt charge, informing the court that Geri had also violated the court order when she spoke to me a year earlier while picking Steven up for summer holidays.

"But she's not charged with anything," said Waurynchuk.

"Well," I said dejectedly, but cautiously, "if the complaint is not dropped then I am prepared to go ahead." I felt if we got to the matter of the breach, the judge would have to address my request for a postponement until I could find legal counsel.

"Well, now, we don't negotiate by hijacking anyone here," Judge Waurynchuk said, no doubt trying to support the court's right to proceed.

"Well, I was hijacked into this very courtroom without a lawyer in 1993, by this justice system while on day parole, and have been so again today!" I said defiantly, astonished by the judge's self-serving statement, especially since this was now the second time I had been intimidated into attending the Fernie courtroom under threat of a bench warrant.(When I looked at the court transcripts later, my statement had been deleted from the transcript, leaving only the phrase,"Well, I--.")

"We are prepared to proceed, to prove a very elementary breach of the restraining order," said Majic, craftily inserting himself into the conversation. "Mr. Mitchell has already conceded that he did, in fact, have contact with Geri Mitchell. And if Mr. Mitchell's prepared to concede that he did, in fact, breach the order, then we can get on with the balance of these applications."

Again I informed the court that I would be seeking legal counsel, but Judge Waurynchuk would have none of it. "We're proceeding with these matters today!" said the judge irritably.

"I have no counsel, your Honor."

"It doesn't matter whether you have counsel or not."

I dejectedly lowered myself into my chair, and Geri was called to the stand. George Majic asked her about the incident at the post office. What they were trying to portray was obvious. "Was he stopping you from getting out of the post office?" asked the lawyer.

"Yes, I was feeling very intimidated by that," Geri replied.

"The history of your relationship involves certain acts of violence that occurred approximately six years ago."

"Yes."

"In which there was a vicious and violent assault on an acquaintance of yours, is that correct?"

"Yes," Geri replied.

"Are you afraid of Mr. Mitchell's violent tendency?

"Yes, I am."

"And why are you afraid?"

"Excuse me," I said in disgust. "I object, your Honor."

"What's your objection?"

"Violent tendencies?" I said, punctuating my question by cocking my head.

"The objection is overruled!"

"Has he ever threatened you personally with physical harm prior to the incident involving this individual, this acquaintance of yours?" Majic went on.

"Throughout the years of our marriage, um, that was a threat, that he would kill me or whoever I was with if I left him."

"And I also understand that when Mr. Mitchell was on parole, one of the conditions of his parole was that he not come into Fernie, is that correct?"

"Yes," Geri answered.

"And I understand he violated that particular provision, is that correct?"

"Yes."

"And his parole was revoked?" said Majic.

"That's right," replied Geri.

Majic concluded and turned towards me.

The hijacking was complete. I had driven 1,000 kilometres to protect myself from a bench warrant, only to find myself being forced to defend myself in proceedings that could see me incarcerated. And I had to do so without any prepared cross-examination.

Unsure where to begin, I decided to try and get Geri to explain the violent tendencies that her lawyer had referred to, asking her to be specific.

Majic immediately objected, but he had no need to worry. Judge Waurynchuk took matters into his own hands. For several minutes he conducted his own prosecution with all the vigor he could muster. He solicited from Geri much of the same innuendo and suspicions that the criminal justice system had managed to put into the record. I tried to interject, but Judge Waurynchuk pushed aside my attempts, relenting only after he had exhausted himself.

I tried to rehabilitate myself, but almost immediately, Judge Waurynchuk found new life. He declared any cross-examination about past abuse irrelevant, demanding instead that I stick to the incident at the post office.

"I understood that she was saying she spent sixteen or seventeen years in a violent and threatening marriage," I argued. "Am I not allowed to question her on that?"

"No, no," shouted Waurynchuk. "The charge is that you breached a term of the court order."

"So she's allowed to give her testimony and I'm not allowed to question her on that?"
"You can give your own evidence on it if you'd like to."

"I'm not allowed to question her on those points?" I asked.

"What happened in the seventeen years of marriage, or sixteen and half years of marriage, has no relevance on the restraining order."

In frustration I moved on to the matter of the assault that Majic had mentioned. "Were you aware that just a couple of days before the assault, the victim was harassing and threatening me?"

Majic looked at the judge. "Your Honor," he prompted.

"The question is not relevant or material to the issue here today," interjected Waurynchuk, cutting me off.

I searched for another question, and asked Geri to explain what she meant when she talked about emotional abuse. "I want to give you the opportunity to explain that."

"Objection, your Honor," said Majic. "The facts were stated and this has all the earmarks of badgering of this woman who is not on trial."

"The objection is upheld," said the judge. "Next question."

I stopped, glared at up at the bench, then turned back to the witness. "When you're talking about this abuse and threats--"

"Mr. Mitchell!" shouted Judge Waurynchuk.

Determined and undeterred, I swallowed my anger and pushed onward. "Are you talking about verbal abuse?"

"Mr. Mitchell, she's already gone over that. Move on to another subject, please."

"And I wish to question her on it," I pleaded.

"She's already testified to that. Now move on."

"And I...I wish to question her on it."

"Your questioning is over on that, Mr. Mitchell."

"I haven't been allowed to question her on it yet!" I said, showing my frustration, which rose considerably when Judge Waurynchuk said, "You sure have. She testified as to the fact that you blamed her for everything, that you accused her of having affairs, you were controlling and showed a lack of trust in the relationship, quote, unquote. Now get on to another subject. You're stuck with those answers."

Frustrated and growing more incensed by the judge's obvious attempt to smother my cross-examination, I moved on and attempted to expose the facts surrounding the revocation of my parole in 1994, which had been based on the accusation that I was out on parole, plotting and seeking revenge.

"You will not ask..." Judge Waurynchuk squealed, "...you will not..." He turned to Geri, who was sitting rigidly in the witness chair. "Don't answer the question. It's not relevant. Next question please!"

"While I was on parole, something you talked about," I said, looking sarcastically at the judge, "is it not true that I asked the kids to ask you, and make you aware, that I wished to come in and take them to Sparwood?"

"Objection, your Honor," said Majic.

"Objection is upheld. The question need not be answered. Your question is struck. Next question."

"You were aware I was coming to Sparwood, were you not?" I said, now paying little heed to the judge.

"Objection, your Honor," said Majic, who had remained standing.

"Mr. Mitchell, I have warned you. You're going to jail on the next line of questioning that relates to this."

With my frustration mounting, I moved onto the post office incident. "Is it not true that I held the door open for you?"

"That's right, you opened the door."

"Did I impede you from leaving?"

Contradicting the answer she had given her lawyer, Geri replied, "No, there was witnesses there so I felt I could safely leave."

"Did I give some indication that I was going to threaten or harass you?"

"Your presence is threatening and harassing," Geri replied. "Your questioning me when you're not to even speak to me is threatening and harassing."

"What did I say to you on that occasion?"

"You wanted to know who was telling lies about you," replied Geri, who then tried to suggest I was making gestures with my arms as she crossed the street.

"In fact, I asked about the comment you made to Jeff, where you told him that you had also seen things written that you felt were written just to make people feel better about what they were doing. I was asking as to the truth about that, and that's all I said, is that not true?"

"Yeah," Geri answered.

"And then I continued on down to my apartment, is that not true?"

"I don't know. I got into my car and I drove away."

"So you didn't see me at all after you stepped off the sidewalk, passing me, is that correct?"

"I got into my car and I closed the door," she stated, this time leaving out any insinuation that I had gestured at her as she crossed the street.

Satisfied that I had managed to redeem myself concerning the day at the post office, I decided to try once more to expose the correctional service's vindictive revocation.

"Mr. Majic had asked you about my coming into Fernie and having my parole revoked."

"Objection, your Honor," said Majic.

I looked up at Judge Waurynchuk. "Mr. Majic had stated this. This was in his questioning."

"We've already dealt with this line of questioning," said Majic, who again stood.

"Your question," inquired Waurynchuk.

I turned to Geri. "Is it not true that I had asked the kids for permission to come in and take them to Sparwood, and you gave them that permission on that occasion?"

"Objection," said Majic.

"She can answer the question, your Honor," I shot back.

"How many times have I told you, to not get into that area, sir? See, you couldn't care less about anything else. You want to go after her with regards to the parole revocation. You want to go after this witness and badger this witness about history."

"No, I'm not, your Honor," I said, wondering if the judge realized the truth surrounding the revocation would harm the correctional service's image.

"Well then, quit asking questions about it or you'll find yourself in jail!"

After the series of objections from Majic and Waurynchuk, and the threat of more jail time, I finally gave in. "That's absolute garbage! I'm not going to continue on with any questioning. I'll stop, and this court can do whatever it wants. I'll go find a lawyer!"

Judge Waurynchuk jumped at the opportunity I handed him, and quickly adjourned the hearing, calling for a lunch break.

After some thoughtful reflections over a cup of coffee and a doughnut, I concluded that I should at least ask Geri about the false affidavit that said I had been wearing a balaclava on the night of the assault. The way things were going there was the possibility that I would never get another chance.

When court resumed, I informed the bench of my intentions.

George Majic stood up and immediately objected. Judge Waurynchuk swiftly upheld the objection, stating that my cross-examination was concluded.

While I stood, numbed into silence by the courts latest refusal, George Majic hastily requested that the court grant an order that would restrict me from coming within 75 kilometres of Fernie.

Outraged and horrified, I looked at Majic, then back at Waurynchuk. My numbness dissipated with an angry plea that the court not grant such an outlandish request. I knew such an order would certainly support the story line that the justice system wanted to project, but to have my access to Steven restricted based on this deception, was unconscionable.

Over my objections, Judge Waurynchuk granted the order.

What had once been a simple order, interpreted earlier by Waurynchuk, as meaning only that we were not to speak to each other when we passed on the street, had now been increased to the point where I was to be shut out of my former community and separated from my son.

Waurynchuk ended the hearing with an order that my file be transferred to Cranbrook, outside the restricted area. He then gave me a couple of hours to spend with Steven, stipulating that I had to leave town by six o'clock that evening, effectively banishing me from the community at sunset.

Chapter 24

Puppet on a String

Steven and I spent the late afternoon at one of the city parks. I took some time to reflect on the years I had spent in the Elk Valley. I would miss its serene beauty, and the protective peaks of the Rocky Mountains that towered above it.

At five minutes to six I rose from the park bench and took Steven in my arms and hugged him. I promised we would see one another again, and soon.

When I arrived back in Victoria, Jeff and Aimee were visibly upset about the new court order. Their anger swelled when they realized their statements to the court had not been taken into consideration. They quickly wanted to take the stand at a new hearing, offering up their own challenge to the restriction, doing so this time, under oath. I applied for legal aid, and once again the government bureaucracy turned me down. Undeterred, I filed for a court date, and a hearing to appeal Judge Waurynchuk's decision was scheduled for November 24, 1997. Four months later the kids and I drove back to Cranbrook to be heard.

My heart sank when the court posting in the hall indicated that Judge Carlgren was going to preside over the hearing. I recalled how I had stormed out of his courtroom muttering angry words about unethical people sitting behind the benches in this case. "I think we'd probably have better luck in Judge Judy's courtroom!" I quipped to the kids. The comment brought a nervous laugh from Aimee. I acknowledged my daughter with a grin and then lowered myself into a chair next to her and Jeff.

When we were finally called before the bench, D'arcy Mahoney, a lawyer from the firm of Majic/Purdy, informed the court that Geri would not be at the hearing. I did my best to hide my disappointment at being denied the opportunity to question her on the stand. The justice system's fear of being exposed through a prepared cross-examination, even carried out by a layman like myself, had no doubt influenced the decision to keep her away.

I called our 21-year-old son, Jeff, to the stand and asked him about a phone conversation he had with his mother. Jeff turned and faced the judge. "I was talking to her on the phone a few months back and expressed my concerns that I have seen things written on paper that I know are not true about my father. During this conversation my mother mentioned that she too, had seen things that she felt were written in such a way as to make people feel better about what they were doing."

Jeff also gave testimony describing his mother's response to his inquiry about the incident at the post office, this time responding directly to me. "I asked her if you had followed her there, if you had threatened her, if you had raised your voice. She basically just responded with 'that's not the point, that doesn't matter' sort of thing, which I took to mean no."

Jeff went on to support what he had written in his letter to the court, stating that the recent court order only harmed the family. He told the judge that he felt his mother should seek counseling to deal with her obsessed notion that I was out to harm her. He added that she had discontinued joint counseling sessions with him after my parole had been revoked in 1994. Apparently Geri had not appreciated some of the feedback she was getting from the family counselor.

As soon as my son had finished, Ms. Mahoney asked a few trifling questions and then hurried Jeff off the stand.

Aimee was then sworn in. "Did you grow up in a violent or abusive home?" I asked my daughter.

"No," she answered firmly.

"In the sixteen years your father and mother lived together, did you ever witness your father physically or verbally abuse or make threatening gestures against your mother?" I asked, glancing over at Ms. Mahoney.

294

"No, I didn't."

"Now I am going to read a piece of court testimony and then ask you a question on it, okay?" Aimee nodded her understanding, and I turned to Judge Carlgren, feeling a need to explain. "This was court testimony given during the November 2, 1993, family court hearing that you presided over, your Honor."

"And whose testimony is Mr. Mitchell going to be reading?" asked Ms. Mahoney, quickly rising from her chair.

"I am reading a question and answer given by the children's mother," I replied.

"Okay. Well, I object to that," Mahoney said, looking to the judge for help.

Judge Carlgren looked at Aimee. "Don't answer until I've heard what you've been read." The judge looked back at Mahoney. "And I'll hear your objection after."

I turned to Aimee and read a section of the November 2, 1993, transcript, pertaining to a night in 1991, a few weeks before the assault. I had taken Steven to a hockey game, but when I brought him back to Geri's apartment as requested, Geri was not home and the lights were out. I had then taken Steven, who was only eight-years-old at the time, to my apartment, where he spent the night with Jeff and I. At the hearing on November 2, 1993, under examination by her lawyer, Geri said that I had not brought Steven back as instructed.

When I questioned her under cross-examination that day, she said she had not been home: **"Because I went to get my daughter, because she didn't feel comfortable in the car with you, and she asked me to pick her up. That's why I was not waiting when you returned, was to provide her with transportation that she felt comfortable with."**

Aimee had also been at the hockey game that evening, attending with a friend whom she was going to spend the night with. We had talked between periods, and as I now read her mother's previous testimony, Aimee listened intently.

"Did you make that statement to your mother?" I asked.

Aware of Judge Carlgren's instructions, Aimee looked up at the bench. "Can I answer?"

"Do you have an objection to that, Ms. Mahoney?" asked the judge.

"No," the lawyer reluctantly replied, shifting nervously in her chair.

"No, I didn't!" answered Aimee, emphasizing her disgust at the insinuation that she was afraid of her father. Satisfied that I had exposed the falseness of another piece of innuendo that had been put into the record, I asked Aimee about the day we spent bowling in Sparwood in 1994. "That was on Easter Monday, do you recall that?" I asked.

"Yes," Aimee answered.

"Had you discussed this with your mother, and did she give you permission to spend this day with your dad?"

"Yeah."

"Can you recall your mother's reaction to you spending this day with your dad? Was she upset, express any anger or fear?"

"No."

"How many days in advance of this trip was your mother aware that your dad was coming into town, and that you and your brothers had made plans for this day? Was it a couple of days in advance? Do you recall?"

"At least," Aimee replied. "I'm not sure of exact."

"During the period your dad was living in Cranbrook, from January '94 until April '94, did you ever witness your father molest, harass, or threaten your mother?"

"No!" Aimee said emphatically. I glanced over at the other counsel table. Mahoney's head was tilted towards the floor.

"Did your mother ever give you reason to believe that she was being molested, harassed, or threatened by your father during this period?" I asked, looking back at Aimee.

"No."

"Were you suffering and unhappy in your family home during the years and times your father and mother lived together?"

"No, I was not."

"You love your mother, don't you?" I asked, wanting to give my daughter the chance to express her love.

Relieved, Aimee replied, "Of course!"

"If you believed for one minute that your father was a danger to your mother, would you hesitate to tell this court so?"

"No."

"Do you believe your father is any kind of threat to your mother?"

"No."

Having now heard both Jeff and Aimee's testimony, Judge Carlgren reduced the 75-kilometre restriction to 25 kilometres, explaining that the new restriction would at least allow me to return to the area. Although I would still have to live outside Fernie, I could move to Sparwood, only 20 minutes away, which was close enough to maintain close contact with Steven.

The change was not what I had hoped for. There were no provisions that allowed me to attend any of Steven's activities in Fernie if I returned to the valley. However, Judge Carlgren indicated that if I came back to court after a year, I could likely have the restriction lifted altogether.

With the matter settled pretty much in our favor, the kids and I returned to Victoria and got on with our daily lives. We were soon preparing for Christmas, now less than a month away.

But then, Aimee, informed me that her mother had asked her to go on a trip to Mexico for the holidays. I was surprised to say the least. Steven had told me Geri's hours had been cut at the clinic and that she was doing the clinic's laundry at night, just to make ends meet. In addition to the cost of the trip to Mexico, even though Aimee was paying her own travel expenses, Geri was also going to pay for Steven's plane fare to Victoria, where he would spend that time with Jeff and me.

I initially suspected the trip to Mexico with Aimee was designed to allow for healing time between daughter and mother. However, it appeared there may have been more to it.

On December 17, three days before Steven was to arrive, I answered a knock on my apartment door in Victoria. A woman asked me to identify myself, and after doing so, she handed me a large envelope. I opened the package to find a copy of a "Notice of Motion" with a provincial court registry stamp that indicated the motion had been filed on December 12. The document stated that Geri's lawyers would be asking for Judge Carlgren's ruling to be set aside until an appeal could be heard. The application would be made at the Cranbrook courthouse on December 19 at 9:30 a.m., only two days away.

The package also contained an affidavit signed by Dianne Lynn Mace of the Fernie Women's Resource Center. I recalled Mace being present in the courtroom during Jeff and Aimee's testimony in November. I sat down and carefully read her statement.

> I have worked with Geri Mitchell on the issue of her abusive marriage and the ongoing harassment to which she has been subjected since Mr. Mitchell was released from prison in 1993. Mr. Mitchell had been uncooperative with following the mandatory counseling in prison. On Ms. Mitchell's request, in March of 1993, I wrote a letter to the Parole Board, asking that Mr. Mitchell serve the rest of his sentence, as he had continually breached the restraining order in place, by phoning her more than the order allowed, and by not following through with the counseling he was ordered to take in prison.

Dianne Lynn Mace's affidavit continued to vilify me, repeating numerous false accusations and innuendos, including the statement that I was wearing a balaclava on the night of the assault. I then read that Geri had received funding through the Workers' Compensation Board, supposedly to pay for counseling for her and the kids.

The affidavit had the mark of the correctional service all over it. I considered the possibility that the money from the Workers' Compensation Board had been a payoff for her ongoing support of the justice system's negative portrayal of me -- money that might well have been arranged through the Victim Assistant Coordinator's Office, possibly as a means to help pay for a sudden holiday to Mexico.

And the authors and bearers of these documents, including the law firm of Majic/Purdy, most certainly knew I had to be at the Victoria airport on the morning of December 20, to pick up Steven.

I frantically called the court registry in Cranbrook and complained bitterly about the short notice. The court registrar, Robert Girard, told me if I wanted to have the hearing postponed the judge needed a written request from me before he would consider doing so. I told Girard that I would fax such a request to the registry, indicating my wish to question Dianne Lynn Mace under oath. He promised he would put my request into the file when he received it, and point it out to the judge. Early on December 18 I tried to fax the statement from a public outlet, but it repeatedly failed to make a connection. When I called the registry in Cranbrook about the problem, I was told their fax machine was down.

Unconvinced, I rushed over to the provincial legislature and relayed my problem to Claire Vessey, who now worked as an office assistant with the Liberal opposition. Claire attempted to send my response through her office fax. She also had no success.

I asked her if she would call, and inform the registry that the Liberal caucus had been trying to get a fax through for some time. She did so, and was put on hold briefly before someone came back on the line and suggested she try again.

Claire had no sooner hung up the phone, when the memory mode on the fax made the connection. I stood over the machine and watched with delight as it printed out a record of the successful transmission. I hurried back to my apartment and called Robert Girard, who reluctantly acknowledged the existence of the fax, telling me to call back at noon the next day after the matter had been put before the judge.

I anxiously waited till noon on the 19th, then called. In stunned silence I listened as Robert Girard told me the hearing had gone ahead, with Judge Waurynchuk granting an order that suspended Judge Carlgren's ruling until an appeal could be heard.

I eked out a hoarse whisper, asking if the judge had seen my fax about the short and unfair notice, and my request for a two-week postponement.

300

Girard assured me the judge looked at it, but had decided that the other party's concerns should be dealt with promptly. It appeared that Judge Wauynchuk's anger at me had colored his ruling. He apparently left the impression that Geri was in imminent danger from her lunatic ex-husband, and that was the reason he was proceeding in my absence.

Waurynchuk's ruling on December 19, 1997, effectively allowed two false affidavits to be entered into the provincial court record that day, without either one being questioned, Lynn Mace's affidavit and another that I was totally unaware of. The manipulative second affidavit was one that Ms. Mahoney had quietly prepared and had Geri sign on December 18, 1997. Filled with falsehoods and innuendoes, much of it supporting Mace's affidavit, was also slipped into the file.

The following morning, still unaware of the second affidavit, I drove out to the airport in Victoria and picked up Steven. As upset as I was with the family court ruling in Cranbrook, I was determined to enjoy the holidays with my two sons.

Unfortunately, I still had to work over the holidays, and it was during one of those days, right after Christmas, that a woman approached me while I was straightening stock in an aisle.

"Excuse me, are you David Mitchell?" she asked.

"Yes, can I help you?" I answered.

"I have a package for you," she replied, placing it in my outstretched hand before quickly retreating. I looked down at the bulky envelope and realized I was holding more legal correspondence.

I opened the package and pulled out a notice for another court hearing. This one confused me. It didn't appear to have anything to do with the appeal of Judge Carlgren's order. Instead it was a notice informing me that a petition had been filed in the Supreme Court. Geri's lawyers were apparently seeking an order that would prevent me from pursuing matters against her, without first getting permission from the courts to do so. The document showed a scheduled hearing date of January 5, 1998, only a week away.

I quickly put two and two together. If Geri's lawyer's succeeded with their appeal to have the restriction moved back to 75 kilometres, and they were also successful with this new application, then my search for answers in a court of law could be over.

After protecting Geri from my cross-examination on November 24, 1997, and after hearing my children's testimony on that day, the law firm of Majic/Purdy had initiated an all-out attack.

Convinced I would not receive any help from legal-aid, I hastily informed my boss that I would need time off to make a quick trip back to Cranbrook. There was no way they were going to hold another court hearing without me, especially this one!

Geri, who had now returned from Mexico, refused to let Steven ride back to Cranbrook with me. At her request, I put him on a plane on January 2, and the following morning I began the long trip back across the province. As much as I missed having my son with during the drive, half way through the trip I was thankful that Steven was home, safe and sound. I had to drive all night through a dangerous snowstorm in order to arrive in Cranbrook early enough on January 4 so I could throw together a presentation for the court.

At nine the next morning, January 5, I arrived at the courthouse. Robert Girard recognized me as I stepped up to the counter and asked him what courtroom I should be in.

"What are you doing here?" he asked nervously.

"I received a notice about some petition in the Supreme Court."

Girard hesitated and then stammered, "I didn't see your name on the list to be heard today. Let me go check the files." He excused himself and disappeared into the back room, reappearing a few minutes later with a piece of paper, which he laid on the counter. In bold type was the word PRAECIPE. Underneath it I read, "Required: To adjourn the hearing of the Petition to January 19, 1998 before the Justice in Cranbrook, because service was not effected in time." The document was dated December 31, 1997, and was signed by D'arcy Mahoney. According to the registry stamp, it had been filed on January 2, three days ago.

I angrily gripped the counter. "My God! What are these people doing? What are they talking about? They just went ahead with a hearing where I had received less notice than this!"

I took a couple of deep breaths and decided I would make use of my otherwise wasted trip. I filed for another family court hearing, requesting that any court orders restricting my access to Steven be dismissed. My reasoning was simple. If I failed in my attempt to stop the petition in the Supreme Court, I believed that a family court hearing already scheduled could not be affected retroactively.

I was assigned a court date of April 29, 1998. I then asked to speak to the Supreme Court Justice about receiving compensation for my otherwise wasted drive across the province. I was granted a brief appearance in Justice Fraser's courtroom and was told my request would be addressed in two weeks when I came back on January 19 for the petition hearing.

Chapter 25

A Fight for Justice

When I arrived back in Victoria, spent and frustrated, I prayed that I could find a shred of decency amongst members of the legal community. I applied for legal-aid, and although I was granted a lawyer to fight the other party's appeal of Judge Carlgren's ruling, I received no help in fighting the Petition, the reason given, I was told I had little chance of succeeding against that particular action.

I got in touch with the Victoria law firm of McCullough Parsons, and spoke with a lawyer by the name of Zofia Porter. She readily agreed to represent me on the appeal, saying she would let me know when they had a court date set.

Two weeks later I drove back across the province and entered the Supreme Court, ready to challenge Majic/Purdy on the petition that was designed to stop me from taking any further court action against my ex-wife.

D'arcy Mahoney presented Geri's case with some desperation, trying to convince the court that my applications over the last couple of years were nothing more than harassment. She went so far as to suggest that I was only forcing my ex-wife into court for the purpose of upsetting her.

When Mahoney concluded her argument, Justice Fraser asked for my response. I slowly and deliberately picked up a binder I had brought with me, and explained to the judge that I was holding a booklet of documents that showed how the law firm of Majic/Purdy, had made repeated trips into court, obtaining Ex-parte orders in my absence.

My presentation caught Ms. Mahoney off guard, and she vehemently objected, stating she had not been given any notice that I was going to present this particular evidence before the court. Her response was amusing to say the least, and only managed to put a spotlight on the legal system's accustomed practice of pushing documentation through the courts in my absence, without fear of having it challenged. Something I suspected would have continued if I had not shown up at the scheduled hearing two weeks earlier.

However, this time, to my delight, Justice Fraser dismissed Ms. Mahoney's objection, and I quickly addressed him with a passionate plea for justice. "My Lord, we are here in this courtroom today, not because I am a danger to inflict any kind of physical harm on my ex-wife. We are in this court today because individuals within our justice system feel exposed, and fear a book I am writing that highlights their lack of integrity, honor, and respect for the basic principles of fair and honest justice, and our Charter of Rights."

I'm not sure if it was my strong words that had any bearing on the judge's decision, but he ruled that the petition would unduly restrict my rights to pursue family court matters and dismissed Ms. Mahoney's application.

When Justice Fraser turned to my request for compensation for my trip across the province two weeks earlier, Mahoney, sheepishly told the court that she had tried to notify me by phone, without success.

I let the judge know I had an answering machine, and that there had been no such message. However, the court gave Ms. Mahoney the benefit of the doubt, suggesting she had at least tried and my request for compensation to cover the earlier trip was turned down. I buried my disappointment at the added financial burden, and accepted my victory as it was, which I had little time to savor. An hour into the return trip, my car broke down and I was forced to sell it for bus fare to get back home. With the three recent trips across the province taking its toll on my vehicle and depleting me financially, the next bit of news I received was all the more devastating.

In February, I was laid off work in the wake of knowledge that a superstore was coming into the Victoria area. My fight against the appeal in the Supreme Court now became more important than ever, as it would determine whether I could return to the Elk Valley and look for employment.

I sensed I was playing against a stacked deck and decided to talk once again to Jody Paterson, the *Times Colonist* columnist I had confided in during my day parole in Victoria in 1993. Jody recalled our meeting at the halfway house that year, and now, after listening to my story, wrote an article that appeared in the paper on February 20, 1998, "Tangled roots of 'justice' spread quickly into a life term of misery."

Around the same time, I also received a date for the appeal, April 7, 1998. Over the next six weeks, Zofia Porter and I went over the case. Then like well-timed clockwork, the chimes of poor man's justice rang out once again.

One week before the hearing, Porter told me that she could not attend the hearing, and that another lawyer from the firm had been appointed to handle the case. I wondered how the young man, James Dunlap, could possibly come to understand the case well enough to effectively represent me after just one week.

However, at the hearing a week later I began to suspect his incompetence did not arise out of a lack of preparation time, or diminished intelligence. It appeared to me that he was simply holding back. At one point I became so frustrated that I asked for a break in the proceedings. I took the young lawyer into a side room and we had a heated exchange. Finally, at my request, Dunlap reluctantly agreed to ask the court to take into account the testimony from Jeff and Aimee that Judge Carlgren had heard, testimony that I was certain had persuaded the judge to lower the restriction from 75 to 25 kilometres.

When we went back before Justice Melnick, Dunlap told the judge about Jeff and Aimee's earlier court appearance, the case concluded, and the Supreme Court Justice reserved his decision.

Now out of work, and with only the family court hearing left to be heard on April 29, I moved back to my mother's place in Vanderhoof and anxiously waited.

306

When I returned to Cranbrook three weeks later for the family court hearing, Robert Girard handed me the Supreme Court's April 7 decision. I was not overly surprised to read that the other side had won its appeal. Justice Melnick had cut my legs out from under me. Despite Jeff and Aimee's testimony, his ruling stated that I needed a change in circumstances, which he said, I had not provided to Judge Carlgren, whom therefore had erred in reducing the distance to 25 kilometers. Justice Melnick ruled that a change of circumstances meant I had to show proof of employment in the Fernie area before I could return. Therefore, the earlier 75-kilometre restriction ordered by Judge Waurynchuk was to remain in place.

I stuffed the ruling into my briefcase, dismissing it as irrelevant. I was headed into a new family court hearing, and my recent unemployment was a definite change in circumstances. One that I believed the family court should, and could hear. It was one thing to be fully employed, and looking for work in the Elk Valley from a distance, but it was quite another to be unemployed and having my physical rights to seek employment curtailed.

I strode into the courtroom and stumbled from surprise when I noticed Geri had accompanied her counsel to court. But I quickly gathered my thoughts together when our case was called before the bench and I immediately asked that all restrictions be lifted.

Judge Carlgren replied that he was inclined to believe that the April 7 Supreme Court decision, just handed down, prevented me from proceeding any farther in family court. I immediately suspected Justice Melnick's ruling had been deliberately designed to sabotage my efforts at this particular hearing. I remained steadfast, and argued to Judge Carlgren that my recent unemployment constituted a change of circumstances that the family court had not had the opportunity to consider previously. Somewhat grudgingly, Judge Carlgren agreed and I was allowed to proceed.

I was sworn in and immediately expressed my sympathy for the many battered women in our country, adding my support for the legitimate actions taken by our society to protect the victims of spousal abuse. I then condemned the justice system for dishonestly portraying me as a violent wife abuser. I challenged Mahoney to produce evidence that supported the false accusations and innuendos that had been used to support the 75-kilometre restriction, laying out fact after fact surrounding the false and misleading documentation used in the case. Including the important fact that I had no record of spousal abuse and that our three children had given sworn testimony, rebuking what the system had implied. I concluded my presentation with a reminder to the court that even the present counsel, Ms. Mahoney, had not challenged the children's testimony during her cross-examination on November 24, six months earlier.

When it came time for cross-examination, Mahoney, who had sat stone faced and silent through my testimony, came prepared, knowing she could not challenge me on the evidence surrounding the justice system's deception. Instead, she focused on the subject of maintenance, a last-minute application that had been brought to court that morning to be used as a diversion. When she finished her presentation, Mahoney indicated that Geri was now prepared to take the stand, but, suspiciously, my ex-wife escaped that fate yet again, when Judge Carlgren gave Ms. Mahoney an out. The judge said he had already decided that there had been no change in my circumstances, making it clear he would not make a new or similar ruling to his earlier one, suspecting it would once again be overturned. Carlgren, following Justice Melnick's lead, declared that my unemployment was not enough; stating that I needed to have a job waiting for me in the Elk Valley before the court would drop the restriction. Therefore, he concluded, there was no need for Geri to testify and face cross-examination.

Although I now knew the ruling was going against me, I asked if I could read my closing statement, a request Judge Carlgren could not deny.

After addressing the court for fifteen minutes on the subject of judicial integrity, I closed with, "On behalf of the Mitchell family, I ask the court to bring an end to seven long years of suffering, heartache and abuse of a decent Canadian family."

As I resumed my seat, the judge made his ruling. He took the arrears of maintenance that had accumulated during my imprisonment, and cleaned it off the books, while leaving the 75-kilometre restriction in place.

I sadly returned to Vanderhoof, unsure what the future would bring. To my dismay it did not take long to find out. A month later, while trying to call my yougest son, Steven, the automatic operator informed me that my ex-wife's phone number was no longer in service. After a couple of days of frantic searching, I was stunned and shocked to learn that Geri had quit her job in Fernie and moved to Terrace, BC, dragging Steven out of school in the process. What appeared to be even more unbelievable, was the fact that the city of Terrace was situated much closer to Vanderhoof than Fernie was. In fact, to arrive at their new community, Geri had driven through Vanderhoof with Steven in tow!

When I finally got the chance to talk with my youngest son on the phone, it was clear that he was upset by the sudden move that had taken him away from his friends in Fernie.

I felt uneasy about driving into Terrace to see him, fearful that I might be set up again if the 75-kilometre restriction had followed Geri to the new community. I waited a month for the summer holidays to arrive, then took a break from writing and bought Steven a bus ticket to Vanderhoof. When we were reunited, Steven quickly informed me that he wanted to spend more time with me. We discussed the possibility of my moving to Terrace while I looked for work, but that idea also made me uncomfortable.

Since Geri no longer lived in Fernie, I decided to apply to have the restriction barring me from that community lifted. If Steven made a decision sometime in the future to live with me, we could then go back to Fernie where he could finish his schooling amongst a crowd of long time friends. The move would also make it easier for me to do more interviews for my book.

I called the Cranbrook court registry and received a hearing date of August 21. The registry, lending a helping hand, contacted

Geri through the court registry in Terrace, as she had to be notified of my application.

On August 21, 1998, I went back to court in Cranbrook for what I thought would be a simple matter of having my banishment from Fernie lifted. When I showed up at the courthouse, however, I was confronted with a new application from Geri, who surprisingly, was present in the courtroom. Apparently the no-contact order had not followed her to her Terrace, and now, after four months, she was asking that the restriction be changed to do just that. What I thought was going to be a simple hearing quickly turned into a war of words between a familiar adversary, Judge Waurynchuk, and myself. Fully aware that a move to Fernie with Steven was not certain, especially in the immediate future, and that my access to him in Terrace might now be restricted after an apparent reprieve of four months, I battled vehemently against the new restriction. I pulled out a notarized statement Steven had signed for the courts. The last paragraph read: "I would like to see my father be free of any kind of restrictions put in place by the courts that either the justice system or my mother could use against him that would interfere with my relationship with my father."

Waurynchuk, aware that Steven now lived in Terrace, glared down at me from the bench and asked me why I wanted to have the restriction from Fernie removed. Considering the Fernie order was supposedly in place for my ex-wife's protection, his inquiry appeared to confirm my lingering suspicions that I had been run out of the Elk Valley community because of the interviews I had been conducting.

By now, I had long suspected Judge Waurychuk had been involved in some of the backroom discussions that had taken place in my case, and I decided to lay it all on his lap. "Besides, giving me an opportunity to look for work, a move back to Fernie will also allow me to conduct more interviews for my book," I said defiantly.

Judge Waurynchuk flushed, then indicated that nothing would have happened to me if I had just gone into Terrace without making this new application.

When all was said and done, it appeared that it had been my request to have the restriction from Fernie lifted that had moved the justice system back into action.

Judge Waurynchuk angrily stated, "Cancellation of the 75 kilometer restriction from the community of Fernie, that is amended to read, 'Terrace, in all purposes."

Still uncertain about any future plans Steven and I may have, I lashed out at the judge, stating I would defy his new court order concerning Terrace. Waurynchuk in turn launched into a tirade, describing me as a dangerous and out-of-control human being whose whereabouts should be monitored by the northern authorities in the province. Then, topping off his dramatics, he turned to Geri and announced that, for her protection, she was to remain in the courtroom until I had left the building, after which the sheriffs would escort her to her car.

I left the courthouse shaking my head in disbelief, no longer suspicious, but convinced that the justice system was determined to destroy my credibility. My first parole officer, Dennis Larose, had been right. I was taking on a three-headed monster in my fight against the courts, corrections, and parole.

After returning to Vanderhoof, I received a copy of Judge Waurynchuk's order through the mail. It now left me wondering and confused about my legal right to even return to Fernie. It stated that my application for cancellation of the restrictive order regarding Fernie had been dismissed.

I filed another application in the Supreme Court, asking to have the new restriction applying to Terrace, lifted, hoping it would clear everything up. After months of stumbling through the legal court process, on March 11, 1999, I gave a four-hour presentation of my case before Justice Thackray in Smithers, BC, a town located between Vanderhoof and Terrace. I briefly mentioned the vindictive revocation of my parole and the false affidavits. I led the court through the manipulation and deceitful tactics that the lawyers had engaged in throughout the criminal and family court process over the years.

When I finished, Justice Thackray told Geri that if he had to rule at that moment, he would rule in my favor, and drop the restriction. However, he adjourned the hearing and gave her a chance to respond on May 21, 1999.

When I returned to Smithers in May, a couple of women I had never seen before accompanied Geri into the Victim Service's office located across from the courtroom. After an inquiry, staff at the registry informed me they were from the Victim Assistance Coordinators office, likely from the community of Terrace.

When the proceedings began, the two women sat in the gallery, and Geri started to address the court.

Because the style of proceeding were arguments from counsel table there was no sworn testimony. No doubt with this in mind, Geri quickly produced some unsworn statements from a couple of friends, and another from herself, statements that had allegedly been given to the RCMP in Fernie. I glanced through the copies I was handed. They indicated I had been harassing and stalking Geri for years. I then noticed the statements had been dated prior to the July 1997 court hearing that dealt with my supposed breach of Judge Waurychuk's court order. I recalled that two of these close friends of Geri's had been sitting in the courtroom during that hearing.

Justice Thackray was now being asked to believe that these close friends (who were supposedly terrified that she was in imminent danger) had sat quietly in court that day, and never offered to give testimony under oath.

The fact was, if their statements were authentic, they would never have stood up under cross-examination, even a layman like myself could see that. They were loaded with conjecture and causal speculation and held no substance at all. (My suspicions about the statements grew to even greater heights, when Steven later told me that his mother had visited these people just prior to coming back to court in Smithers.)

312

After producing these unsworn documents, Geri then tried to submit a recent doctor's report that allegedly showed evidence of a long-term disability she had been living with, supposedly due to the single slap in the marriage that had happened almost twenty years earlier.

When I asked for a copy of the document, she objected. When the court informed her that I was entitled to a copy, she withdrew the alleged report.

I informed the judge that I would take the time to go through any statements she did submit, if the court felt it necessary. However, Justice Thackray wasted no time. He made it clear that he was not giving any weight to them, so, I instead read my closing statement.

My Lord, I ask this court to do its duty. I ask the court to exercise the legitimate mandate given to it by the citizens of our country. A mandate that ensures each and every citizen a fair and just decision. I ask the court to protect our constitution and a citizen's right to due process.

This is a bond between a father and son, that although emotionally has never wavered, physically it has been unfairly restricted through unwarranted vengeance and an unconscionable vindictiveness, initiated by others. ...Steven wishes to have a closer relationship with his father, and asks the court to grant him his wish.

I plead with this court not to punish myself, or my son any further, by searching for rules of law that have been unethically raised as shields against truth and justice. I ask the court to protect a father who has been forced to proceed into the legal arena where he is technically unschooled, but passionately speaks out in defense of what he believes our justice system should stand for. Fair and equitable justice for all our citizens!

The hearing concluded and Justice Thackray reserved his decision. After I returned to Vanderhoof, Steven called to let me know that as soon as school was out, he was coming to live with me, no matter what the court ruled. While waiting for the decision, and still uncertain about Fernie, we decided a move to Victoria would give Steven the opportunity to spend time with his older brother and sister.

On June 9, 1999, after Steven and I had made the move to Victoria, Justice Thackray wrote a decision that set aside the Terrace restriction. His defining words were, "This is an extraordinary injunction. There had to be sound reasons to grant it. There weren't. To maintain it there must be compelling reasons. There aren't."

Steven had been eight years old when I had first went to prison. It had been another long and difficult eight years since. I quietly asked myself, "IS THE NIGHTMARE FINALLY OVER?

Chapter 26

A Civil Suit

The move to Victoria was everything I hoped it would be. The kids and I spent a great deal of time together. Games of tennis and par three golf became regular family activities. However, as the months passed it became apparent that the turmoil of the last decade had left several deep wounds.

After some inquiries, Steven was afforded help through youth counseling. However, at the same time, the government bureaucracy told me it was my responsibility to come to terms with what I saw as the abusive nature of the justice system, and then get on with my life as it was. Accepting the degrading manipulation of the judicial process was one thing, but walking away from it was quite another. If I was ever to find any lasting peace, I knew I had to confront the demons that continued to hold me captive.

Justice Thackray's comment indicated that he felt I had also been dealt with unfairly. Convinced that I was in a no-lose situation, I sought out legal counsel, hoping to find someone willing to help me pursue a lawsuit against the Attorney General of Canada. But after giving me only minimal assistance in organizing my Statement of Claim, the legal community closed its doors on me, citing an inability to come up with any funds.

In spite of my distrust of the courts I remained undaunted. I filed the claim on my own, adding Geri as a respondent in the case. By forcing her onto the stand, I hoped to expose the false affidavits that had made their way into the family court file, thereby adding more support to my case.

My claim made several accusations, most of them centered around the justice system's manufactured documentation, and the psychological abuse I was subjected to during my incarceration. The most notable accused the Attorney General of violating part 1 of the Charter of Rights under section 7. The Charter read: "Everyone has the right to life, liberty and security of the person and the right not to be deprived therof except in accordance with the principles of fundamental justice." This was the part of the Charter I felt I could use against the correctional service and the National Parole Board's vindictive revocation of my parole in 1994.

During the discovery stage of proceedings I was deluged with hundreds of documents from the Attorney General's office, much of it duplicated in two separate files. As I was going through the massive pile of paper, one particular report caught my attention.

In May 1993, Doug Hampson, the private counselor who had come into the Ferndale Institution to see me at the request of a friend, had left me a copy of his assessment report. He had also given a copy to my case management team. As I now stared at the assessment that had been given to case management, and was now included in the government file, I was stunned by some inferences I did not recall seeing in the copy Doug had given me.

I quickly rummaged through my own file and found my copy of the document. I laid the two side-by-side and immediately realized that the government's copy was three paragraphs longer.

I went back to the assessment Doug had left me, and read it carefully. It began with an explanation of how I had sought him out for counseling on numerous occasions, demonstrating an eagerness to understand others and myself better. Doug also described the ongoing frustration I was experiencing as a result of the many reports written by the justice system. His assessment ended with:

> As I have met with Mr. Mitchell, I have not perceived him to be in denial about his offence nor do I sense him harboring a bitterness about his conviction. From my perspective, the real issue for Mr. Mitchell is his overwhelming sense of being misunderstood. If there are any questions concerning this report please do not hesitate to contact me.

I then turned back to the government copy, and what should have been the same ending. It read:

> As I have met with Mr. Mitchell, I have not perceived him to be in denial about his offence nor do I sense him harboring a bitterness about his conviction.

From my perspective the real issue for Mr. Mitchell, at this time, is his perception of being misunderstood and the emotions that accompany that perception. Mr. Mitchell desires to be understood, and when he perceives that he is being misrepresented his anxiety level rises. As Mr. Mitchell becomes more stressful, his perception of reality can become distorted and consequently this can precipitate erratic behavioral patterns (insomnia, irritability, missing appointments, etc).

There was also an entirely new paragraph that contained Doug's closing remark. It read:

In sessions we have discussed how to effectively manage the emotions of anger, stress, and depression; we have role played appropriate communication skills and techniques; we have contemplated insight on how to address his current situation. I believe that as Mr. Mitchell learns to express himself appropriately and work through the emotions that at times overwhelm him, he will better equip himself for life experiences in the future. If there are any questions about this report please do not hesitate to contact me.

I was stunned by the alterations in the document. I was well aware that this was a case where the justice system would be pleased to have evidence that a counselor from outside the institution had suggested that I could be distorting reality and had been uncooperative.

I considered the possibility that the justice system had recently changed the assessment, unaware that I had a copy. I also sensed Ferndale case management's manipulative presence in the report. The fact was; Doug and I never had any scheduled one on one appointments. My case manager at Ferndale, Carter Alexander, had turned down my request to speak to an institutional counselor. Doug Hampson's initial trips into the prison to see me had been as a visitor. It was only after he had been hired to do group therapy sessions in Ferndale that I had sought him out on my own time while he was free from his duties at the institution.

I immediately called Doug and arranged for us to meet at the Tsawassen ferry terminal on the mainland, just south of Vancouver. After looking at the two documents, he acknowledged that the Correctional Service's copy had been altered and agreed to testify.

Meanwhile, keeping up my end of the discovery process, I gave counsel for the Attorney General, copies of the diary notes that I was going to bring into the case. In the package, I also included some transcripts of the taped interviews I had conducted for the book, letting counsel know that I was going to enter them into evidence as well.

Government counsel quickly filed a motion to have the suit dismissed, while arguing that if the case went ahead they wanted the interviews barred from the proceeding.

I responded by telling the court that I was prepared to go before the media and talk about another cover-up. I couldn't be certain how much my threat had to do with the court's decision, but it set aside the Attorney General's motion to dismiss the case. However, the judge also made no ruling on whether the interviews would be allowed into evidence and the trial began in the spring of 2001, without any ruling on their admissibility.

I began my case by addressing the bench and reading a statement informing the presiding judge, Justice Sing, that this was not a story about guilt or innocence. I had assaulted a man; there was no doubt about that. This I said, was a story about deception and manipulation, about coercion and the abandonment of due process. It was a case about abuse of power and a lack of integrity throughout the judicial system.

When I finished, to my dismay, Justice Sing indicated he wanted to restrict the case to the period between my sentencing hearing, May 1992, and my warrant expiry date, October 1995.

I politely questioned the restriction. With Geri as a respondent in the case, I believed I had the right to tell my story from start to finish. And if the head and the tail of the story were to be cut off, it would severely harm my ability to link everything together in a cohesive manner.

However, Justice Sing remained adamant that the case would be restricted, citing the fact, that most of my claim centered on conduct involving the correctional and parole services. He left me with the impression that any further argument on my behalf could see the case thrown out before it got off the ground.

I realized that if I wanted to expose the abuse surrounding my incarceration, putting what I could into the record was imperative, so I agreed to proceed as the court wished.

The case moved forward and I offered up for evidence the original copy of Doug Hampson's report and the correctional service's altered copy, both dated May 8, 1993. I told Justice Sing that I hoped to call Doug to the stand in a few days and expose the dishonesty behind the alterations in the documents.

After court ended for the day, I phoned Doug to give him a date for his testimony. Doug hesitated, then informed me that he might have had a laptop computer with him on that particular day at the institution, and might have changed the report himself -- he could not be sure. I was unable to hide my disappointment, even when Doug made it clear that the new inclusions I had shown him in the government's copy did not represent his personal experience with me.

Doug went on to say that he had talked with a lawyer who told him that he should not testify if he couldn't be certain whether or not he had made the changes himself.

I was not prepared to force the hand of someone I considered a friend, so I went back to court and withdrew the two reports from evidence. However, I was troubled as I pondered the abrupt turnaround in Doug's willingness to help. Could it have been the intimidating prospect of testifying against a powerful bureaucracy for whom he still did contract work for?

Pushing my setback aside, I moved on, submitting other institutional documents that had been used to enhance and support the character assassination done on me while I was in the custody of the government. During a break in proceedings, however, the court clerk became concerned that I did not understand how documented evidence was tagged for the record, which determined what the judge would look at later on. She indicated that I could not knowingly submit documents that were false, if I did, I would be agreeing with the content they held. Confused and without any instructions on how to enter them into evidence, with the understanding that they were false and misleading, I reluctantly asked that they be removed from evidence as well.

During my sworn testimony, I also entered my early diary notes from the Matsqui Induction Center into evidence. After I did so, Justice Sing indicated it was not necessary for me to enter my remaining diary notes. He explained that if my verbal testimony was not disputed, than the mere fact that I was reading my diary into the record was enough. I accepted the judge's explanation, feeling somewhat confident that the other side would be forced to put witnesses on the stand if they were going to dispute anything I said on record.

With my case restricted to the time surrounding my federal sentence, the most grievous injustice, I felt, was the manufactured reports that had been used to support the revocation of my parole. The most damming of these was the National Parole Board's own document that said I had been out in the community, plotting and seeking revenge.

I had proof that my counselor at that time, Kevin Kennedy, had never made this incriminating declaration which had been attributed to him in the document. The fact was; my investigation and my fight in family court following my release from prison told an entirely different story.

Hoping to expose the government's deception, I set out to prove my case by first giving evidence about the false affidavit George Majic had entered into the family court record on behalf of Geri, right after my parole suspension in 1994. This particular affidavit, which suggested I had been harassing Geri and the kids while on parole, also held a blatantly false statement that indicated I had been wearing a balaclava on the night of the assault in 1991.

I then read into the record much of the institutional documentation that had been used to support the revocation of my parole and my eventual transfer to higher security. With my emotions rising, I choked back tears as I talked about the night I tried to take my own life while languishing in the hole at the Matsqui Penitentiary.

After highlighting these reports that suggested I was a dangerous man out to seek revenge on my ex-wife and the world, I produced the correctional service's follow-up document. With some obvious satisfaction, I read from the case management report that had been used to justify my transfer to minimum security, just prior to my statutory release in 1995. This report, which had been written after months of reports declaring that I was a danger to society and needed extensive treatment, now showed Corrections Canada patting itself on the back, telling the world it had just completed a much-needed and successful rehabilitation, only months before my imminent release.

I then accused Corrections Canada and the parole service of using victim services as a means to expand its power base into the community. Government counsel swiftly rebuffed that idea, stating there was no direct connection between corrections and victim services.

I challenged the Attorney General's declaration, quickly producing an internal document I had found amongst the government's files I had been sent. It was a letter dated August 3, 1993, and had been given to Geri by the National Parole Board, encouraging her to produce a victim impact statement. The document made reference to Marilyn McNeil, identifying her as the Victim Coordinator at the Ferndale Institution. The document proved, McNeil, was wearing two hats while I was incarcerated at Ferndale, as she was also the head of case management. McNeil, had also been one of the staff members involved in the theft of my mail, specifically the supporting letter from the guard at KRCC in Kamloops (I had already mentioned that fact during my testimony).

I watched the color drain from the faces of the two young government lawyers who sat sullenly at their counsel table. When their lingering silence continued, I ended what had been an emotional two weeks on the stand by asking that the taped interviews now be allowed into evidence.

Justice Sing promptly refused my request, stating that I had the right to call these people as witnesses. This was something I hadn't counted on. I had wanted these people on the stand, but I had believed all along that my questioning would happen during a cross-examination, when, and if, the government called them to the stand to oppose my testimony.

I informed the court that I had tried to contact Judy Chouinard and Kathy Roy at the Manchester House, but was told they were both on holidays. I suspected the truthfulness of that particular information, but what I was certain of, was the fact that everyone in the courtroom knew I had no financial means to pay for a plane fare and a hotel room for even one witness, let alone several of them.

Justice Sing brushed my predicament aside and asked counsel to begin its cross-examination.

I was not surprised when my sworn testimony went unchallenged. I waited patiently and answered politely while government counsel, and Geri's lawyer hurried through some pointless rhetoric, dealing with dates and confirmation concerning documents, before releasing me from the stand.

I then listened as the government attorney submitted an application asking to have the case dismissed. They started out by attacking my statement of claim that held a dozen or more statements, identifying my arguments in short form. One of the first they went after was my claim that the justice system had improperly identified my ex-wife as the victim. They argued:

> Within the meaning of subsection 2(1) of the Corrections and Conditional Release Act, a victim is defined as follows: means a person to whom harm was done or who suffered physical or emotional damage as a result of the commission of an offence, and for the purposes of information sharing under subsections 26(2) and 142(3), a victim is defined as a person who satisfies the National Parole Board that harm was done to the person, or that the person suffered physical or emotional damage, as a result of an act of an offender, whether or not the offender was prosecuted or convicted for that act, and that a complaint was made to the police or

prosecution or an information was laid under the Criminal Code.

Ironically, the government's argument supported my earlier suggestion, that corrections and parole had used its vast power to promote legislation that gave it considerable clout in the area of victim services. In their own words they were using legislation that allowed them to indiscriminately define who was, or was not, a victim. The legislation let the correctional and parole service portray inmates and parolees as guilty of a criminal act, even if they had never been charged in a court of law.

And the legislation not only allowed the National Parole Board to declare Geri as a victim of my crime, due to the alleged emotional trauma she suffered as a result of my assault on her lover, but it also allowed the justice system to give her victim status under the degrading impression that she had been an abused spouse, a false allegation that the correctional service had used against me throughout my sentence, and something that had taken me years to challenge in family court.

The Attorney General also argued that the case should be dismissed because I had let too much time pass before filing the lawsuit. The lawyers then suggested that the correctional service's reports were just opinions, and were not actionable in a court of law. They also suggested that the only damages I had suffered were hurt feelings.

Of course there was no mention of Ferndale case management's deceptive ploy of toying with my emotions during my parole suspension. This specific emotional abuse had left me with the haunting memory of an attempted suicide while imprisoned at the Matsqui Penitentiary.

But despite my overwhelming sworn testimony, Justice Sing said he had not heard anything that would support any specific charges of abuse as far as this particular hearing went. He then made it clear that he felt my case rested on my claim under the Charter of Rights.

Not wanting to have the case stalled, or possibly even dismissed, I followed his lead and indicated that I was prepared to drop the other specific charges and proceed under the charter. My conciliatory act caught Justice Sing by surprise and he hastily tried to assure me that he had not made up his mind on any of the other claims. He said he would allow for a break in the proceedings, asking that I take the time to go over my statements, explain each, and then come to a decision on how I wanted to proceed.

Justice Sing rose and left the courtroom, and I immediately let out my frustration. "If he doesn't think there was any abuse, then I might as well walk out of here right now," I muttered out loud, unable to hold back my disgust at his inference that the other claims were without merit.

The court clerk overheard my grumble and suggested I stay and take the judge's advice by focusing on my claim under the Charter of Rights. I considered the possibility that Justice Sing might be duping me into dropping my other arguments, therefor enabling a defense for the justice system later on. He had after-all, given me no reason why he felt my other claims were not viable. I pondered over my situation and then calmed myself, deciding I would give the judge the benefit of my doubt about his intentions. It was true that many of my charges in the statement of claim arose out of a series of events, a systematic policy of degradation and abuse. And on top of the documentation that had been removed from evidence, many of the others had never come to light because they existed outside the period of my incarceration and my testimony.

And although I knew a cross-examination of witnesses would help support all my allegations, I hadn't cross-examined anyone yet, because the case had not proceeded that far.

Feeling somewhat lost and confused, I quickly realized I was in over my head as far as legal knowledge went. What constituted evidence, and what did not, clearly eluded me in technical terms. I was also leery of the judge's suggestion that he had not made up his mind on the many other charges. Something still told me those words had been uttered, simply to give an appearance of fairness to any probing ears.

My trepidation was supported by the fact that I had been denied the right to use the taped interviews that would have been extremely damaging to the government. Included in the interviews was the admission by my former parole officer that the revocation of my parole had been supported with false and misleading documentation. I had also received no explanation as to why my sworn testimony had not been enough to support my claims, especially when none of it had been disputed under cross-examination.

However, I concluded that if I wanted the case to proceed with a degree of civility between Justice Sing and myself, I would have to agree to proceed in the manner he had suggested, besides, I was convinced that my claim under the charter covered about everything anyway. And I was even more confident I could show that the revocation of my parole had been nothing more than a vindictive act initiated by Corrections Canada.

When Justice Sing returned, crippled by an uneasy feeling that I was being led around by the nose, I informed the court that the citizens of Canada could read my book and determine for themselves whether there had been any abuse by the justice system in this case. With that, I reluctantly agreed that there was no evidence to support my other claims, at least for the purpose of this particular hearing, something Justice Sing had made reference to while addressing the other counsel table. With my point made, I then agreed to proceed on my claim under the Charter.

Justice Sing however, continued to wander through the charges I had already agreed to drop. After responding to some of his statements, my suspicions rose. He now appeared to be focused on getting me to agree that there had been no abuse at all. This went beyond his earlier reflection, when he had indicated that if I dropped my many other claims, I was only agreeing that I had not shown evidence to proceed with them for the purposes of this particular hearing.

"I agree only because I was not allowed to present the evidence," I said, emphasizing that point as I went through the claim with the judge.

"Well then it's not evidence," responded an irritated Justice Sing, perplexed that I had inserted the qualifying remark.

I shrugged off his comment and turned my attention to the Charter, emphasizing Part 1, section 7, using it to support my claim of an unjust revocation and imprisonment. If the judge was prepared to continue with the case along this path, I felt I would finally get the chance to force my accusers onto the stand. With that in mind, I brought up what I felt was the most damaging evidence I had against the government: the National Parole Board's revocation document.

I went through the board's decision with Justice Sing, exposing it for what it was, a deceptive document meant to support the vindictive actions of those involved in my revocation. I highlighted the assessment of risk that declared I had been dismissed from counseling while still on parole because I had been using the sessions to vent and plot revenge.

My interview with Kevin Kennedy, the Cranbrook community counselor, clearly showed that both these allegations were false. Kevin had made it clear during our taped interview that he never terminated our sessions, and that I had never given him any indication that I was out plotting or seeking revenge against anyone.

Although the government had prevented me from using that taped interview with Kevin, they had overlooked one important piece of evidence. I now pulled out my ace: another document I had found amongst the government files during the discovery process. With obvious satisfaction, I read out Kevin's last comment in the first paragraph of a closing assessment he had forwarded to Corrections Canada, given to them shortly after my sentence had expired in 1995. "Sometime after our last visit on February 17, 1994, Mr. Mitchell was remanded back to prison for reasons that have never been completely qualified or explained to me."

I stared hard at Justice Sing before speaking boldly. "If Kevin Kennedy had told these people that I was out plotting and seeking revenge, he most certainly would have known why I had been sent back to prison!" I said emphatically.

A look of embarrassment leapt across Justice Sing's face.

The reason was obvious. The evidence clearly showed that my former parole officer, Dennis Larose, and the National Parole Board, had used Kevin Kennedy to support the board's most damaging reason for revoking my parole. Larose's special report, written on April 5, 1994, the very same day I was taken back into custody, read: "Mr. Kennedy was unable to make any progress with moving David beyond 'venting' and 'plotting revenge.'"

However, despite my sworn testimony pertaining to this overwhelming evidence, coupled with the fact that Kevin Kennedy had been the only counselor I had seen during this period of my parole, Justice Sing inferred that the National Parole Board's decision might be referring to a different counselor altogether. Then, without giving any meaningful support for this off-the-cuff assumption, the judge hastily ended the discussion, stating he would come back the next morning with a decision on whether or not the case would go forward.

The following day I sat in resigned silence as Justice Sing upheld the Attorney General's motion and dismissed the case, while suggesting that I find something else to do that would be more productive than writing my book.

My disappointment was somewhat muted. I had come into court knowing full well that the justice system only had two paths it could take. Its decision not to search for the truth was disheartening, but not devastating. Watching the justice system deny me the opportunity to question my accusers, only highlighted the undeniable. The court's decision only supported my contention that our courtrooms are *not* a place where a search for truth rules the day. Rather they are forums where rules and regulations are used to manipulate and suppress the purest meaning of justice.

As I sat, lost in my thoughts, Justice Sing indulged himself in one last bit of business. Although the Attorney General had verbally declared it was not seeking court costs, he demanded that government counsel now ask for it, which counsel did, to the tune of $24,000.

And Geri, who had never made an appearance in the courtroom, and had once again escaped having to answer any tough questions under cross examination, including an explanation regarding the false affidavit, was awarded the right to seek court cost. That amount, according to her lawyer, rested in the neighborhood of $17,000.

This was particularly troubling to me. Neither my children nor I could see any evidence that she had been paying any legal fees. However, for a decade she had managed to have lawyers working overtime on her behalf, year after year, protecting her from having to answer to the false affidavit and other related matters.

Her family court lawyers had even managed to file two applications in the Supreme Court -- one for a Petition and another for an Appeal -- which would easily exceed a cost of $10,000. And now another lawyer, Bruce Webber, had just taken on her defense in a civil suit.

When Jeff questioned his mother on how she was paying for her lawyers, and she refused to answer, I was not overly surprised. I had suspected all along that the Canadian taxpayers were unwittingly covering her legal fees. It was certainly an arrangement that would benefit both the justice system and my ex-wife.

My thoughts returned to the bench and I remained seated as Justice Sing rose and headed for his exit. In my dire financial state, I concluded his demand that the government pursue court costs, was the justice system's way of letting me know it was prepared to interfere in any income I derived from the sale of my book.

So a decade after that frightful night in October 1991, the case came to an end. And on September 27, 2001, I conducted my last interview for the book. While sitting beside my friend Richard Engel, a man who had remained by my side throughout my imprisonment, I questioned the one other person I had put my trust and faith in during my incarceration.

I quickly sensed that Doug Hampson was trying to walk a delicate line, wanting to be fair, but not certain what explanation he could accurately support involving the altered document.

Although Doug was unsure if he had changed his report, he indicated he could not dismiss that possibility. He went on to say that he recalled Carter Alexander asking him to submit a report.

And after giving it to Carter (on the same day he had given me a copy), Doug had a vague recollection of Carter making statements about my association and interaction with case management.

When I thought about the date, May 8, 1993, on Doug's report, I realized it coincided with Carter Alexander's return to the Ferndale Institution after his drug and alcohol rehab. My diary notes showed that he had very quickly become confrontational with me during this period, and had attempted to sabotage my parole.

So although Doug could not recall exactly what questions or statements Carter made, the altered report strongly indicated Carter had suggested to Doug that I had been distorting reality and engaging in other erratic behavior. Doug said that he might well have been asked to put his answers to Carter's questions or statements into the report, which could explain the difference between the one he had given me, and the one the government had on file. However, Doug made it clear that he did not perceive me personally, as being someone who was distorting reality.

Let me say at this point that I do not wish to question the integrity of a man I consider a friend. My explanation of Doug's apparent confusion and his inability to recall changing, or not changing the report is not a difficult one to understand. As he said, it was years ago. And there is absolutely no doubt that my diary notes support the fact that Carter was extremely manipulative when it came to producing reports on me. I cannot say if Doug was manipulated into altering his report, or even if he in fact made the changes himself. What I can say with certainty is that he was aware of the considerable struggle I was engaged in with case management at Ferndale.

In 2003, almost 2 years after the civil case had concluded, the Attorney General of Canada, after my refusal to sign papers acknowledging court costs, reinitiated court proceedings that highlighted their costs, and left with a court ruling that held me financially responsible, pending my ability to pay. Geri, who also had to show proof of her legal fees, made no such request for compensation. An action that supported my belief that her legal fees were being taken care of by a justice system that was not only ethically challenged, but morally corrupt.

Chapter 27

The Bill of Integrity

When I look back at the criminal, civil, and family court process' I experienced, the deception and manipulation that remained hidden behind a veil of justice is something that still frightens me today. There is no doubt that backroom deals are an everyday occurrence throughout our justice system. Many argue that our courts would be overwhelmed if it were not for the plea-bargaining process. Ironically, that is an argument I agree with. However, as a society we must make sure the process is open, honest, and fair.

I would also argue that the legislation in the Corrections and Conditional Release Act, which allows the National Parole Board to define who are victim's of crime, is nothing short of an act of lunacy. It is a horrific abuse of power that undermines due process and puts citizens' legal, civil, and human rights at risk. For this reason alone, "due process" in the initial court proceedings must be protected. This is also why any plea-bargain agreement must be supported with full disclosure in a court of law, where the public can be given all the factual circumstances surrounding any given case.

Unfortunately, the plea-bargaining process as it is used today has the ability to abuse society in two ways. The rich, the powerful and even inmates who support case management can plea-bargain for shorter sentences or easier prison time. This can victimize society and the true victims of crime all over again.

On November 28, 1998, an article in the editorial section of the *Hamilton Spectator*, "Plea Bargain review in order," outlined concerns surrounding the fast-track prosecution, conviction, and sentencing of a self-confessed hitman. The article highlights how conviction and sentencing can be arranged through backroom deals, outside the domain of full public disclosure. In the article, a well-known hitman, allegedly provided evidence to the Crown, identifying those who had hired him. The agreed-upon sentence allowed the hitman to become eligible for parole after serving only thirteen years for a crime of multiple murder.

The article also went on to describe how the Karla Homolka case prompted public outrage about plea-bargains being negotiated behind closed doors. In this case, the victims' families never had a say in the agreement, and Homolka was given a twelve-year sentence for manslaughter. This case also involved multiple deaths, with two young girls losing their lives.

On the other hand, the process can victimize poorer citizens who must rely on legal-aid or public defenders. They can easily be overcharged and then intimidated or manipulated into agreeing to a lesser charge. This is most often done by offering shorter sentences, coupled with promises of early release through parole.

My personal experience with plea-bargaining shows how these backroom deals, without any signed agreement, can allow the justice system to avoid accountability, and hide its deception.

Since my release from prison I have written a private members bill, the Bill of Integrity. The purpose of the bill is to build integrity and bring balance to the plea-bargaining process. It's built on the principle of due process and is meant to ensure that society's rights are protected, along with an accused citizen's right to a fair and just sentencing procedure.

The bill, as written, would require the accused, the defense attorney, the prosecutor, and the victim to sign off on a plea-bargain. The agreement would have to show the charge, the agreed upon evidence, and the length of sentence sought. It would then have to be endorsed by the judge, who would add his or her signature. However, if the judge felt the agreement did not serve the interest of the public, he or she could opt not to endorse the agreement and send the case to trial.

I first passed the bill onto Canada's official opposition party in February 1999. John Reynolds, MP for the Reform party (now of the Alliance party), took the bill to their justice team for its consideration. The members concluded that the bill would not be appropriate as written, but gave no indication they were willing to suggest any changes. The only viable reason I could see for not proceeding rested in their argument that my bill gave victims the power to veto a plea-bargain. They argued this would paralyze our legal system. But this matter could easily be taken care of by making the victim's signature voluntary, either for or against, with the judge still making the final determination.

It is worth noting that nowhere in the official opposition's response did it address the manipulation that can occur in our open-ended plea-bargaining process.

I also sent a copy of the bill to my local Member of Parliament, David Anderson, of the governing Liberal party. In May 2002, Justice Minister Martin Cauchon responded to my proposed bill. He acknowledged that there were no specific provisions in the Criminal Code regarding the plea-bargaining process. He also stated that a judge is bound to pass sentence, taking into consideration any mitigating or aggravating factors, but he failed to recognize how these factors can be distorted, manipulated or suppressed, which is the problem with the open-ended plea-bargaining process.

The justice department indicated it would not proceed with the Bill of Integrity. Mr. Cauchon stated, "I believe that the vast majority of dealings between Crown attorneys and defense counsel are already characterized by the utmost of professional honesty, courtesy, and integrity in criminal court proceedings."

It is clear from these responses that politicians will shy away from legislation that will help protect society's legal and human rights if it means forcing the justice system into accountability. It is clearly hypocritical for a country like Canada, which takes pride in promoting its democracy as a model of equality, to speak of individual freedoms while restricting poorer citizens' rights to fair and honest justice. It gives way to neither, an honorable society, or a just one.

My criticism of the plea-bargaining process, and a need for the Bill of Integrity, is also supported by the Auditor General of Canada. The Auditor General's 2002 report on the criminal justice system highlights the significant challenges the system faces. Section 4.37 states: "The practice of plea-bargaining has been criticized. It has the potential to undermine the integrity of the criminal justice system, in part because disclosure of the basis for agreements and accountability for the decisions have been inadequate."

Whether you believe the legal profession proceeded with honor in my case or not, the Bill of Integrity would help promote a stronger sense of fairness in our society by holding those who administer justice to a higher standard, while making them accountable.

On the other end of the spectrum, society must also be wary of how an unhealthy plea-bargaining process affects parole in a negative way. First, it increases the probability that false or misleading documentation can go into a judicial record, unchallenged. Whether this happens as a result of manipulation, or because of a lack of empathy on the part of lawyers or judges, is irrelevant. It happens, and it allows the correctional service to abuse the parole process in several ways, including the unethical process of defining victims of crime, as I have already mentioned.

Society can be abused by the parole system in other ways as well. In 1997, Clifford Olson, a notorious child serial killer, was paraded across Canada in a spectacle that created a furor of angry resentment towards Canada's prison population. This case more than any other shows how the justice system can feed the fears of society and re-victimize everyone. Relatives of Olson's victims' wept while listening to government prosecutors read out victim impact statements. And for what purpose? To let society see how the parole process protects society in a case where the individual has absolutely no hope of parole? I suspect this shameless display was a calculated way to promote the growth industry of corrections and parole, by showing a perceived fairness, yet toughness to the public?

The history of parole and the evolution of the Correctional Service of Canada has been filled with turmoil. [The following information was gathered from the National Parole Board web-site] On August 11, 1899, the Canadian Parliament enacted the Ticket of Leave Act. It was designed to lower prison costs by releasing first-time offenders who were deemed unlikely to re-offend. There was no requirement that a certain amount of prison time be served before the offender applied for release, and there was no provision for supervision when an offender was released. The only requirement was that the offender register with, and report to the local police authority. And only the Governor General could grant a ticket to leave.

Seventy-one people were granted tickets to leave (licences) in 1899. Five were revoked and seven forfeited their licence. The other 59 went on to complete their sentences in the community. Over the next decade the ticket to leave appeared to be a resounding success.

In the early twentieth century, some people began to believe that the relatively new science of psychology could solve social problems and change criminal behavior. Others remained skeptical. The skeptics began to attack the ticket to leave process, claiming it was driving up the crime rate, even though the Remission Branch, which ran the fledgling parole system, released statistics, that showed only 2.2 percent of prisoners granted a ticket of leave between 1899 and 1922, had committed an offence while on leave.

Between 1932 and 1938 the number of rules and regulations in the penitentiary system increased from 194 to 1500. This meant it was almost impossible for a prisoner to avoid committing some offence. Abuses, even some atrocities, went unchallenged because the penitentiaries were a world apart, a secret kingdom cut off from the rest of the community. The Canadian public was indifferent to the plight of prisoners and quite willing to leave the distasteful chore of dealing with them to the authorities.

After a series of prison riots, Agnes Macphail, the first female Member of Parliament, demanded an inquiry into the penal system. The Conservative government attempted to discredit her allegations of abuse in the system, but in 1935 the Conservatives were defeated, and the new Liberal government created a royal commission to investigate the allegations. Justice Joseph Archambault headed the commission and wrote a report that condemned, and recommended several changes. One proposal called for a prison commission that would have full authority over the management of penitentiaries, and act as an independent federal parole board.

In 1947, Major General Ralph B. Gibson was appointed Commissioner of Penitentiaries. Conscious of the Archambault report and its demands that the penal system become more humane, Gibson began to hire teachers and psychologists, and to develop training courses.

In 1948, the Remission Service, hired its first social worker. Through the 1950s, the Remission Service and parole were restructured, leading to today's modern prison industry. Private after-care agencies like the Salvation Army and the John Howard Society were used to introduce supervision into the correctional and parole process.

In 1959, the Ticket of Leave Act was repealed and the Remission Service abolished. The old legislation was replaced by the Parole Act of 1959, and the National Parole Board was created in statute, allegedly as an independent paroling authority.

In the 1960s, day parole was incorporated into the correctional process. The National Parole Service, which had been responsible for case preparation and supervision under the NPB, now took a leading role in the Penitentiary Service, merging under one Commissioner of Corrections. New parole officers were hired for community supervision and the prison system became inundated with caseworkers and social workers.

Pressure to play the game with this new type of guard (case managers) caused friction in the prison population. Resentments grew. Rights of inmates became a major theme of internal reviews and commissions of inquiry. Finally, the National Parole Board's discretionary authority came under so much fire it was forced to make changes to its rules and regulations. In 1977, these changes were enshrined in amendments to the parole act and under the mantle of seeking fairness, the NPB reorganized, and once again expanded. By the mid 1970s the Board was on the verge of becoming a quasi-judicial body with extended powers in the criminal justice system.

Despite some of the procedural safeguards put into place to protect inmates' rights to fair and open parole hearings, the Supreme Court of Canada was unmoved. The Chief Justice blasted the Board, calling it a tyrannical authority with unprecedented power that threatened people's liberty.

The stinging attack brought on further changes in the correctional and parole system. The National Parole Service and the Penitentiary Service became one entity, the Correctional Service of Canada (CSC). The assimilation of the modern day prison industry was now complete. Prisons warehoused inmates as a slow process of assessments, programs, and day and full parole moved prisoners through the system, and into the community under supervision.

Prisoners quickly found themselves caught in a trap. Good conduct during incarceration was no longer enough. Now inmates were forced to take programs at the discretion of case managers. If they refused they were threatened with less than favorable assessments that would scuttle their parole.

A growing number of prisoners refused to play the intimidating parole game, opting instead to wait for Statutory Release (Formally known as mandatory release. Achieved after an inmate has served two thirds of his/her sentence). To offset the problem of inmates refusing to play the parole game (which corrections blamed on inmate resentment at being released on parole with conditions attached) the Board threatened specific prisoners, telling them they would be re-arrested at the prison gate when leaving after two-third's of their sentence had been served. (The practice was referred to as, "gating")

These prisoners were then urged to challenge the practice, and in 1983 the Supreme Court ruled gating was illegal. To get around this, in 1985 the Solicitor General introduced a bill that allowed for prisoners to be detained beyond their Statutory Release date. The system used the highest profile case it could find to gain support -- Clifford Olsen. In 1986 the Parole Act was amended accordingly, and correctional staff now had the ability to threaten inmates with "detention."

Empowered with a growing number of rules and regulations, the correctional service moved into high gear as the prison population continued to grow. They used social sciences to develop prediction scales that indicated whether an offender could be expected to complete the parole period without committing another offence. Assessment of risk became the correctional service's buzz phrase.

In 1992, the same year I entered the federal correctional system, legislation repealed the Parole Act of 1959 and the Penitentiary Act of 1961. They were replaced with the "Corrections and Conditional Release Act." The National Parole Board and Corrections Canada touted the CCRA as a comprehensive act that promoted fairness and integrity. Ironically, I became one of its first tests!

The authors of the act claimed it was the result of many years of work, integrating research findings, the knowledge and experience of correctional workers, and the views of many ordinary Canadians. The alleged reforms reflected three major themes -- public safety and reintegration, openness and accountability, and procedural fairness. The act required prisoners to serve longer periods of time inside the institutions before they became eligible for day parole. It also provided a role for victims.

In the mid 1990s Willie Gibbs was hired as chairman of the National Parole Board. He was a psychiatric social worker who had worked his way through the correctional service, starting out as a parole officer. Gibbs quickly initiated a change in the structure of NPB members. Today the Board resembles a round table of promoted correctional officers and others with previous ties to the criminal justice system. The Correctional Service of Canada now has a death grip on the parole system in Canada, and its accountability to Canadian citizens is more questionable than ever.

Let's look at some of the myths that support the use of parole as it now exists.

1) It is safe and humane.
2) It will reduce the prison population.
3) It is cost effective.

Now consider the following:

[1] Most people do not respond positively to threats and personal attacks on their character, but these are exactly the methods that have been adopted by our prisons. The group-think mentality I described earlier in the book, is commonly used to bully inmates into behaving. Case management's degradation of inmates draws out the anger of prisoners, which in turn, is then used to justify imprisonment while case managers put in place, the hoops, inmates must jump through to prove they are rehabilitated. This practice is neither safe nor humane!

[2] When parole was instituted into our legal system, with a promise to the public that time spent in prison would be reduced, the power brokers in the prison industry began a propaganda campaign for longer sentences. Desensitizing the public by highlighting the most vicious and frightening cases

became a common theme that group-labeled all inmates. The end result saw frustrated, angry, and dysfunctional men and women being released back into society, with little or no positive rehabilitation to fall back on. The fact is; inclusion of parole in our legal system has kept people tied to our institutions for longer periods of time, adding to an ever-increasing pool of parolees who continue to flood in and out of revolving prison gates.

[3] With people tied to the system longer (mostly the poor and less affluent in society), costs have skyrocketed. Parole is not cost effective!

With this in mind, it is no wonder that politicians and the bureaucrats working within the correctional service are trying to perform a balancing act like no other. The dramatic increase in prison sentences due to the concept of parole has become a disaster! The NPB and the Correctional Service of Canada find themselves in a constant fight, trying to numb the conscience of society through the promotion of safe community supervision. The awareness of parole has also infected the legal profession and the courts with indifference. Today the front end of the judicial system relies on parole to take care of any shortcomings in the legal process.

The reality is, parole has become a social trap that imprisons people longer and wraps fear and uncertainty around society. The idea that it would not affect our courts and sentencing has proven to be false. Instead, parole has become a dangerous and cancerous growth in our judicial system.

Let's look at the benefits of an open and up-front sentencing procedure:

[1] The preservation of our Charter of Rights.

[2] Prison time that fits the crime. (The public would no longer have to live in fear of early release for violent serial killers and sexual predators. Ticket to leave could be re-enacted and made available through the courts on humanitarian reasons for life sentences. At the same time, shorter sentences could be handed down for the majority

of crimes without the courts having to take into consideration the parole factor.)

[3] Both society and the incarcerated citizen would know where they stand, which would relieve tension in both these areas without forcing people to wade through the emotional abuse that the parole game brings onboard.

[4] A signed plea bargain, that included an agreed upon sentence would bring about a reduction in court costs and in time spent at the appellant court level.

In 2000, I learned there was to be a debate in Victoria on the topic of justice in Canada. I attended what I thought was going to be a public form on corrections and parole, only to realize I was witnessing something much different. Almost all the people present appeared to be there by written invitation. With an abundance of past and present employees of the justice system among the 50 to 60 participants, the exercise, which lasted two days, was clearly a self-promotion put on by the National Parole Board and Corrections Canada. It was the first of about a dozen so-called "town-hall meetings" to be held across the country.

The Board used the forum to seek public support for its increased participation and growth in the criminal justice system. My observations were supported by a few others who felt overwhelmed by the high percentage of correctional and parole staff who made up the majority.

In January 2003, I was searching the web, when I came across a title that spurned an immediate interest in me, "Parole and Public Safety: A Public Form. Final Report." The report was the National Parole Board's carefully crafted assessment of these town-hall meetings. The observations I had made, and the conclusion I had arrived at three years earlier, were confirmed. The National Parole Board and the Correctional Service of Canada were actively seeking to expand their powers into the community. Not only did the report shamefully promote the NPB and CSC, but there was also a definite indication that the public was in favor of the Board's intrusion in our schools, something that would give CSC and the NPB a classroom setting of unrestricted self-promotion. The report also suggested the public was in favor of giving the NPB and CSC a heightened say in a new restorative justice system. In the report, the Board saw itself as a champion of victim services, and indicated the public wished to see it expand deeper into that area as well.

As this underground judicial system continues to mass and grow, unabated, the public could one day see restorative justice legislation bypass the court process altogether, paving the way for the prison industry to incarcerate people through a further dismantling of due process, something that should frighten all citizens.

In closing, let me say that there is nothing evil or vindictive about being tough on crime. With that in mind I would like to leave you with these words: While we search for equality in due process, let us never forget that honest and fair justice is measured through the strength of our justice system's integrity, and its commitment to the truth. We must turn back from the concept of better safe than sorry and follow that path, wherever it takes us.

The End

Made in the USA
Las Vegas, NV
30 June 2023

74027333R00193